THE AMERICAN
CANCER SOCIETY
COOKBOOK

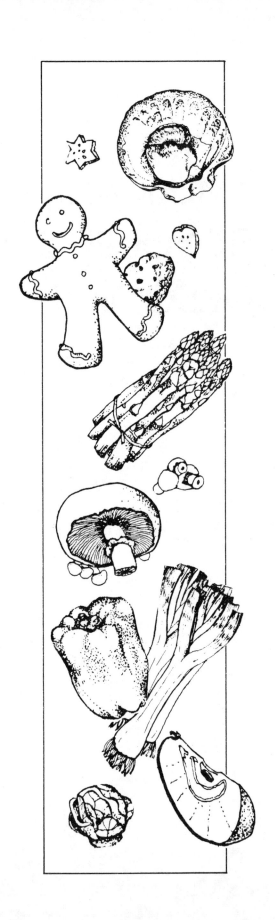

THE AMERICAN CANCER SOCIETY COOKBOOK

ANNE LINDSAY

in consultation with Diane J. Fink, M.D.

HEARST BOOKS

New York

An earlier edition of this book was published in Canada in 1986, in cooperation with the Ontario Division of the Canadian Cancer Society, as *Smart Cooking* by Macmillan of Canada, a division of Canadian Publishing Corporation.

Photographs by Fred Bird
Photograph of Orange-Ginger Chicken by Mark Bird

Illustrations by Penelope Moir

Library of Congress Cataloging-in-Publication Data

Lindsay, Anne.
    The American Cancer Society cookbook.

    Rev. ed. of: Smart cooking.
    Bibliography: p.
    Includes index.
    1. Cancer—Risk Reduction—2. Recipes.
I. Fink, Diane J. II. Lindsay, Anne. Smart cooking. III. American Cancer Society. IV. Title.
RC268.L56   1987   641.5′63   87-28203
ISBN 0-688-07484-7

Printed in the United States of America

First Revised Edition

6 7 8 9 10

BOOK DESIGN BY BERNARD SCHLEIFER

CONTENTS

INTRODUCTION

FOOD—that basic necessity and pleasure—has become a little scary. For years the media have been bringing us bad news about one item after another: Cholesterol clogs our arteries, too much salt gives us hypertension, too much sugar causes any number of problems, and, it sometimes seems, *everything* causes cancer. Small wonder that, faced with this barrage, many of us give up, throw our fate to the gods, and dig into the barbecued ribs and chocolate cream pie.

But recently researchers have come out with some exciting and encouraging new information. An evolving body of scientific evidence suggests that by making some rather simple changes in our eating habits, by choosing foods consistent with healthy eating from every point of view, we may not only do good things for our general health, heart, and waistline, but may reduce our cancer risk as well.

Scientists estimate that as much as 80 percent of cancers in the world are caused by environmental and life-style factors. One of the most important of these may be diet, which may account for perhaps as much as 35 percent of all cancers, except those of the skin.

Researchers have suspected for decades that diet had something to do with cancer, but only in the last few years have they zeroed in on this area. The results of their work to date seem to show that some things we eat—fat, for example—may increase the risk of certain cancers such as colon and breast, while others, such as fiber, may have a protective effect, especially for cancer of the colon.

This doesn't mean that a perfect cancer-preventing diet for everyone can now be prescribed; that may never be possible. The research is still so new, and both cancer and nutrition are so complex, that it may be years before anything can be said with greater certainty about the cancer/diet connection.

Much research still needs to be done and many questions need to be answered. One difficulty is that it usually takes twenty to thirty years after exposure to a cancer-causing agent before a statistically significant increase in cancer rates can be detected; and the interpretation of both epi-

5

demiological and laboratory data is very difficult and often controversial.

Cancer research is now at the point vis-à-vis diet and nutrition that it was with smoking thirty years ago. The American Cancer Society decided then that the evidence against smoking, though limited, was sufficient to justify warning the public about the potential dangers. They have similarly concluded now that the data linking diet and cancer is convincing enough to justify issuing some general dietary guidance. These are similar to background statements issued by the National Research Council of the National Academy of Sciences, and the National Cancer Institute.

AMERICAN CANCER SOCIETY DIET GUIDELINES

1. Avoid obesity.
2. Cut down on total fat intake.
3. Eat more high-fiber foods, such as whole-grain cereals, fruits, and vegetables.
4. Include foods rich in vitamins A and C in the daily diet.
5. Include cruciferous vegetables, such as cabbage, broccoli, Brussels sprouts, kohlrabi, and cauliflower, in the diet.
6. Be moderate in consumption of alcoholic beverages.
7. Be moderate in consumption of salt-cured, smoked, and nitrite-cured foods.

Before the guidelines are explained, a little background:

The research leading to these recommendations was carried out using several methods of investigation.

1. Descriptive epidemiology is the study of the occurrence of disease in populations. The most important are those comparing cancer occurrence or death rates among countries or among persons migrating to other countries.
2. Analytic epidemiology consists of epidemiologic studies that examine the diets of cancer cases with the diets of control groups (noncancer patients).
3. Studies in laboratories involve two kinds of research: experiments with animals, and experiments that test the effects of chemicals on bacteria or other cells or organisms. Chemicals that cause genetic changes (mutations) are immediately suspect.
4. Interventional studies compare the cancer rates of control groups, which follow a normal diet, and test groups, which follow a modified diet.

Much of the weight of evidence comes from epidemiological research, which suggests a link between diets in modern, affluent countries and several cancers, especially those of the colon and the breast, and also the endometrium (lining of the uterus) and the prostate. Our diet, though it has virtually eliminated many deficiency diseases, such as scurvy, rickets, and pellagra, appears to encourage the development of others. For example, a survey of the international incidence of colorectal cancer (cancers of the colon and rectum) and breast cancer shows striking differences between Western and developing countries: In the African communities studied, for instance, colorectal cancer accounted for only about 2 percent of total cancer cases, and breast cancer rates were also low; whereas in America, colorectal cancer is the second most common cancer for men and women combined, and breast cancer is the most common cancer in women.

Additional evidence has come from the study of migration patterns. Groups of people who move from an area with a low incidence of a certain cancer to one with a high incidence (or vice versa) eventually develop the cancer rate of the new country, depending on how long it takes them to adopt the new life-style and diet. Japanese immigrants to Hawaii, for example, are developing a Western cancer pattern: high for colon and breast cancer, low for stomach cancer—the reverse of the Japanese pattern. The same is true of East European immigrants to North America and southern Europeans to Australia.

Although it is easy enough to demonstrate a statistical association between some kinds of diet and some cancers, it is extremely difficult to establish a casual relationship and to nail down which components of diet, if any, are the villains and which are the white knights. Nevertheless, research has pointed to certain dietary factors as most likely to play a role in cancer.

FAT

Of the dietary elements studied so far, high fat intake may be an important factor in increasing cancer risk. Research data from both population and laboratory studies tend to implicate high fat consumption, especially in cancers of the colon, rectum, prostate, and breast—among the most common cancers in the country.

Some of the evidence is controversial, however. For example, many studies have shown that breast cancer may be associated with fat consumption. Breast cancer rates are low in countries where fat intake is also low (Thailand,

Japan, Mexico) and high where intake is high (United States, Canada, Denmark, New Zealand). And laboratory studies tend to confirm that rats fed a high-fat diet may have a high rate of mammary tumors. But other studies have failed to connect high fat consumption with breast cancer. A recent four-year study that tracked the diets and subsequent breast cancer incidence of 89,538 American nurses did not support this link. It's possible however, that this lack of correlation may be explained by other factors, such as the time frame being too short, or the fact that the group with the lowest average fat intake had 32 percent of calories in fat; the effects of a lower percentage are not known.

Scientists have speculated that fat may have an initiating effect on some cancer development and perhaps a promoting effect on others. (In cancer, some agents appear to act as initiators, causing genetic changes in cells. Others act as promoters, furthering the malignant development of changes already initiated.) Exactly how fat works in these ways, however, is still unclear.

To date, research has not definitively pinned down the role of different types of fat, such as saturated, polyunsaturated, cholesterol, in cancer promotion; total fat intake seems to be the most important factor. But, some recent research suggests that olive oil, a monounsaturated oil, may be less harmful than other fats (which might explain why in Greece and Spain, where diets are high in fat—mostly olive oil—breast cancer rates are low); and certain fish oils rich in omega-3 fatty acids (such as cod, halibut, salmon) may in fact be beneficial. Research continues in this area.

OBESITY

Research indicates that the significantly overweight (those 40 percent or more above ideal weight) have a higher cancer risk—as much as 50 percent, according to some studies. Whether it is the weight itself or the foods eaten that is responsible for the increased risk is not clear. A twelve-year study conducted by the American Cancer Society indicated that marked obesity is associated with a much higher death rate from cancers of the endometrium, gallbladder, cervix, ovary, colon, breast, and prostate than that found in people of average weight. Other studies have confirmed that being overweight increases the incidence of endometrial and breast cancers in women after menopause. Earlier lab studies had shown that maintaining animals at normal weight or lower both reduced their cancer rates and lengthened their lives.

ALCOHOL

Heavy drinkers have an unusually high risk of cancers of the mouth, esophagus, larynx, and throat. If they also smoke, the risk increases dramatically. In addition, excessive alcohol causes liver damage, which may lead to liver cancer. Recent studies appear to link alcohol intake with increased risk of breast cancer; even as few as three drinks per week may increase risk; other studies have shown no excess risk from moderate drinkers.

NITRITE, NITRATE, SALT, AND SMOKE

Nitrite, which is added to cured meats (bacon, sausages, cold cuts) to prevent botulism, can enhance the formation in the digestive system of nitrosamines, which have caused stomach and esophageal cancer in lab animals. In countries where people eat a lot of salt-cured and pickled foods, such as Japan and China, or where nitrate and nitrite are common in food and water, such as Colombia, incidence of stomach and esophageal cancers is high. It is encouraging to note that in response to such data, the American meat industry has substantially reduced the amount of nitrite in prepared meats and is looking for better methods of meat preservation.

Nitrates, which are converted to nitrite in the body, are found naturally in many foods, but nitrate-containing foods (such as spinach and beets) are not thought to present a problem. Some nitrate-containing foods also contain vitamin C, which blocks the conversion of nitrite into nitrosamines. It may be that nitrite poses a problem only when the diet is low in vitamin C. But whatever the full story turns out to be, cured meats are high in fat and salt, so it seems prudent to limit intake of these foods. (High salt intake may be related to stomach cancer.)

Smoke ingested from conventionally smoked hams, sausages, fish, and other meats may pose a risk in that they may contain tars or other substances, similar to those inhaled from cigarettes, that are potential carcinogens. Again, food processors have responded by switching to "liquid smoke," thought to be less hazardous, in preparing smoked foods. A similar cooking method that may pose dangers is barbecuing. When fat drips onto a wood or charcoal fire, carcinogens such as benzopyrene may form and be deposited on the food by the smoke or flames. This theory, however, has not been verified in epidemiologic studies.

FIBER

Among the dietary elements that have been proposed as possibly protective against cancer, fiber is one of the most controversial to researchers. Fiber is that part of cereals, fruit, and vegetables that is not digested or is only partially digested. It is the "bulk" that cereal commercials laud for its ability to "aid regularity." It certainly helps prevent constipation, but some evidence seems to show that it may also play a part in reducing the risk of more serious bowel disorders.

The positive data come mostly from international epidemiological studies, which seem to support an association between high-fiber diets and low incidence of colorectal cancer and other diseases of the colon. One of the characteristics of diets in Western countries, where risk of colorectal cancer is high, is low fiber, whereas the opposite is true in Third World countries.

The Seventh-Day Adventists in California present a useful comparison study for researchers, since they share with other Americans the same environment and economic affluence but have much lower rates of colorectal and lung cancers. Many of them follow an ovolactovegetarian diet (no meat, but including eggs and milk products), which emphasizes high-fiber fruits, vegetables, and whole-grain cereals. However, it's possible that other factors may be involved in producing the data, such as the fact that Seventh-Day Adventists discourage smoking and alcohol use.

Pinning down the fiber connection has proved maddeningly elusive. Further population and lab studies have yielded confusing data, suggesting that the relation between dietary fiber and cancer is a complex matter that requires much more study.

Nevertheless, several theories have been put forward that attempt to explain how fiber might protect against colorectal cancer. One is that fiber, particularly cereal fiber, increases the bulk of waste products by absorbing water, thereby diluting the concentration of carcinogens in the bowel. Another is that fiber may bind bile acids or alter the proportion of bacteria in the colon, thus preventing bacteria from metabolizing the acids into cancer-promoting end products.

There are several kinds of fiber, and it is not clear which, if any, may be protective. Scientists also aren't certain whether it is the fiber itself or the presence of the fiber interacting with other components in foods that might be the protective factor. Thus fiber supplements are not the answer to getting more fiber in the diet. The way to increase fiber intake is to eat more high-fiber foods, which can be a wholesome substitute for high-calorie and fatty foods.

VITAMINS A AND C

Several studies have shown that vitamin A-containing foods may lower the risk of cancers of the larynx, esophagus, lung, and bladder. In some of these studies, people recorded the food they ate, and the vitamin A content was calculated; other studies measured vitamin levels in the blood. Cancer rates of the low- and high-level groups were then compared. Laboratory studies also show that vitamin A reduces the incidence of certain cancers in animals. Scientists believe that vitamin A may be an agent that can reduce the tendency for malignant cells to multiply.

There are two forms of vitamin A in foods: preformed retinol (the vitamin itself), found in such foods as liver and milk, and beta-carotene, a compound that converts to vitamin A in the body, found in dark green and deep yellow-orange vegetables and fruits. Most of the research to date has involved foods containing carotene. Scientists are not sure whether it is the carotene or some other component in the foods that is the active element.

Epidemiological studies have indicated that vitamin C-containing foods appear to protect against gastric and esophageal cancers. These studies have been similar to those involving vitamin A: The subjects' intake of the vitamin was calculated from the foods they ate rather than from measured quantities of the vitamin. Again, it is not certain whether it is the vitamin itself or some other component of vitamin C-containing fruits and vegetables that is protective. However, biochemical experiments with animals and with cells have shown that vitamin C inhibits the conversion of nitrites into carcinogenic nitrosamines, which indicates that vitamin C may be effective in dealing with that potential cancer threat.

Cancer researchers strongly discourage people from attempting to meet their needs for vitamins A and other vitamins and minerals by taking supplements except in some instances when prescribed by a physician. Pills are not a good substitute for foods, which are very complex mixtures of fiber and essential nutrients, some of which may also be important in cancer prevention. High doses of vitamins such as Vitamin A can be dangerous.

CRUCIFEROUS VEGETABLES

One of the surprises in diet/cancer research has been the lowly cabbage: It and its relatives may protect against some cancers of the gastrointestinal tract. Both epidemiological and laboratory studies show the cruciferous vegetables (such as broccoli, cabbage, Brussels sprouts, and cauliflower) may reduce the incidence of cancers of the colon, stomach, and esophagus. In animal experiments, they seem highly effective in inhibiting the effects of carcinogenic chemicals. As a bonus, most are a good source of fiber and certain vitamins.

ADDITIVES AND OTHER AREAS OF INVESTIGATION

Several substances, such as food additives, vitamin E, selenium, artificial sweeteners, and coffee, have received a great deal of media attention for their possible positive or negative link with cancer. Although they are being investigated, there is no clear evidence about them one way or the other.

USING THE DIET GUIDELINES

In the following pages, there are dozens of suggestions and hundreds of recipes to help you plan a healthier style of eating. The underlying message is: Eat a variety of foods in moderation. Cut down on fat and eat more fiber.

1. *Avoid obesity.*

Since being significantly overweight (40 percent above ideal)) seems to increase cancer risk, it is important to keep your weight as close as possible to ideal. Maintaining normal weight will also benefit your general health and decrease your risk of other serious diseases, such as heart disease and diabetes.

The best way to lose weight—you've heard it before, but it's still true—is to eat less and exercise more. It is the safest method (no dangerous starvation diets), the one most likely to be permanent (no drastic changes you won't be able to keep up), and it has extra benefits (toned muscles, more energy). Other points to remember:

- Check with your physician about the best weight-loss plan for you.
- Lose weight slowly, about two pounds a week. Anything more puts you in danger of losing essential lean tissue, such as muscle.
- Eat smaller portions.
- Eat less fat. Fat is concentrated calories. One gram of fat has more than twice as many calories as one gram of protein or carbohydrates, so reducing fat intake is the quickest way to cut down on calories. Some fat is essential for nutrition, though, so don't try to eliminate it completely. (See pages 13 & 14 for fat-cutting suggestions.)
- Cut out or cut down on alcohol. Alcohol is the second most concentrated source of calories (see page 19) and is strongly associated with increased cancer risk. And the

nutritional benefits of alcohol are negligible.
- Avoid foods that are high in sugar.
- Exercise within your own capability.

CHOOSE TO LOSE

Instead of	Calories	Choose	Calories
doughnut	235	plain muffin	120
peanuts (1/2 cup)	420	popcorn, unbuttered (2 cups)	108
fried chicken (3 ounces dark meat with skin)	240	roast chicken (3 ounces white meat, skin removed)	145
mayonnaise (2 tablespoons)	120	low-cal mayonnaise (2 tablepoons)	40
ice cream (1/2 cup)	135	low-fat yogurt (1/2 cup)	75
chocolate bar (2 ounces)	285	frozen yogurt, chocolate-coated (1/2 cup)	127
rib roast (4 ounces)	300	lean flank steak (4 ounces)	200
spareribs (4 ounces)	450	lean pork tenderloin (4 ounces)	275
whole milk (1 cup)	150	skim milk (1 cup)	85
chocolate cake, iced (1 piece)	310	angel food cake, plain (1 piece)	121

2. Cut down on total fat intake.
Most Americans have been living a little too literally off the fat of the land: About 40 percent of the calories we consume are from fat. The National Academy of Sciences has recommended that we reduce dietary fat to 30 percent of calories. And more recent studies suggest that even this may not be low enough.

We're talking about cutting down on fat—not cutting it out completely. We still need some fat to add flavor and richness to foods, and for the constant manufacture of new cells. Fatty deposits serve as reserves of energy and protect our vital organs. Fats are also carriers of the fat-soluble vitamins A, D, and E.

You can measure fat in terms of both weight (e.g., grams) and energy (e.g., calories). One gram of fat supplies 9 calories (1 gram of protein or of carbohydrate supplies 4 calories).

It's not easy to change the habits of a lifetime, but reducing fat intake to 30 percent of your total calories needn't be an exercise in penance. If you normally eat about 2,000 calories a day, for example, 40 percent of which is fat (800 calories ÷ 9 = 88 grams), the reduction

13

to 30 percent (600 calories ÷ 9 = 66 grams) would mean cutting out only 200 calories, or 22 grams of fat. That amounts to 1 tablespoon of butter and 1 tablespoon of mayonnaise. To find out how many grams of fat you should cut in a day, refer to Appendices, page 243.

Since saturated or animal fats are associated with increased risk of heart disease, it makes sense to start there. If you don't have time for complicated calculations, the four easiest ways to reduce fat are:
- Trim fat off meats.
- Use less butter, margarine, and oil.
- Eat fewer rich desserts (such as pastries, whipped cream).
- Adjust your cooking methods. Steam, poach, oven-broil, or bake instead of frying.

And don't underestimate the fat hidden in foods such as baked goods, meat dishes, sauces, and salad dressings. (See Tables C, D, and E on pages 245–249 for the fat content of several common foods.)

Much of the fat we eat can be reduced without sacrificing taste. The following are fat-containing foods you might eat in a typical day, with some leaner substitutions. You don't have to make them all every day; just aim to reduce your fat intake.

CUT THE FAT

Instead of	Choose	Grams fat saved
Fried egg (9)*	Boiled or poached egg (6)*	3
2 pats butter on toast (8)	1 pat butter (4)	4
Cream in coffee (3)	2% milk in coffee (0)	3
Hamburger (20)	Tuna sandwich (11)	9
Salad with French dressing (6)	Salad with diet dressing (2)	4
Ice cream (8)	Low-fat yogurt (2)	6
8 ounces round steak (30)	4 ounces round steak (15)	15
Asparagus with Hollandaise sauce (18)	Asparagus with lemon (0)	18
15 french fries (12)	Baked potato with 1 pat butter (4)	8
Apple pie (18)	Apple crisp (8)	10
Tea with cream (3)	Tea with 2% milk (0)	3
2 ounces potato chips (1 small bag) (24)	3 cups unbuttered popcorn (2)	22
Almond Danish pastry (15)	Bran muffin (4)	11
*grams fat	Total grams fat saved	116

3. *Eat more high-fiber foods, such as whole-grain cereals, fruits, and vegetables.*

American diets tend to be low in fiber, so this one may take some work. It's not enough simply to switch to whole wheat bread, though this is a good start. Nutritionists vary in their estimates of how much dietary fiber is optimal for general health, but most agree it's wise to increase intake gradually to avoid any possibility of discomfort. Such problems as gas can be easily overcome by changing your diet gradually, over the course of a week or so, and drinking plenty of liquids every day—8 to 12 cups of water, milk, juice, or other beverages.

Remember, it's essential to get your added fiber from fiber-rich foods, not from supplements. And when you're stepping up your intake, don't go overboard. Excessive amounts of fiber might interfere with calcium and iron absorption. As is generally true in diet, moderation is the key.

CHOOSE SEVERAL FIBER-CONTAINING FOODS EACH DAY

Excellent sources	Good Sources
(4.5 grams or more per serving)	(2 to 4.4 grams per serving)

BREAD AND CEREALS

Bran and other cereals and breads containing 4.5 grams or more fiber per serving (read product labels)	Cereals and breads containing 2 or more grams fiber per serving (read product lables)

VEGETABLES

Beans, baked, canned (½ cup)	Corn, kernels (from 2 ears)
Beans, soaked and boiled (½ cup)	Peas, green (1/2 cup)
Lima beans, boiled, drained (½ cup)	Spinach (1/2 cup)
	Sweet potato (1)
	Lentils, boiled (1/2 cup)
	Potato, baked (1)
	Parsnips (1/2 cup)
	Brussels sprouts (8)
	Beans, green or yellow (1/2 cup)

FRUITS

Prunes, dried, raw (6)	Avocado (1/2)
Apricots, dried halves (6)	Blueberries (1/2 cup)
Figs, dried (2)	Dates (10)
	Raspberries (1/2 cup)
	Raisins (1/2 cup)
	Apple, raw, with skin (1)
	Orange (1)
	Pear, raw, with skin (1)

NUTS

Almonds (1/2 cup)	Walnuts (1/2 cup)
Brazil nuts (1/2 cup)	
Peanuts (1/2 cup)	

Note: Nuts and avocados have a high fat content, so they shouldn't be used very often as a source of fiber.

Some foods that seem to be likely candidates for high-fiber status are in fact poor sources: brown rice, corn-flake cereals, lettuce, green peppers, and grapes are some examples.

Add extra fiber to your diet with:
- bran in meat loaf
- raisin-bran muffins
- oatmeal toppings on fruit crisps
- lentils or legumes in soups
- legumes in salads (chick-peas, kidney beans)
- wheat germ in muffins, on cereals
- fresh fruit for breakfast instead of juice

4. *Include foods rich in vitamins A and C in your daily diet.*
Your mother was right when she told you to eat your vegetables; they are among the few foods that can be unreservedly recommended. Fruits are another. Many fruits and vegetables are important sources of vitamins A and C, which may be protective against certain cancers. With their enormous variety, they can offer almost every other essential nutrient and fiber as well, and most of them are fat and calorie bargains.

Dark green and deep yellow vegetables and fruits are rich sources of vitamin A (in the form of carotene), so choose them often.

EAT YOUR GREENS—AND YELLOWS

Excellent sources of carotene	Good sources of carotene
broccoli	apricots
cantaloupe	beet greens
carrots	nectarines
spinach	peaches
squash	tomatoes
sweet potatoes	watermelon

See also lists of excellent vitamins A and C recipes, pages 252–253.

Everyone knows that citrus fruits (oranges, grapefruit, lemons, limes) are high in vitamin C, but when you select fruit juices such as apple, grape, or pineapple, or fruit drinks, remember to look for the statement "vitamin C added." Several vegetables are also rich sources of vitamin C. Because vitamin C isn't stored in the body, it's important to include vitamin C-rich foods in your daily menu.

VITAMIN C—MORE THAN JUST CITRUS

Excellent sources

apple juice (vitaminized)
broccoli
Brussels sprouts
citrus fruits and juices
green and red peppers
strawberries

Good sources

cabbage
cauliflower
potatoes (baked or
  steamed)
rutabaga
tomatoes and tomato juice

CAUTION: Vitamin C is perishable. Heat, light or exposure to air can destroy it, and it dissolves in cooking water. To preserve it:
- Cover and refrigerate juices after opening.
- Prepare foods just before cooking.
- Cook vegetables with their skins on.
- Steam or bake (don't boil) fruits and vegetables.
- Keep cooking times as short as possible.
- Eat fruits and vegetables raw as often as possible.

5. *Include cruciferous vegetables, such as cabbage, broccoli, Brussels sprouts, kohlrabi, and cauliflower in your diet.*
Not only are these vegetables packed with vitamins and minerals, but they seem to have an extra protective effect against cancer risk. Have several servings of these vegetables each week.

CABBAGES ARE KINGS

broccoli
Brussels sprouts
cabbage

kohlrabi
rutabaga
cauliflower

6. *Be moderate in consumption of alcoholic beverages.*
"Moderate" consumption is generally interpreted as two standard drinks per day or two bottles of beer. It should be noted, however, that a recent study seems to show that more than three drinks per week may increase the risk of breast cancer.

Alcohol, especially when combined with smoking, is implicated in increased risk of several cancers. It's also a source of "empty" calories: It supplies 7 calories per gram (or about 90 calories per 5 ounces dry white wine; 104 calories per 1½ ounces 80-proof Scotch; 150 calories per 12 ounces beer, 95 calories for light beer; 193 calories per 8 ounces gin and tonic; 335 calories per 4 ounces eggnog).

Instead of alcoholic drinks, consider switching to other beverages: fruit or vegetable juices, mineral water or club soda with lime or a dash of angostura bitters.

7. *Be moderate in consumption of salt-cured, smoked, and nitrite-cured foods.*
Since smoked hams and fish, cold cuts, sausages, and other cured foods seem to be associated with cancer risk, it's wise to cut down. Even if it is later found that adequate intake of vitamin C and better methods of preparing meats reduce the risk, cured foods are high in fat and salt, which are linked to cancer and hypertension.

MENU PLANNING

All recipes in this book have been chosen on the basis not only of good taste but of good health. They are high in fiber, low (or lower than usual) in fat, and rich in vitamins and minerals, and they emphasize fruits and vegetables, whole-grain products, and the lean kinds and cuts of meat and fish. Sugar and salt have been kept to a minimum. Some of the recipes are classic favorites, which you will recognize, adapted to reflect the goals of the American Cancer Society Diet Guidelines.

Use the recipes for everyday meals or for entertaining. Suggested menus are included throughout the book and are listed in the index.

To help you plan your own menus, each recipe gives you the number of calories and grams of fat per serving, as well as fiber, vitamin, and mineral ratings. Remember the daily requirements:

- 20 to 30 grams of fiber
- fat intake not to exceed 30 percent of total calories. (To calculate your fat allowance in grams, refer to Appendix, page 243)

All recipes in this book were analyzed and tested using 2% milk, low-fat yogurt, and 2% cottage cheese.

The Four Food Groups

When planning menus, try to include foods from each of these groups at every meal. The four food groups and recommended daily servings are:

1. Fruits and vegetables (including green and deep yellow vegetables): 4 or 5 servings (serving size ½ cup)

2. Breads and cereals (including pasta, rice, muffins): 3 to 5 servings (serving size: 1 slice bread, muffin or roll; ½ to 1 cup cereal, cooked rice, macaroni)

3. Milk and milk products (including cheese, yogurt): 2 to 4 servings (serving size: 1 cup low-fat milk, yogurt or cottage cheese; 1½ ounces cheddar cheese)

4. Meat, fish, poultry, and alternates (such as peanut butter, beans, lentils, low-fat cheese): 2 servings (serving size: 2 to 3 ounces cooked lean meat, fish or poultry; 4 tablespoons peanut butter; 1 cup cooked dried peas, beans or lentils; 2 ounces cheddar or cottage cheese; 2 eggs [but do not exceed 3 a week]). Three ounces of cooked meat means a piece of sirloin steak about 4 x 2 x ½ inches.

Liquids: A daily intake of 8 to 12 cups of liquid (including soups, juices, and beverages) is recommended.

To see if you need to adjust your eating habits, keep track of your diet for several days. Figure out the amount of fat and fiber you are eating, and whether you are eating the recommended servings from the four food groups.

Once you are familiar with which foods are high in fat and fiber and which are low, you can plan your menus with this in mind. For example, if you have a meal with a rich dessert, compensate by choosing other foods low in fat for the rest of the menu: use low-fat salad dressing and broiled chicken instead of a creamy dressing and fried steak. If you aren't getting enough fiber, add a bran muffin, fresh fruit or raw vegetable to your diet.

Once you get used to your new way of eating, you will be able to estimate how you are doing without a lot of calculating.

Comparing Menus

Breakfast

Instead of

orange juice

cheese omelet (2 eggs, cooked in butter)

croissant with jam and 1 pat butter or margarine

coffee with cream

Choose

whole orange (more fiber)

bran cereal with low-fat milk

whole wheat toast and jam

low-fat milk, or coffee with low-fat milk

Fast-Food Lunch

Instead of

hot dog

french fries

milkshake

Choose

slice of pizza with green peppers and mushrooms

Italian vegetable salad with low-fat dressing or lemon juice

low-fat milk

Dinner

Instead of

roast pork and gravy

hash brown potatoes

carrots with butter

lettuce salad with creamy dressing

lemon meringue pie

3 glasses wine

coffee with cream

Choose

lean pork tenderloin with meat juices

baked potato with low-fat yogurt and chives

carrots with parsley and lemon

spinach salad with diet dressing

whole wheat roll

lemon sherbet

1 glass club soda

coffee with low-fat milk

These menus are relatively low in calories. To suit higher calorie needs, serve larger portions and add milk, breads, or snacks.

Everyday Family Meals	Grams Fiber/ Serving	Grams Fat/ Serving	Calories (% Calories from Fat)
Breakfast			
Grapefruit (½)	.72	trace	45
Swiss Fruit Muesli (page 241)	5.83	2	237
Milk (skim, 1 cup)	0	trace	90
Lunch			
Oven-toasted cheese sandwich (with skim-milk cheese) (1½ ounces) on whole wheat bread (2 slices)	4.24	4	226
Carrot sticks (½ cup)	1.68	trace	20
Peaches, packed in water (½ cup)	1.16	trace	39.5
Cinnamon Coffee Cake (page 226)	.58	3.8	172
Dinner			
Chicken Dijon (page 98)	0	3.89	190
Brown rice (¾ cup)	1.32	2.5	112
Steamed asparagus (1 cup)	1.15	trace	16
Whole wheat roll	1.89	1	125
Butter (1 teaspoon)	0	4	36
Rhubarb Crumb Pie (page 228)	2.76	3.6	234
Milk (skim, 1 cup)	0	trace	90
Totals with skim milk	21.3 grams	25.8 grams	1678 (13.8%)
Totals with 2% milk	21.3 grams	35.8 grams	1756 (18%)
Totals with whole milk	21.3 grams	43.8 grams	1812 (22%)

Everyday Family Meals	Grams Fiber/ Serving	Grams Fat/ Serving	Calories (% Calories from Fat)
Breakfast			
Orange (1)	2.62	trace	65
Breakfast Bran-and-Fruit Mix (page 237) (includes ½ cup)	6.65	7	219
with fresh blueberries	5.4	0.5	45
Slice whole wheat toast (1)	1.8	0.5	73
Jam or jelly (1 tsp)	0	trace	18
Lunch			
Tri-Color Bean Soup (page 58)	8.95	0.4	120
Whole Wheat Irish Soda Bread (page 193) with 1 teaspoon butter	2.9	5.7	179
Yogurt (low-fat, ½ cup)	0	3	85
Almond-Apricot Squares (page 196)(2)	3.4	8	154
Dinner			
Marinated Flank Steak (page 111)	0	9	200
Mashed Potatoes with Onions (page 180)	1.81	2	123
Broccoli and Sweet Pepper Stir-Fry (page 167)	2.75	2	40
Poached Pears with Chocolate Sauce (page 205)	2.6	8	168
Milk (skim, ½ cup)	0	0	45
Totals with skim milk	39 grams	38.9 grams	1498 (23%)
Totals with 2% milk	39 grams	48.9 grams	1576 (28%)
Totals with whole milk	39 grams	56.9 grams	1632 (31%)

Everyday Family Meals	Grams Fiber/ Serving	Grams Fat/ Serving	Calories (% Calories from Fat)
Breakfast			
Orange juice (½ cup)	0	trace	64
Bran flakes (¾ cup) with fresh strawberries (½ cup)	5.5	1.39	145
Refrigerator Bran Muffin (page 188) (1 medium)	3.42	5.5	116
Jam or jelly (1 teaspoon)	0	trace	18
Milk (skim, 1 cup)	0	trace	90
Lunch			
Bermuda Bean Salad (page 89)	8.28	3.5	201
Whole Wheat Raisin Scone (page 194) (1)	2.43	8	220
Prune Cake with Lemon Icing (page 213)	2.58	1.25	182
Milk (skim, 1 cup)	0	trace	90
Banana (1)	3.9	trace	100
Dinner			
Sole Fillets with Lemon and Parsley (page 129)	0	7	117
Brown Rice	.82	0.5	105
Steamed green beans	1.95	trace	16
Spinach Salad with Buttermilk Herb Dressing* (page 85)	7	12	250
Chocolate cake	1	9.5	271
Totals with skim milk	36.8 grams	48.6 grams	1985 (22%)
Totals with 2% milk	36.8 grams	58.6 grams	2063 (26%)
Totals with whole milk	36.8 grams	66.6 grams	2119 (28%)

*These figures are for the large main-course-size serving of salad; the smaller side-salad size has 4 grams of fat and 83 calories.

Everyday Family Meals	Grams Fiber/ Serving	Grams Fat/ Serving	Calories (% Calories from Fat)
Breakfast			
Stewed prunes (3)	9.98	0.5	156
Shredded Wheat (1)	2.2	trace	80
Boiled egg (1)	0	6	79
Slice whole wheat toast (1)	1.79	0.5	73
Butter (½ teaspoon)	0	2	18
Milk (skim, 1 cup)	0	trace	90
Lunch			
Chicken sandwich on whole wheat (2) with lettuce or alfalfa sprouts and mayonnaise (1 teaspoon)	4.64	6	295
Celery sticks (½ cup)	.95	trace	9
Tangerine (1)	2.20	trace	40
Wheat Germ Crispy Cookies (page 199) (2)	.9	6	114
Milk (skim, 1 cup)	0	trace	90
Dinner			
Old-Fashioned Meat Loaf (page 114)	0.3	9.5	186
Baked potato (1 medium)	4.04	trace	91
Steamed Brussels sprouts (½ cup)	2.38	0.5	29
Lemon-Ginger Carrots (page 165) (½ cup)	2.54	4	69
Butter (1 teaspoon)	0	4	36
Apricot Clafouti (page 223)	2.05	4.4	162
Totals with skim milk	34 grams	43.4 grams	1527 (26%)
Totals with 2% milk	34 grams	53.4 grams	1605 (30%)
Totals with whole milk	34 grams	61.4 grams	1661 (33%)

EATING OUT

There's no reason to throw away your diet resolutuions when you eat out or travel. The American Cancer Society Diet Guidelines are flexible enough to accommodate almost any dining situation. Superhuman willpower is not required, only knowledge and foresight—and a little ingenuity.

- Beware of high-fat foods: don't order a succession of rich dishes. Concentrate more on fruits, vegetables, and whole-grain foods.
- If you over-indulge on a special occasion, eat moderately for the rest of the day and for a few days after.
- Many restaurants now offer low-calorie or light meals—some even specialize in creating exciting gourmet versions (sometimes called alternative or spa cuisine).
- Ask to have a fried dish steamed or broiled; ask for salads with the dressing on the side so you can serve yourself; ask to have meats served minus rich sauces or gravy. Many restaurants are becoming accustomed to such requests.
- Split a dish, or several dishes, with your dining companion; many restaurants will serve the two half-portions on separate plates.
- Choose a couple of appetizers instead of an entrée, or order soup and a salad.
- Choose clear instead of cream soups.
- Butter bread or rolls sparingly, or not at all.
- Choose fish or chicken dishes, and avoid those with cream sauces.
- Cut all the fat off meats.
- Avoid sautéed and deep-fried foods.
- If choosing a high-fat food, ask for a small portion.

Breakfasts

Choose:
- fresh fruits and juices
- whole-grain breads and cereals, muffins
- poached or boiled eggs (if concerned about cholesterol, limit to 3 per week)
- pancakes or waffles as long as they're not fried in a lot of fat—ask about this—and don't add butter yourself
- yogurt with fresh fruit
- low-fat milk instead of cream or whole milk with cereals and coffee or tea

Avoid:
- Danish pastries or croissants
- bacon, sausages, ham
- too much butter or margarine

Lunches and Dinners

Choose:
- pretzels or unbuttered popcorn rather than peanuts
- salads—add the dressing yourself or ask for a wedge of lemon. Choose from the salad bar: include spinach, corn, kidney beans, chick-peas.
- low-fat cottage cheese
- clear soups
- pasta dishes with tomato-based or wine-based sauces rather than sauces made with cream, oil, or butter
- chicken or fish dishes, broiled or poached (light sauce only)
- fresh fruit desserts, sorbets and sherbets

Avoid, or choose occasionally and in moderate amounts:
- alcoholic drinks (other possibilities are tomato juice, soda, or mineral water)
- quiches (pastry is high in fat)
- pâtés and avocados (high in fat)
- french fries
- butter or sour cream on baked potatoes (ask for yogurt and chives or green onions)
- fatty cuts of beef, pork, and lamb (especially in large servings), duck and goose
- high-fat cheeses (cheddar, cream cheeses)
- barbecued foods
- breaded foods (they're usually fried)
- peanuts and potato chips (substitute raw vegetables)
- smoked and heavily salted foods: ham, salami, herring
- chocolates (instead, choose fruit-jelly candy)
- mousses and rich desserts (chocolate, cream)

COOKING METHODS

Cooking methods to avoid or use with caution:

It's important to avoid frying because it adds extra fat and calories. In addition, some cooking methods, such as barbecuing, grilling or smoking, may be harmful. To barbecue safely, wrap food in foil or place it high above the coals and cook slowly. It has been suggested that chemicals that are possibly cancer-causing may form when food is charred. This is another reason to avoid frying, especially at high temperatures.

Cooking methods to choose:

Baking, roasting (use rack), oven-broiling (don't burn or char), microwave cooking, boiling, steaming (see pages 139 and 172), poaching, stewing, and stir-frying (see page 104) are good methods. They require little or no additional fat.

Cooking equipment you need:

- steamer: either the double-boiler type or a basket
- heavy nonstick skillet
- heavy Dutch oven

To preserve vitamins in cooking:

Some vitamins are destroyed by heat; others dissolve in the cooking water. To preserve them as much as possible:
- Cook vegetables quickly just until tender-crisp.
- Use as little water as possible and have it boiling before adding vegetables.
- Use any leftover cooking liquid in soups or stews.
- Use cooking methods that require very little or no liquid at all: microwaving, baking, steaming, foil-wrapped in oven and stir-frying using a small amount of oil.

To reduce fat in cooking:

- Many recipes begin by sautéing vegetables such as onions in butter. In most cases you can reduce the butter at least by half, often to 1 teaspoon; add a few tablespoons of white wine or water and cook the vegetables slowly over low heat. This method brings out the flavors just as effectively as the traditional method.
- If oil, margarine, or butter is needed for flavor, add it at the end just before serving; you will get the most flavor for the least amount of fat.
- It is very important to use heavy pans, nonstick where possible. This is one of the best ways to cut down on fat without having foods burn or stick.
- Cut off all visible fat before cooking and drain off fat during cooking; make stews or soups using meats or stocks a day in advance and refrigerate overnight—fat solidifies on top and can be easily lifted off.
- Instead of butter or oil for flavor, use herbs and spices, onions or garlic, ginger, lemon juice, mustard.
- Buy the best-quality vegetables in season; they will have the best natural flavor and won't need as much butter or salt.
- Use vegetable purées as a sauce rather than butter-based sauces.
- Use a rack in the roasting pan so that the meat doesn't sit in fat.
- Remove the skin from fowl before cooking or eating.

- Choose lean cuts of meat, such as flank steak or sirloin tip. Avoid prime rib and pork loin.
- Serve 4-ounce portions, or less, of meats; you can extend them and make them more interesting by cooking them with vegetables in stews, soups, and stir-fries or with pasta.
- Cut meats into thin slices; it will look like more.
- Reduce oil in standard marinades, or omit oil altogether (see Marinated Leg of Lamb with Coriander, page 123; Marinated Flank Steak, page 111).
- Use skim or 2% milk instead of whole; yogurt instead of sour cream; wine instead of butter or oil.
- Avoid desserts made with whipping cream; choose desserts based on milk or yogurt.
- Avoid dessert pastries; choose fruit crisps or crumble instead (e.g. instead of double-crust pie, choose an apple crisp or crumble).
- If you're making muffins, cakes, or other rich desserts, compare various recipes for fat or oil content and choose the one with the lowest amount.
- Use dessert recipes calling for cocoa rather than chocolate, as long as the cocoa recipe doesn't have additional fat.

Shopping

Check the labels on cans and other containers: they often give the fat and fiber content in grams per serving, plus other nutritional information. When the ingredients are given on a label, they are listed in order of amounts by weight, beginning with the largest amount. Sugars are often listed by kind (invert sugar, glucose, sucrose) and it may be difficult to determine the total amount of sugar.

Choose:
- calorie-reduced or low-fat soups and salad dressings
- low-fat yogurt, milk, ice cream, and cheese (see Tables D and E, pages 248 and 249)
- low-fat or whipped butter or margarines for spreading (use regular hard margarines or butter for baking)
- lean types and cuts of meat (see Table C, page 245)
- angel food cakes; Social Teas, Fig Newtons, gingersnaps, arrowroot
- turkey that hasn't been injected with fat, i.e., regular grades, not self-basting
- dark green lettuces or spinach (not iceberg lettuce)
- whole wheat or stone-ground breads, pita bread, crackers, English muffins, pasta
- whole-grain cereals, cereals with bran or high fiber (see Table F, page 250)

- bran muffins
- fresh fruits and vegetables

Avoid:
- processed meats: hot dogs, bologna, salami
- high-fat meats and poultry: duck, goose, regular ground meat, sausages, spareribs (see Table C, page 245)
- bacon (very occasionally choose lean ham or Canadian bacon)
- breaded and fried frozen meats and fish, e.g. fish sticks
- tuna fish packed in oil (instead choose tuna packed in water)
- avocados
- doughnuts, Danish pastries, croissants, pies, pastries, cakes, cookies, brownies
- cereals with sugar and low fiber
- chocolates
- peanuts, potato chips

Guidelines for Rating the Recipes as Sources of Nutrients

To assess the nutrient rating of a single portion of food, we established the criterion that each serving of food must provide the following amount of each nutrient to qualify as either a good or an excellent source.

Nutrient	Good Source	Excellent Source
Vitamin A (IU)	600	1200
Thiamine (mg)	0.25	0.45
Riboflavin (mg)	0.40	0.75
Niacin (mg)	2.50	4.50
Vitamin C (mg)	7.5	15.0
Calcium (mg)	150	300
Phosphorus (mg)	150	300
Iron (mg)	2.0	4.0
Dietary fiber (g)	2.0–3.9	4.0 +

All recipes in this book were tested and analyzed using 2% milk, low-fat yogurt, and 2% cottage cheese.

APPETIZERS

SCRUMPTIOUS snacks and cocktail party tidbits are irresistible, and first courses are often the most innovative and interesting part of a meal. What's more, they can add valuable nutrients to your diet. But beware, they can also be nutritional hazards.

Pâtés, peanuts, potato chips, savory-filled pastries, and mayonnaise-based dips are high in fat and should be avoided. Instead, choose crudités (raw vegetables, higher in fiber and vitamins) with a yogurt- or cottage-cheese-based dip, or savories with a bread casing (lower in fat than pastry cases). Appetizers such as Shrimp Wrapped with Snow Peas or Teriyaki Beef Rumaki will be favorites with any crowd and are also low in fat. The recipes in this section of the book will help you plan menus for entertaining that are low in fat and calories.

Appetizer courses in restaurants can be wonderfully appealing and nutritious. Because some restaurant entrées are very large, appetizers are often just the right size to substitute for a main course.

Shrimp Wrapped with Snow Peas

This colorful, delicious hors d'oeuvre is very easy to prepare. Serve any remaining snow peas with a dip or spread, or split them down the center and fill with cottage cheese. This dish is unusually low in fat and calories. Serve with any of the dips in this book. (See color photograph.)

4   cups water
1   thick slice of onion
1   clove garlic, halved
1   bay leaf
2   stalks celery with leaves
1   pound large raw shrimp in shells (about 18)
¼   pound snow peas

In large saucepan, combine water, onion, garlic, bay leaf, and celery; bring to a boil. Reduce heat and simmer for 5 minutes; add shrimp and simmer, uncovered, for 3 to 5 minutes or until shrimp turn pink. Drain immediately and chill under cold water. Remove shell and black intestinal vein from each shrimp.

Trim snow peas and blanch in boiling water for 2 minutes or just until peas are pliable. Drain and plunge into a bowl of ice water to prevent further cooking and to set color. Drain.

Wrap a snow pea around each shrimp and secure with a toothpick. Arrange on serving platter or stick into head of cauliflower. Cover and refrigerate until serving time. Makes about 18 (4 servings).

Calories per piece: 14
Grams fat per piece: 0.1
Fiber: Good
Snow peas are a good source of vitamin A and fiber.

Crab-Stuffed Mini-Pitas

Small pita bread rounds (less than 2 inches in diameter) provide quick and easy containers for countless fillings. The packaged varieties are available in the bread sections of some supermarkets and specialty stores. Choose the whole wheat ones for more flavor and fiber. (See color photograph.)

1	**7-ounce package whole wheat mini-pitas**
½	**pound crab meat (canned, fresh, or frozen)**
2	**tablespoons finely chopped scallion**
½	**cup Parsley Dressing* (page 95)**
½	**teaspoon lemon juice**
	Salt and freshly ground pepper
	Leaf lettuce

Cut pita breads in half. Drain crab meat thoroughly. In bowl, combine crab meat, scallions, Parsley Dressing, lemon juice, and salt and pepper to taste; and mix lightly. (Add more parsley Dressing to taste.) Line pita bread pockets with lettuce. Spoon crab meat mixture into each pita. Refrigerate until needed. Makes 40.

Calories per piece: 16
Grams fat per piece: 0.2
Fiber: 0.26 grams per piece

Although crab meat is very low in fat, it does have cholesterol, which may be of concern in relation to heart disease. In this recipe it works out to a small amount (less than 6 milligrams cholesterol per pita). If this is a concern, use salmon or tuna instead.

Variations:

• Use pita rounds with any of the salads in salad section of book.

• Line pita with alfalfa sprouts and fill with a spoonful of Hummus (page 40); top with Garlic Dip (page 36).

• Substitute cooked or canned salmon or tuna (not tuna fish packed in oil) for crab.

• Line pita with lettuce and fill with Eggplant Caviar (page 39) or Spinach Dip (page 37).

*Make the full recipe of Parsley Dressing and use the rest of it as a dip—it's delicious!

Crab-Cucumber Rounds

Crisp cucumber slices, instead of pastry or bread, make refreshing low-calorie, low-fat canapé bases.

1   **seedless English cucumber**
1   **6-ounce can crab meat**
2   **tablespoons low-fat sour cream**
2   **tablespoons chopped chives or scallion**
    Salt and freshly ground pepper
    Paprika

Run tines of fork lengthwise along cucumber to make decorative edge on slices. Cut cucumber into slices ¼ inch thick.

Drain crab meat thoroughly. Mix with sour cream, chives, and salt and pepper to taste. Place small spoonful of crab mixture on each cucumber slice. Sprinkle with paprika. Cover and refrigerate for up to 4 hours. Makes about 36.

Calories per round: 4.3
Gram fat per round: 0.2

Diet Hint: Reducing fat content in hors d'oeuvres

• Instead of pastry cases, use: bread cases—see Stuffed Mushroom Croustades (page 34)—or whole wheat mini-pita rounds.

• To hold fillings, use hollowed-out cherry tomatoes, canned lichees, and cucumber slices.

• Avoid pâtés and mayonnaise-based dressings.

Hidden Fat in Foods

We all know that foods such as mayonnaise, whipped cream, and cheddar cheese are high in fat. Here are some other foods that are also deceptively high in fat.

	Grams fat/serving
Peanuts (½ cup)	36
Potato chips (1 small bag)	24
Corn chips (1 small bag)	20
Half an avocado	19
Eggnog, nonalcoholic (1 cup)	19
Peanut butter (2 tablespoons)	16
Olives, black (6 medium)	14
Pâté de foie gras (2 tablespoons)	13
Ice cream bar, chocolate-coated (2 ounces)	10
Chocolate bar (1 ounce)	9
Chocolate chip cookies (3 small)	9
Popcorn with butter (1 cup)	8
[Popcorn without butter (1 cup)	0.7]
French fried potatoes (10 pieces)	7
[Boiled or baked potato	trace]
Olives, green (8 medium)	6
Egg yolk	5

Green Bean Crunch

For a salty, crunchy snack that's low in fat and calories, try Green Bean Crunch instead of peanuts or potato chips. It's sure to be appreciated by dieters who crave salty foods. You can add other raw vegetables such as carrots, kohlrabi, fennel, and turnip.

1½	*pounds green beans*
½	*small head cauliflower*
1	*cup water*
1	*onion, chopped*
1	*large clove garlic*
1	*tablespoon lemon juice*
¼	*cup soy sauce*
¼	*cup water*
1	*tablespoon sunflower oil*
1	*tablespoon sesame seeds*
8	*large leaves Boston lettuce*

Remove stem end of green beans. Cut cauliflower into small florets. In large saucepan, bring 1 cup water to a boil; add onion, garlic, lemon juice, beans, and cauliflower. Reduce heat, cover, and simmer until vegetables are tender-crisp, about 8 minutes; drain, and discard garlic. Combine soy sauce, ¼ cup water, and oil; pour over vegetables. Cover and refrigerate for at least 1 hour.

Place sesame seeds on pie plate and toast in 325°F oven for 5 minutes or until golden brown.

Just before serving, toss vegetable mixture; remove from marinade. Arrange lettuce leaf on each plate. Spoon vegetable mixture onto lettuce and sprinkle with sesame seeds. Makes 8 servings.

Calories per serving: 45
Grams fat per serving: 1.7
Fiber: Good
Vitamin A: Good
Cauliflower is a good source of vitamin C.

Spinach-Stuffed Mushrooms

Fresh white mushrooms are delicious raw. Remove their stems and they're easy to stuff. If you're having a party, make the full recipe of Spinach Dip (page 37) or Parsley Dressing (page 95); use 1 cup as a stuffing for ½ pound mushrooms or cherry tomatoes, and the rest as a dip. They're a low-fat, low-calorie appetizer.

Stuffed Cherry Tomatoes

Cherry tomatoes are a colorful, fresh-tasting addition to an hors d'oeuvres platter. To stuff, cut off the top of each tomato, hollow out some of the pulp, and fill with Hummus (page 40), Spinach Dip (page 37), or Creamy Fresh Dill Dip (page 38).

Cherry tomatoes are a good source of vitamins A and C and are low in fat.

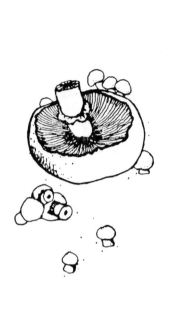

Stuffed Mushroom Croustades

These mushroom appetizers are so delicious, they just melt in your mouth. You can also use the croustade cases—thin bread slices molded into little cups—for other savory fillings; they're much lower in fat and calories than pastry. (See color photograph.)

24   **thin slices bread**
24   **medium-size white mushrooms**

STUFFING:
   1   **cup fine fresh whole wheat bread crumbs**
   1   **large clove garlic, finely chopped**
  1/4 **cup finely chopped fresh parsley**
      Salt and freshly ground pepper
   4   **teaspoons butter or margarine**
  2/3 **cup grated part skim mozzarella cheese**

Using 2½-inch cookie cutter or glass, cut out 24 rounds of bread. Press bread rounds into small muffin tins. Bake in 300°F oven for 20 to 25 minutes or until light brown. Remove from oven and let cool. (Croustades may be prepared in advance and stored in covered container for about 1 week or frozen for longer storage.)

Wash mushrooms and dry with paper towels; remove stems (save for use in soups). Store mushrooms in refrigerator until needed.

Stuffing: In food processor or mixing bowl, combine bread crumbs, garlic, parsley; and salt and pepper to taste; process until combined. Add butter and process just until mixed. (If mixing by hand, use soft or melted butter.) Spoon some stuffing into each mushroom cap; top with grated cheese.

Just before serving, place a mushroom into each bread case. Place on baking sheet and bake in 400°F oven for 10 minutes or until hot. If desired, turn on broiler for last minute. Serve hot. Makes 24.

Calories per piece: 93
Grams fat per piece: 2
Fiber: Two pieces are a good source of fiber.

Teriyaki Beef Rumaki

Wrap tender strips of marinated beef around crunchy water chestnuts for a delectable hot appetizer. The number and size of water chestnuts in a can will vary from brand to brand. To be on the safe side, buy an extra can. If they're very large, cut in half. Use enough meat just to cover the water chestnuts and overlap slightly so it can be secured with a toothpick. (See color photograph.)

<table>
<tr><td>³/₄</td><td>pound sirloin, round, or flank steak
(about ¹/₂ inch thick)</td></tr>
<tr><td>¹/₄</td><td>cup soy sauce*</td></tr>
<tr><td>1</td><td>clove garlic, finely chopped</td></tr>
<tr><td>1</td><td>tablespoon finely chopped onion</td></tr>
<tr><td>1</td><td>tablespoon granulated sugar</td></tr>
<tr><td>1</td><td>teaspoon Worcestershire sauce</td></tr>
<tr><td>¹/₂</td><td>teaspoon ground ginger</td></tr>
<tr><td>1</td><td>10-ounce can water chestnuts</td></tr>
</table>

Place meat in freezer for about 30 minutes or until firm for easier slicing. Cut off any fat. Slice meat across the grain into very thin strips about ¹/₈ inch thick and 3 inches long.

In a bowl combine soy sauce, garlic, onion, sugar, Worcestershire, and ginger. Add meat and stir to coat strips evenly. Marinate for 30 minutes at room temperature, stirring occasionally, or overnight in refrigerator.

Drain meat. Wrap one strip around each water chestnut and secure with toothpick. Arrange on baking sheet or in shallow glass serving dish. Broil for 3 to 4 minutes or until piping hot and cooked medium-rare (or microwave on High for 3 to 4 minutes, rotating dish ¹/₄ turn halfway through cooking time). Makes about 25.

Calories per piece: 37
Grams fat per piece: 0.8
Four pieces of rumaki are a good source of iron.

Cocktail Party for 25

Plan on 6 to 8 pieces per person. Multiply recipes according to number of guests.

Teriyaki Beef Rumaki
Crab-Stuffed Mini-Pitas (page 31)
Parsley or Watercress Dressing with raw vegetables (page 95)
Mushrooms stuffed with Spinach Dip (page 37)
Shrimp Wrapped with Snow Peas (page 30)
Salmon Mousse with Dill (page 41)

*Use naturally brewed light or sodium-reduced soy sauce for lower sodium (salt) content. Alternatively, you can dilute regular soy sauce with equal parts water.

Garlic Dip

Serve as a dip with raw vegetables, or as a sauce over baked potatoes, slided tomatoes or cucumber, steamed green beans, or fish fillets.

1½ **cups low-fat yogurt**
¼ **cup chopped scallions or chives**
2 **cloves garlic, finely chopped**
1 **tablespoon vegetable oil (optional)**
½ **teaspoon granulated sugar**

In bowl, combine yogurt, onions, garlic, oil, and sugar. Mix thoroughly. Cover and refrigerate until needed. Makes about 1½ cups.

	Per 1 tablespoon (with oil)	Per ¼ cup (with oil)
Calories:	24	96
Grams fat:	2	7

⅓ cup dip is a good source of calcium.

Variation:

Curry Dip: Add 1 teaspoon each curry powder and cumin to Garlic Dip. Amount of onions and garlic can be reduced.

Diet Hint: Reducing fat content in finger foods, snacks, and first courses

Instead of	Choose
Guacamole or mayonnaise	Low-fat cottage cheese- or yogurt-based dips
Peanuts and potato chips	Unbuttered popcorn and pretzels
Buttery crackers	Whole wheat crackers
Crackers with cheese	Pita bread
Oysters Rockefeller	Raw oysters
Cocktail sausages or frankfurters	Lean meats
Meat pâté	Vegetable pâté
Cream soup	Gazpacho or consommé
Pasta with cream sauce	Pasta with tomato sauce
Mayonnaise-dressed salads (egg, potato)	Green salads with yogurt dressing
Bloody Mary	Tomato juice

Spinach Dip

Perfect for dipping vegetables, this is also delicious as a filling for mushrooms and cherry tomatoes or as a dressing for salads and chilled cooked vegetables. Spinach is an excellent source of fiber and vitamin A (carotene). (See color photograph.)

1   **10-ounce package frozen chopped spinach, or 1 pound fresh**
1   **cup low-fat sour cream or low-fat small-curd cottage cheese**
½   **cup low-fat yogurt**
½   **cup finely chopped fresh parsley**
¼   **cup finely chopped scallions (including tops)**
1   **teaspoon salt**
  Freshly ground pepper

If using fresh spinach, trim tough ends. Boil or steam spinach until wilted; drain thoroughly and chop. If using frozen, squeeze by hand to remove all moisture or wrap in paper towels and squeeze.

In bowl, mix together spinach, sour cream, yogurt, parsley, scallions, salt, and pepper to taste. Cover and refrigerate for at least 4 hours or overnight to blend flavors. Makes 2 cups dip.

	Per 1 tablespoon (made with sour cream)
Calories:	10
Grams fat:	0.5
Vitamin A:	Good
Folacin:	Good

Spinach is an excellent source of fiber and vitamin A.

Serve with broccoli, snow peas, asparagus, carrots, turnip, green beans, cauliflower, and/or cherry tomatoes for good to excellent fiber.

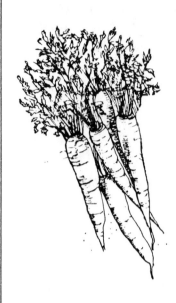

Crudités with Creamy Fresh Dill Dip

Prepare a colorful selection of raw vegetables—cauliflower, carrots, red, yellow, and green peppers, snow peas, baby corn, zucchini, Belgian endive, green and yellow beans, celery, fennel; cut them into strips suitable for dipping and arrange on a large platter with dip in center. (See color photograph.)

4	*carrots*
2	*sweet red, yellow, or green peppers*
½	*small cauliflower*
2	*Belgian endives*
¼	*pound mushrooms*

CREAMY DILL DIP:

¼	*cup chopped fresh dill or 2 teaspoons dried dillweed**
2	*tablespoons chopped fresh parsley*
1	*cup low-fat cottage cheese*
3	*tablespoons low-fat yogurt*
	Salt and freshly ground pepper

Cut carrots and peppers into strips. Separate cauliflower in florets. Separate endive leaves. Halve mushrooms if large. Refrigerate until serving time.

Creamy Dill Dip: Chop dill and parsley in food processor; add cottage cheese, yogurt, and salt and pepper to taste. Process with on-off turns to mix. Refrigerate.

At serving time, arrange vegetables on platter. Place dip in center. Makes 10 servings (about 1¼ cups dip).

Per 1 tablespoon of dip
Calories: 12
Grams fat: 0.25
Fiber will vary depending on vegetables (see chart, page 251).

*If using dried dillweed, add 3 tablespoons more chopped fresh parsley.

Compare: Dip made with:	Per 1¼ cups	
	Calories	Grams fat
low-fat yogurt	143	3.4
low-fat cottage cheese	230	4.4
sour cream	416	40
mayonnaise	1,616	179

Eggplant Caviar

Often called Poor Man's Caviar, this Mediterranean dip is delicious with raw vegetables or as a spread with melba toast.

1	eggplant (about 1¼-pounds)
3	scallions, finely chopped
1	large clove garlic, finely chopped
1	large tomato, peeled and chopped
½	stalk celery, finely chopped
¼	cup finely chopped green pepper (optional)
1	tablespoon fresh lemon juice
2	teaspoons vegetable oil
½	teaspoon salt
¼	teaspoon freshly ground pepper

Prick eggplant in several places with a fork. Place on baking sheet and bake in 400°F oven for 45 minutes or until soft, turning once or twice during baking. Let cool, drain off liquid, then peel and chop finely.

In mixing bowl, combine eggplant, scallions, garlic, tomato, celery, and green pepper if using; toss to mix. Add lemon juice, oil, salt, and pepper; mix well. Cover and refrigerate for at least 1 hour to blend flavors. Makes 3 cups.

	Per 1 tablespoon	Per ¼ cup
Calories:	5.8	23
Grams fat:	0.3	1.2

½ cup of Eggplant Caviar is a good source of fiber.

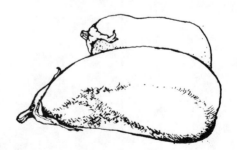

	Per ¼ cup	
Compare:	**Calories**	**Grams fat**
Chicken liver pâté	276	26.4
Eggplant Caviar	23	1.2

Hummus (Chick-Pea Dip)

Serve this Middle Eastern classic with pita bread or vegetables as an appetizer or for lunch snacks, or a picnic. For a casual dinner, add vegetable soup to the menu.

¼   **cup tahini (sesame paste)* or peanut butter**
1   **teaspoon cumin or more to taste**
½   **teaspoon salt**
2   **large cloves garlic, finely chopped**
3   **tablespoons lemon juice**
3   **tablespoons hot water**
1   **19-ounce can chick-peas (garbanzo beans), drained**
    Chopped fresh parsley (optional)

In small bowl, combine tahini, cumin, salt, and garlic; while stirring, slowly pour in lemon juice, then hot water. Purée chick-peas in a blender or a food processor, or pass through a food mill; add tahini mixture to purée and process or mix well. Taste and add more cumin and salt if desired. Spread hummus on dinner plate and sprinkle with chopped parsley. Makes 1½ cups.

	Per 1 tablespoon	Per ¼ cup
Calories:	75	300
Grams fat:	2	8
Fiber: Good—¼ cup: 3.4 grams		

Summer Lunch or Picnic

White wine spritzers
Whole wheat pita bread filled with Hummus (page 40), topped with alfalfa sprouts or shredded lettuce, and sliced tomatoes or sweet red peppers and a spoonful of low-fat yogurt seasoned with curry or cumin.
Strawberries

*Tahini is a sesame seed paste available in health food stores. If not available, substitute peanut butter.

Salmon Mousse with Dill

This smooth and creamy spread looks pretty when unmolded and surrounded with crackers, melba toast, or fresh vegetables. And because it's made without whipping cream and mayonnaise, it's low in fat and calories. If sockeye salmon is available in your area, buy it for its bright red color.

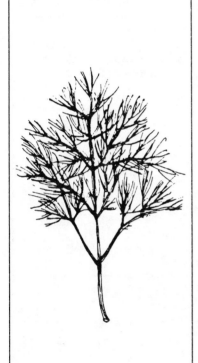

1	envelope unflavored gelatin
½	cup water or clam juice
⅓	cup finely chopped fresh dill or 1 teaspoon dried dillweed
2	tablespoons grated onion
1	tablespoon lemon juice
1	teaspoon salt
	Dash Tabasco sauce
¾	cup low-fat yogurt
½	cup low-fat sour cream
½	cup finely chopped celery
2	7¾-ounce cans salmon, drained

In small saucepan, sprinkle gelatin over cold water or clam juice; let stand until softened, about 5 minutes. Warm over medium heat until gelatin is dissolved. Let cool to room temperature. Stir in dill, onion, lemon juice, salt, Tabasco, yogurt, sour cream, and celery. Refrigerate until mixture begins to set.

Remove skin from salmon (but not bones—they're an excellent source of calcium); mash salmon with a fork or process in a food processor. Mix into gelatin mixture. Spoon into 4-cup mold. Cover and refrigerate until firm, at least 3 hours.

Unmold onto serving plate and surround with crackers, melba toast, or fresh vegetables. Makes about 4 cups.

	Per 1 tablespoon
Calories:	18
Grams fat:	1

First Courses

When planning menus, first decide on the main course. If it is low in fat and calories, you can then consider a hearty or cream soup or a more filling first course such as pasta or fish; if the main course is high in fat and calories, choose a light green salad or a clear soup for a first course. Many of the recipes in the book make wonderful first courses. Here are some suggestions.

Soups

Any soup recipe in this book can be a first course, but if it is a filling soup, serve in smaller amounts.

Salads

Roasted Red Pepper, Mushroom and Melon Salad (page 70)
Spinach and Red Cabbage Salad with Blue Cheese Dressing (page 71)
Greek Salad (page 87)
Arugula and Radicchio Salad with Balsamic Vinaigrette (page 76)
Pasta Salad with Sweet Peppers and Dill (page 90)
Julienne Vegetable Salad with Lemon Vinaigrette (page 77)
Artichoke-Tomato Salad (page 73)
Melon with Blueberries (page 214)

Fish

Brochettes of Salmon and Shrimp (page 138) (small portions) with Tomato Salsa (page 156) or Dill Mustard Sauce (page 155)
Mussels Sicilian Style (page 132)
Shrimp Wrapped with Snow Peas (page 30) with Garlic Dip (page 36)

Pasta

Capellini with Clam Sauce and Sweet Red Peppers (page 131)
Linguine with Shrimp and Tomato (page 133)
Fettucine with Fresh Tomatoes and Basil (page 146)
Pasta Salad with Sweet Peppers and Dill (pages 90)

Vegetables

Asparagus with Red Pepper Purée (page 166)
Asparagus with Orange Vinaigrette (page 94)
Baked Leeks au Gratin (page 170)
Corn on the Cob (serve, just picked, as a first course)
Broccoli Frittata (page 142)

Honey-Lime Dip for Fruit

Delicious at the beginning or end of a meal, this refreshing dip can be made with lemon or lime. Choose a colorful variety of fruit: strawberries, grapes, pineapple wedges, apple, mango, papaya, pear, peach, melon, sections of orange, or other seasonal fresh fruit. Arrange the fruit on a large platter with the dip in the center and let guests help themselves.

---

1   cup low-fat yogurt
    Grated peel of 1 lime
1   tablespoon lime juice
3   tablespoons liquid honey

Combine all ingredients and mix well; cover and refrigerate overnight (mixture will thicken upon standing). Makes 1 cup dip (enough for 6 servings).

	Per 1 tablespoon	Per ¼ cup
Calories:	16	64
Grams fat:	0.2	0.8

Fiber (including ¾ cup fresh fruit): Good (will vary depending on kind of fruit)
Vitamins A and C: Excellent (will vary depending on kind of fruit)

Sunday Afternoon Tea

Crab-Cucumber Rounds (page 32)
Watercress sandwiches
Fruit crudités with Honey-Lime Dip
Whole Wheat Raisin Scones (page 194)
Almond Meringues (page 191)
Tea

SOUPS

IF we had to choose only one type of food to exist on, many of us would quickly choose soups. A warming soup in winter is the best comfort food of all, and nothing beats a chilled soup in summer to cool and refresh. Any time of year, with a large bowl of soup for either lunch or dinner we need nothing more than thick crusty bread, perhaps a wedge of cheese or a salad, and fresh fruit for dessert. Some soups, such as Portuguese Collard Soup, Summer Garden Italian Soup with Pesto, or Split Pea Soup, can happily be eaten day after day until a large pot is finished.

Don't forget, when planning your menus, that soups are ideal for lunch or dinner, as either first courses or main courses, for party fare either after the theater or après-ski, or for a midnight meal.

Soups are often a good source of vitamins, particularly A and C, and of fiber. Cream soups are usually a good source of calcium, an important addition for adults who don't drink milk and therefore have difficulty meeting their calcium requirements.

Balkan Beet Cream Soup

Save any leftover cooked beets for this flavorful chilled soup. On a hot summer evening it's perfect for a light meal, along with a refreshing salad and warm bread. (See color photograph.)

½   **cup low-fat sour cream**
½   **cup low-fat cottage cheese**
4   **cups buttermilk**
4   **medium beets, cooked, peeled, and cut in cubes***
2   **hard-cooked eggs, peeled and chopped**
½   **unpeeled English cucumber, diced**
½   **cup chopped fresh parsley**
⅓   **cup sliced radishes**
3   **tablespoons chopped fresh chives or scallions**
Salt and freshly ground pepper

In blender or food processor, combine sour cream and cottage cheese; mix until smooth (or pass through a sieve). Combine with buttermilk; refrigerate.

Just before serving, divide beets among serving bowls. Stir remaining ingredients into buttermilk mixture and pour over beets. Makes 8 large servings (1 cup each).

Calories per serving: 125
Grams fat per serving: 5
Calcium, phosphorus, and vitamin C: Good

Diet Hint: Reducing fat content of soups

When making cream soups, substitute low-fat milk or buttermilk for cream or whole milk, and plain low-fat yogurt or low-fat sour cream for sour cream. You can add whipping cream to a hot soup and boil it without the soup curdling, but you cannot do this with the lower-fat substitutes. Here a little care is needed. It is best to warm the milk or yogurt gradually by slowly adding some of the hot mixture to it, then pouring it into the hot soup. The soup can be reheated, but don't let it boil.

See Table E (page 249) for the fat content of milk, yogurt, and various creams.

*See page 75 for instructions on cooking beets.

Chilled Melon and Yogurt Soup

A hint of ginger and fresh mint heightens the flavor of this light, refreshing summer soup. Serve it as a first course for brunch, lunch, or dinner. Be sure the cantaloupe you use is ripe.

1	**ripe cantaloupe**
1	**cup low-fat yogurt**
3	**tablespoons lemon juice**
½	**teaspoon peeled and grated fresh ginger root or ¼ teaspoon dried ginger**
2	**tablespoons chopped fresh mint leaves**

Cut cantaloupe in half and remove seeds. Scoop out pulp into container of food processor or blender and purée. You should have about 1½ cups purée. Add yogurt, lemon juice, and ginger; process to mix. Refrigerate until serving.

Serve soup in small bowls, topped with a sprinkling of fresh mint. Makes 4 servings (about ½ cup each).

Calories per serving: 80
Grams fat per serving: 0.3
Vitamins A and C: Excellent
Calcium: Good

60-Minute Dinner Party

Chilled Melon and Yogurt Soup
  (page 47)
Chicken with Snow Peas
  (page 105)
Rice
Tarragon Carrots (page 165)
Frozen Lemon Cream (page
  209)

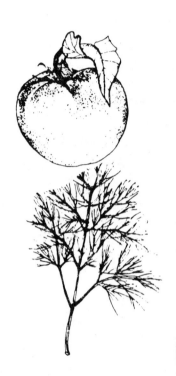

Fresh Tomato-Dill Bisque

Make this soup in the summer and fall when fresh dill is available and tomatoes are at their best.

3	large tomatoes, sliced
1	medium onion, sliced
1	medium clove garlic, chopped
3	tablespoons chopped fresh dill or 2 teaspoons dried dillweed
1	teaspoon salt
¼	teaspoon freshly ground pepper
¼	cup cold water
½	cup cooked macaroni
1	cup chicken stock
¾	cup milk
2	tablespoons tomato paste (optional)

GARNISH:

4 or 5	sprigs fresh dill, chopped
1	large tomato, chopped

In saucepan, combine tomatoes, onion, garlic, dill, salt, pepper, and cold water. Simmer, covered, for 15 minutes.

Transfer to blender; add macaroni and process for 1 minute. With machine running, add stock, milk, and tomato paste (if using). Refrigerate, covered, until thoroughly chilled.

Before serving, taste and adjust seasoning. Garnish each serving with chopped dill and tomato. Makes 4 servings (about ¾ cup each).

Calories per serving: 74
Grams fat per serving: 1.4
Vitamin C: Excellent
Vitamin A: Good

Compare: Fresh Tomato-Dill Bisque made with:	*Grams fat/serving*
low-fat milk	1.4
whole milk	2.8
light cream	8.7
whipping cream	15.4

Split Pea Soup

This is one of America's favorite soups. You can use the leftover bone from a cooked ham; many cooks add carrots and other vegetables. Don't add any salt until just before serving—there is often enough salt in the ham.

1	ham bone from cooked ham
1¼	cups split green peas (12 ounces)
8	cups water
4	onions, sliced
	Salt and freshly ground pepper

Remove any fat from ham bone, but leave meat. In large saucepan, combine ham bone, peas, water, and onions. Bring to a boil and skim off any scum.

Reduce heat and simmer, partially covered, for 1½ to 2 hours or until peas are soft, stirring occasionally. Makes 10 servings (about ¾ cup each).

Calories per serving: 66
Grams fat per serving: 0.2
Fiber: Good

The Taste of Smoked Foods Without Nitrates

The American Cancer Society Diet Guidelines recommend avoiding as much as possible smoked and heavily preserved and salted foods that contain nitrate. (Some nitrate is necessary to prevent botulism.) This means that preserved meats such as bacon, ham, and cold cuts should be eaten in moderation or avoided.

One way to have the taste of ham without eating too much of it is to serve Split Pea Soup, which has only small pieces of ham, as well as flavor from the ham bone.

Gazpacho

This cold Spanish soup is perfect for hot summer evenings. It's easy to make in a blender, but tastes best when the vegetables are chopped by hand.

1 clove garlic
½ small onion, quartered
½ green pepper, seeded and cut in chunks
3 tomatoes, quartered
1 cucumber, cut in chunks*
2 tablespoons wine vinegar
2 tablespoons olive oil
½ cup (approximate) chicken stock or
        water (optional)
     Salt and freshly ground pepper

In blender with machine running, drop garlic into feed tube, then add onion. Turn machine off and add green pepper, tomatoes, cucumber, vinegar, and oil. Blend just until chopped. If soup is too thick, add up to ½ cup chicken stock. Cover and store in refrigerator until serving time. Taste, and add salt, pepper, and more vinegar if necessary. Serve cold. Makes 6 servings (about ¾ cup each).

Calories per serving: 57
Grams fat per serving: 4
Fiber: Good
Vitamin C: Excellent
Vitamin A: Good

*Peel cucumber only if skin is tough or waxy.

Cream of Broccoli Soup

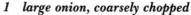

This is a delicious soup either hot or cold. You can top each serving with a spoonful of low-fat sour cream and chopped chives, dill, or parsley.

1   **large onion, coarsely chopped**
1   **medium carrot, sliced**
1   **small stalk celery (with leaves), sliced**
1   **clove garlic, finely chopped**
3   **cups chicken stock**
¼   **cup uncooked rice**
3   **cups coarsely chopped broccoli**
2   **cups low-fat milk**
1   **teaspoon salt**
    Pinch cayenne pepper

In large saucepan, combine onion, carrot, celery, garlic, and chicken stock; bring to a boil. Add rice; cover and simmer for 15 to 20 minutes or until rice is tender. Add broccoli; cover and simmer until broccoli is tender, about 5 minutes. Transfer to blender or food processor and purée (may be done in batches). Return to saucepan; add milk, salt, and cayenne. Serve hot. Alternatively, let cool, cover and refrigerate until serving time. Makes 8 servings (¾ cup each).

Calories per serving: 70
Grams fat per serving: 1.8
Fiber: Good
Vitamins A and C: Excellent

Broccoli is an excellent source of vitamins A and C and of fiber. It's also a cruciferous vegetable, and people whose diets frequently include cruciferous vegetables have been shown to have a lower risk of colon cancer. Other vegetables in this family are cabbage, cauliflower, Brussels sprouts, rutabaga, kale, and turnips.

Fresh Tomato and Basil Soup

This light, flavorful soup is perfect for a first course during tomato season. If fresh basil is not available, use fresh dill; you'll probably want to add more dill than the basil called for here.

1 **tablespoon butter**
1 **large clove garlic, finely chopped**
1 **medium carrot, diced**
1 **medium onion, chopped**
4 **cups chicken stock**
3 **cups diced ripe tomatoes**
3 **tablespoons chopped fresh basil leaves**
   Salt and freshly ground pepper

In heavy saucepan, melt butter; stir in garlic, carrot, and onion. Cook over medium-low heat until onion is tender. Add stock; cover and simmer for 20 minutes. Stir in tomatoes and simmer for 10 minutes. Just before serving, stir in basil and salt and pepper to taste. Makes 6 servings (about 1 cup each).

Calories per serving: 76
Grams fat per serving: 2.9
Vitamins A and C: Excellent
Niacin: Good

Spa Vegetable Soup

One of the easiest and quickest ways of making soup is simply to cook the vegetables in chicken stock. The trick is to have a colorful and interesting variety of vegetables. Here's a suggestion about which ones to use, but you may substitute any you have on hand—squash, turnip, lettuce, potatoes. Add chopped fresh herbs if available.

3	**cups chicken stock**
1	**carrot, diagonally sliced**
1	**cup broccoli florets**
1	**cup cauliflower florets**
½	**cup thinly sliced red cabbage or spinach**
1	**green onion, diagonally sliced**
	Salt and freshly ground pepper

In saucepan, bring chicken stock to a boil; add carrot and simmer for 10 minutes. Add remaining vegetables and simmer until tender. Season with salt and pepper to taste. Makes 4 servings (about 1 cup each).

Calories per serving: 52
Grams fat per serving: 1
Fiber: Good
Vitamins A and C: Good
Niacin: Good

Variation:

Seafood Vegetable Soup: After vegetables are tender, add 1 cup or 4 ounces of scallops, or scallops plus 4 ounces mussels in shell (optional). Simmer for 2 to 3 minutes longer or until scallops are opaque and mussel shells open. (Discard any mussel if shell doesn't open.)

Potage Vert

Here is a low-calorie, attractive green vegetable soup that's quick to prepare if you slice the vegetables in a food processor. For a creamy, thick soup, purée in a food processor or blender.

1   **large onion, peeled and sliced**
2   **celery stalks sliced**
2   **cloves garlic, finely chopped**
¼   **pound green beans, cut in 2-inch lengths**
1   **large carrot, thinly sliced**
6   **cups chicken stock**
½   **head romaine lettuce, sliced, or ½ 10-ounce package fresh spinach**
1¼   **cups frozen peas, thawed**
1   **cup sliced mushrooms (about 4 large)**
½   **teaspoon salt**
    Pepper
    Pinch nutmeg
⅓   **cup finely chopped fresh parsley**
1   **teaspoon dried dillweed or 2 tablespoons chopped fresh dill**

In large saucepan, combine onion, celery, garlic, beans, carrot, and chicken stock. Bring to a boil; cover, reduce heat, and simmer (at a low boil) for 15 minutes or until vegetables are tender. Add lettuce, peas, and mushrooms; cook until tender, 3 to 5 minutes. Add salt, pepper to taste, nutmeg, parsley, and dill. Serve hot. (Soup may also be puréed in food processor or blender and served warm or cold.) Makes 8 servings (about 1¼ cups each).

Calories per serving: 74
Grams fat per serving: 1.3
Fiber: Excellent
Vitamins A and C and niacin: Excellent
Iron: Good

Leek and Potato Soup

The base for this soup freezes well; just thaw, add cream, and serve hot or cold for a first course at a dinner party. For a lunch main course, top soup with garlic croutons and baby shrimp and chopped chives or scallions.

6 medium leeks
1 clove garlic, finely chopped
4 medium potatoes, peeled, cubed
8 cups chicken stock
1 cup light cream or low-fat milk
  Salt and freshly ground pepper
3 tablespoons finely chopped fresh parsley
  or chives

Trim all but about 2 inches of green part from leeks. Cut lengthwise halfway into white part. Spread apart and wash under cold running water. Slice thinly by hand or in food processor.

In saucepan, combine leeks, garlic, potatoes and chicken stock; simmer, partially covered, for 30 minutes or until vegetables are tender. Purée in blender or food processor. (Soup can be prepared ahead to this point; let cool, transfer to freezer containers, and freeze. Reheat gently before continuing with recipe.)

Just before serving, reheat soup; add cream, and salt and pepper to taste. Remove from heat. Sprinkle with parsley. Makes 12 servings (about 1 cup each).

Calories per serving (made with light cream): 91
Grams fat per serving: 3
Vitamin C and niacin: Good

This soup was traditionally made with whipping cream and butter. For a special occasion you might use light cream; otherwise use low-fat milk.

Variation:

Family-Style Leek and Potato Soup: Omit the cream and double the potatoes (don't peel them or you will lose fiber). Serve without puréeing. Leftovers can be puréed and frozen. You can also add any other vegetables such as carrots, green beans, and broccoli to this soup.

Summer Garden Italian Soup with Pesto

Pesto, a pungent Italian sauce made with fresh basil and garlic, adds exquisite flavor to soups, pasta, and vegetable dishes. This version has less oil than most, without any loss in flavor. If fresh basil isn't available, substitute ¾ cup fresh flat-leaf Italian parsley and 2 teaspoons dried basil. The flavor isn't the same but is quite acceptable. Add pesto sauce directly to soup before serving, or top each serving with a spoonful.

1	cup dried white beans
1	tablespoon vegetable oil
2	onions, coarsely chopped
3	tomatoes, chopped, or 2 cups canned, chopped
4	carrots, thinly sliced
2	potatoes, coarsely chopped
4	leeks (white part only), coarsely chopped (optional)
2	large stalks celery (with leaves), coarsely chopped
2	cups sliced green beans
1	medium zucchini, coarsely chopped
¾	cup broken egg noodles or spaghetti
	Salt and freshly ground pepper

PESTO:

2	cloves garlic
¾	cup fresh basil leaves (or fresh parsley leaves plus 2 teaspoons dried basil)
½	cup grated Parmesan cheese
2	tablespoons olive oil
¼	cup (approximate) hot soup liquid

Compare:

This pesto sauce has less than half the amount of fat of most pesto recipes.

Pasta with Pesto Sauce:

If making pesto to serve with pasta, use pasta cooking liquid instead of soup liquid and add enough to make sauce thick, yet pourable. This makes enough pesto for about ½ pound pasta. Return hot, drained pasta to saucepan; add pesto sauce and toss to mix.

Soak beans in water overnight and drain, or cover beans with cold water and bring to a boil; remove from heat and let stand for 1 hour, then drain.

In saucepan, combine beans with enough water to cover; bring to a boil. Reduce heat and simmer, covered, until beans are tender, about 1 hour; drain.

In skillet, heat oil over medium heat; add onions and cook, stirring, until tender, 6 to 8 minutes. Add tomatoes (if using fresh) and cook until soft, 3 to 4 minutes.

In large pot, bring 8 cups water to a boil. Add carrots, potatoes, leeks, celery, onion mixture, and tomatoes (if using canned); simmer for 15 minutes.

Add green beans, zucchini, egg noodles, and cooked white beans; simmer until vegetables are tender, 10 to 15 minutes, adding more water if needed. Add salt and pepper to taste.

Pesto: In food processor, combine garlic and basil; process until chopped. Add Parmesan and olive oil and process until smooth. Add enough warm soup liquid to make mixture the consistency of mayonnaise.

Ladle soup into bowls. Top each serving with a spoonful of pesto. Makes 10 servings (about 1⅓ cups each).

Calories per serving: 162
Grams fat per serving: 5
Fiber: Excellent
Vitamins A and C: Excellent
Iron and niacin: Good

Tomato-Bean Chowder

This comforting soup is perfect for a cold winter day, yet light enough for a summer supper.

> 4 onions, finely chopped
> 2 teaspoons chili powder
> 1 green pepper, seeded and chopped
> 1 28-ounce can tomatoes, undrained
> 4 cups beef or vegetable stock
> 1 19-ounce can red kidney beans, drained
> 1 19-ounce can chick-peas (garbanzo beans), drained
> Salt and freshly ground pepper

GARNISH:
> ½ cup finely chopped fresh parsley

In large, heavy saucepan, combine onions, chili powder, green pepper, tomatoes, and stock; bring to a boil, reduce heat, and simmer for 15 minutes. Break up tomatoes with back of spoon. Add drained beans and peas; simmer for 10 minutes. Add salt and pepper to taste. Garnish each serving with a sprinkling of parsley. Makes 10 servings (1 cup each).

Calories per serving: 233
Grams fat per serving: 2.6
Fiber: Excellent
Vitamin C: Excellent
Iron, vitamin A, phosphorus, and niacin: Good

Tri-Color Bean Soup

This hearty soup is a meal on its own. Serve with homemade bread and a crisp salad.

Rush-Hour Family Dinner

Tri-Color Bean Soup
Spinach Supper Salad (page 85)
Whole wheat rolls
Fresh Fruit

2 **large onions, sliced**
3 **cloves garlic, finely chopped**
4 **cups water**
2 **potatoes, cubed**
3 **carrots, cut in 1/4-inch slices**
1 **19-ounce can pinto beans, drained***
1 **19-ounce can kidney beans, baby lima beans, or black-eyed peas, drained**
1 **19-ounce can chick-peas (garbanzo beans), drained**
1 **teaspoon oregano**
2 **teaspoons basil**
    Salt and freshly ground pepper

In large saucepan, combine onions, garlic, water, potatoes and carrots; bring to a boil, cover, and simmer for 20 minutes or until vegetables are tender. Add all beans, oregano, basil, and salt and pepper to taste. Simmer for 5 to 10 minutes to blend flavors. Makes 12 servings (1 cup each).

Calories per serving: 120
Grams fat per serving: 1.6
Fiber: Excellent
Iron and vitamin A: Good

*If unavailable, substitute kidney beans, baby lima beans, or black-eyed peas.

Red Lentil Soup

Serve this soup with grilled cheese sandwiches or a salad for a quick meal. Be sure to use red lentils, not brown ones.

1   *8-ounce package dried red lentils (about 1 cup)*
3   *onions, coarsely chopped*
5   *cups water*
1   *bay leaf*
1   *large clove garlic, finely chopped*
1   *teaspoon dried thyme or 1 tablespoon chopped fresh*
3   *carrots, scraped and thinly sliced*
3   *tablespoons chopped fresh parsley*
    Salt and freshly ground pepper

Wash and drain lentils. In large saucepan, combine lentils, onions, water, bay leaf, and garlic. Cover and simmer for 1 hour. Add thyme and carrots; simmer, covered, for 30 minutes longer, or until carrots are tender and lentils are soft. Remove bay leaf. Add parsley, and salt and pepper to taste. Serve hot. Makes 8 servings (¾ cup each).

Calories per serving: 96
Grams fat per serving: 0.9
Fiber: Good
Vitamin A: Excellent

Brown or Red Lentils—is there a difference?

Yes. When cooked, red lentils are soft, while brown (or green) lentils retain their shape. Use red lentils for soups, and dishes (such as patties) where you want the lentils to be soft. Use brown lentils in salads, or in dishes where you want the lentils to retain their shape.

When cooked in a soup, red lentils turn an attractive yellow. Brown lentils are unappealing in soups, unless used in a small amount and combined with other vegetables.

Because lentils are a good source of protein, they are often included in meatless meals. One cup is an excellent source of fiber.

Nova Scotia Seafood Chowder

Serve as a main course, along with crusty rolls and a tossed green salad, for an après-ski dinner buffet or an after-theater party. You can make it early in the day to give the flavors a chance to develop. To save time, chop onions, celery, and carrots in a food processor.

2	**tablespoons butter or margarine**
1	**cup chopped onions**
2	**cups chicken stock or clam juice**
1	**cup chopped celery**
3	**carrots, coarsely chopped**
1	**teaspoon salt**
	Freshly ground pepper
1	**pound haddock fillets**
2	**cups whole milk or part whole, part low-fat milk**
⅓	**cup all-purpose flour**
1	**5-ounce can clams, undrained**
¼	**pound cooked small shrimp or lobster meat**

In large saucepan or soup kettle, melt butter; add onions and cook over low heat for a few minutes until soft. Stir in chicken stock, celery, carrots, salt, and pepper to taste. Bring to a boil; reduce heat and simmer, uncovered, for 20 minutes or until carrots are tender. Add fillets, cover, and cook for 5 minutes longer. (The chowder may be prepared ahead to this point and frozen; thaw and reheat before continuing with recipe.)

Stir about half of the milk into the flour to make a smooth mixture. Gradually stir mixture into soup, then stir in remaining milk and simmer until soup thickens slightly. Just before serving, stir in clams and shrimp; heat through. Taste and adjust seasonings. Makes 6 servings (about 1¼ cups each).

Calories per serving (made with whole milk): 225
Grams fat per serving: 6
Calcium: Good
Vitamin A and niacin: Excellent

Vegetable Borscht

Serve small portions of this colorful, bursting-with-flavor soup for a first course, or larger servings for a main course. Any leftover soup may be frozen.

1	*onion, chopped*
2	*large fresh beets, peeled and chopped*
1	*medium carrot, sliced*
1	*large potato, peeled and cubed*
4	*cups beef or chicken stock*
¼	*small head cabbage, shredded*
1	*tomato, chopped*
2	*tablespoons chopped fresh parsley*
½	*teaspoon dried dillweed*
1	*teaspoon salt*
	Freshly ground pepper
1	*teaspoon lemon juice*

GARNISH:

3	*tablespoons sour cream or low-fat yogurt*

In large saucepan, combine onion, beets, carrot, potato, and stock. Bring to a boil; cover and simmer for 30 minutes, skimming foam if necessary. Add cabbage, tomato, parsley, and dill; simmer for 30 minutes longer, or until vegetables are tender. Season with salt, pepper to taste, and lemon juice. Top each serving with 1 teaspoon of sour cream or yogurt. Makes 8 servings (1 cup each).

Calories per serving: 53
Grams fat per serving: 1.4
Fiber: Good
Vitamins A and C: Good

Diet Hint: Sour cream versus yogurt

Sour cream, the traditional garnish for borscht, has 2.5 grams fat per 1 tablespoon. If serving this soup as a main course, or as part of a meatless meal, the fat content is probably not significant, and sour cream may be used. If not, either omit the sour cream, or use low-fat yogurt, which has a negligible amount of fat per 1 tablespoon.

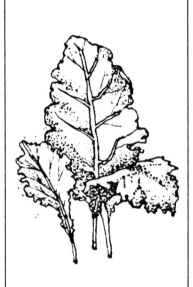

For a very low-fat diet, omit oil. Soup will taste fine.

Variation:

Spinach Soup: Substitute 1 10-ounce package fresh spinach, thinly sliced, for the collard.

*Chorizos are available in many European meat stores or delicatessens. Sweet means they are not hot and spicy. If they aren't available, use a small pepperoni instead.

Portuguese Collard Soup

Collard greens are similar in shape to large beet greens but look like dark green, flat cabbage leaves with coarse stems. This soup is so popular in Portugal that the grocery stores sell plastic bags full of thinly sliced collard leaves.

5   large potatoes, peeled and coarsely
      chopped
1   large carrot, cut in thin slices
6   cups water
14 large collard leaves
2   ounces chorizo (sweet smoked pork
      sausage),* about 3½ inches long
2   tablespoons olive oil
2   teaspoons salt

In saucepan, combine potatoes, carrot, and water; simmer over medium heat, until tender. Use a hand-held blender and purée in pot until smooth. (Alternatively, use slotted spoon to transfer potatoes and carrots to food processor, then blend until smooth. Return potato mixture to pan with cooking liquid and stir until combined.)

Remove tough stems from collard leaves. Thinly slice leaves in food processor or by hand into ⅛-inch strips or less. (Roll up 4 or 5 leaves, put into food processor, and slice crosswise.) You should have about 8 cups lightly packed, sliced collard leaves.

Peel casing from chorizo; slice as thin as possible (1/16 inch). Add sliced collard leaves and chorizo to soup; stir. Simmer, uncovered, for 10 minutes. Add oil and salt. If soup is too thick, add more water. Makes 10 servings (about 1 cup each).

Calories per serving: 185
Grams fat per serving: 6.7
Fiber: Excellent
Vitamins A and C: Excellent
Thiamine, calcium, and iron: Good

Fish Chowder, Family Style

Fresh or frozen fillets can be used in this recipe. Try haddock, or monkfish if it's available; it's sometimes called lobster fish because it tastes so much like lobster.

Super Supper

Fish Chowder, Family Style
Whole wheat buns
Tossed salad
Fresh fruit

2	**tablespoons butter**
1	**onion, finely chopped**
3	**potatoes, diced**
1	**carrot, finely chopped**
2	**cups water**
2	**cups whole milk**
1	**pound haddock, cod, monkfish, or other firm, white-fleshed fish fillets**
1	**cup kernel corn**
1	**teaspoon salt**
1/8	**teaspoon freshly ground pepper**
	Chopped fresh parsley

In heavy saucepan, melt butter; add onion, potatoes, and carrot, and cook over medium heat, stirring occasionally, for 5 minutes. Add water; cover, and simmer until vegetables are nearly tender, about 15 minutes.

Stir in milk, fish (if using monkfish, cut into chunks), and corn; simmer for 5 to 10 minutes, or until fish flakes and is opaque. Add salt, pepper, and parsley to taste. Makes about 6 cups (1½ cups main-course serving; ¾ cup appetizer serving).

Calories per main-course serving: 258
Grams fat per serving: 8
Fiber: Good
Vitamins A and C: Excellent
Calcium, phosphorus, and niacin: Good

Chicken and Leek Chowder

Here's a delicately flavored yet hearty soup. For a stew, simply thicken liquid with flour and add dumplings to top.

1	3-pound chicken
1	onion, coarsely chopped
1	stalk celery, chopped
8	cups water
10	black peppercorns
4	large leeks*
2	large potatoes, diced
3	medium carrots, sliced
2	large stalks celery, chopped
1	tablespoon chopped fresh thyme leaves or 1 teaspoon dried
1	tablespoon chopped fresh tarragon leaves or 1 teaspoon dried
1	tablespoon chopped fresh rosemary leaves or 1 teaspoon dried
2	bay leaves
1	cup kernel corn (frozen or canned)
1	cup lima beans (frozen or canned)
½	cup vermicelli or broken spaghetti
1	tablespoon butter or margarine
1½	cups low-fat milk
⅓	cup all-purpose flour
¾	cup chopped fresh parsley
2	teaspoons salt
	Freshly ground pepper

* If leeks aren't available, substitute 3 onions instead.

Remove as much fat as possible from chicken and discard. In large saucepan or soup kettle, combine chicken, onion, 1 stalk celery, water, and peppercorns. Bring to a boil; reduce heat, partially cover, and simmer for 1 to 1½ hours or until chicken is cooked. Let cool.

Remove chicken from pot and discard skin and bones; cut meat into bite-size pieces and set aside. Strain liquid and refrigerate. When cold, remove hardened fat from surface.

Trim leeks, leaving about 3 inches, or tender part, of greens attached. Cut stalks in half lengthwise and wash thoroughly under running water, holding leaves apart. Slice crosswise into ½-inch slices. In large saucepan, combine leeks, potatoes, carrots, and reserved chicken stock (from cooking chicken); bring to a boil and simmer for 15 minutes, stirring occasionally.

Add chopped celery and chicken meat to soup. Add

thyme, tarragon, rosemary, and bay leaves; simmer for 10 minutes. Add corn, beans, and vermicilli; cook for 10 minutes longer, or until vegetables are tender.

Just before serving, remove bay leaves and add butter. Stir enough of the milk into the flour to make a smooth, thin paste; gradually add to soup, stirring continuously. Add remaining milk, parsley, salt, and pepper to taste. Makes 10 large servings.

Calories per serving: 232
Grams fat per serving: 5.7
Fiber: Good
Niacin, vitamins A and C: Excellent
Iron: Good

Curried Apple and Zucchini Soup

This light cream soup has a lovely, delicate flavor. It's a good choice for a first course at a dinner party.

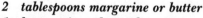

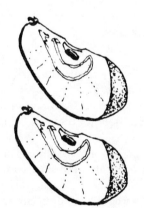

2	*tablespoons margarine or butter*
1	*large onion, chopped*
1	*apple, peeled, cored, and chopped*
1	*to 2 teaspoons curry powder*
4	*cups chicken stock*
¼	*cup uncooked rice*
2	*cups diced, unpeeled zucchini (½ pound)*
½	*teaspoon salt*
1	*cup low-fat milk*

In saucepan, melt butter; sauté onion and apple until soft. Sprinkle with curry powder; cook, stirring, for a few seconds. Pour in chicken stock; bring to a boil. Add rice, zucchini, and salt. Cover and cook until rice and zucchini are tender, about 30 minutes. Pour into blender and blend until smooth. Return to pan and add milk. Heat through. Serve hot. Makes 8 servings (¾ cup each).

Calories per serving: 79
Grams fat per serving: 3
Niacin: Good

Corn and Tomato Chowder with Tarragon

Fresh tarragon is a delightful addition to this soup. If it isn't available, but other fresh herbs are, use them instead (try coriander, also called cilantro, basil, rosemary, or oregano). If you can't find any fresh herbs, use 1 teaspoon dried tarragon.* Serve soup hot or cold.

1   **tablespoon butter**
¼   **cup chopped onion**
1   **clove garlic, finely chopped**
2   **tablespoons all-purpose flour**
1   **16-ounce can tomatoes, undrained**
2   **potatoes, diced**
1   **cup chicken stock**
2   **cups low-fat milk**
2   **cups kernel corn (canned, frozen, or from cooked cob)**
1   **tablespoon chopped fresh tarragon**
2   **tablespoons chopped fresh parsley**
2   **tablespoons chopped fresh chives or scallions**
   Salt and freshly ground pepper

In heavy saucepan, melt butter; add onion and garlic and cook over medium heat until tender. Sprinkle flour into pan and mix well. Stir in tomatoes and bring to a boil, stirring. Add potatoes and stock; boil gently for 15 minutes or until potatoes are tender.

In separate saucepan or in microwave oven, heat milk until hot but not boiling; pour into tomato mixture and stir in corn.

Just before serving, stir in tarragon, parsley, chives, and salt and pepper to taste. Makes 10 servings (¾ cup each).

Calories per serving: 88
Grams fat per serving: 2.3
Fiber: Good
Vitamin C: Excellent
Vitamin A: Good

*For a completely different but appealing flavor, substitute 1 teaspoon each curry powder and cumin for the tarragon.

Buttermilk-Cucumber Bisque

A refreshing beginning to a dinner or a picnic, this cream soup is low in calories and fat.

1	**English cucumber**
½	**teaspoon salt**
1¼	**cups buttermilk**
1¼	**cups chicken stock**
2	**tablespoons finely chopped scallion or fresh chives**
¼	**cup chopped fresh parsley**
	Freshly ground pepper

GARNISH:
> **Thin slices of unpeeled cucumber**

Peel cucumber only if skin is tough or waxed; remove seeds and chop cucumber by hand or in food processor. Place in colander; sprinkle with salt. Let drain for 30 minutes; pat dry.

In pitcher or large bowl, combine buttermilk, chicken stock, scallions, parsley, pepper to taste, and cucumber. Refrigerate for 2 to 8 hours. Taste and adjust seasoning if necessary. To serve, ladle into bowls; garnish with cucumber slices. Makes 4 servings (about 1 cup each).

Calories per serving: 46
Grams fat per serving: 1.1

SALADS

SALADS are achieving a new status in our meals, and deservedly so. Rock-hard tomatoes and flavorless iceberg lettuce are finally being pushed aside by crisp romaine and tender, buttery Boston lettuce. We now have so many wonderful fresh ingredients to work with that there has been a breakthrough in imaginative combinations of foods—the Melon and Bean Salad (page 82) is absolutely superb. In fact, we could feast on salads for months and never taste the same one twice. Red radicchio lettuce and nutty arugula are special treats to excite your palate. Pasta salads (now much more than macaroni with mayonnaise), Greek Salad, Chick-Pea with Red Onion and Tomato, plus many others, are wonderful as a main course as well as a side salad.

Moreover, health-conscious gourmets realize that salads are a good way to get fiber, vitamins, and minerals into our diet. When combined with high-fiber vegetables, such as spinach, beans, and chick-peas, and tossed with a low-fat dressing, such as Yogurt-Basil (page 95) or Blue Cheese Dressing (page 94), they are low in calories and fat, and high in fiber. This follows the American Cancer Society's recommendations for a low-fat, high-fiber diet.

Roasted Red Pepper, Mushroom, and Melon Salad

Roasted peppers have a rich flavor and a soft yet firm texture. If time is short, use the peppers raw. This salad is spectacular as an appetizer or for lunch. For a special occasion use shrimp.

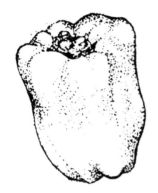

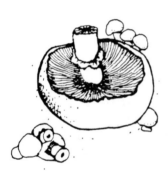

1	**large sweet red pepper**
1	**head Boston lettuce**
1	**honeydew melon or cantaloupe**
12	**white mushrooms**
2	**tomatoes, sliced**
½	**pound cooked salad shrimp (optional)**
1	**cup Orange Vinaigrette (page 94)**

Place red pepper on a baking sheet; roast in 375°F oven for 18 minutes; turn and roast on other side for 18 minutes longer, or until pepper is soft and blistered. Place pepper in paper or plastic bag; close bag and let pepper steam for 10 minutes. Using fingers and small knife, peel skin from pepper (it should come off easily); seed pepper and cut into strips.

Wash lettuce leaves; dry in spinner or with paper towels and refrigerate until needed. Cut melon in half; discard seeds. Peel and cut melon into wedges. Slice mushrooms.

Line 8 individual salad plates with lettuce leaves. Arrange wedges of melon in center; place red pepper strips on top of melon, mushrooms on one side, tomato slices on other, and shrimp (if using) over remaining lettuce. Drizzle Orange Vinaigrette over each salad. Makes 8 appetizer servings.

Calories per serving: 82
Grams fat per serving: 0.8
Fiber: Good
Vitamin C: Excellent
Vitamin A, iron, and niacin: Good

Spinach and Red Cabbage Salad with Blue Cheese Dressing

Red cabbage on dark green spinach is a striking color combination. Team it with Blue Cheese Dressing to add extra flavor and a creamy texture. (See color photograph.)

3	**cups packed spinach leaves (5 ounces)**
1	**cup grated red cabbage**
²⁄₃	**cup Blue Cheese Dressing (page 94)**

Wash spinach; discard tough ends and tear large leaves into 2 or 3 pieces. Just before serving, toss spinach with cabbage and dressing. (Alternatively, line individual plates with spinach; arrange cabbage in rings on top. Place spoonful of dressing in center of each plate.) Makes 4 servings (about 1 cup each).

Calories per serving: 56
Grams fat per serving: 2
Fiber: Good
Vitamins A and C: Excellent

Menu-Planning Tip for Busy Cooks

Once a week, make a large amount of a hearty soup, such as Tri-Color Bean Soup (page 58), Summer Garden Italian Vegetable Soup with Pesto (page 56), or Nova Scotia Seafood Chowder (page 60), and a salad that keeps well, such as Bermuda Bean Salad (page 89), Tabbouleh (page 74), or Chick-Pea Salad with Red Onion and Tomato (page 88). Along with thick fresh bread or toast, you'll be ready for rush-hour meals. Or serve either the salad or the soup with open-face grilled sandwiches, such as part-skin mozzarella on whole wheat buns sprinkled with oregano for a fast, nutritious meal.

Broccoli Buffet Salad

Serve this colorful winter salad as a first course, or as a main course with an omelet, soup, or grilled meat or chicken. It's ideal for a buffet table because you can make it ahead. For a variation, make the salad with Tomato-French Dressing (page 96) instead of the vinaigrette.

1	**1-pound bunch broccoli**
1	**red onion, thinly sliced and separated into rings**
¼	**pound small mushrooms**
¼	**pound feta cheese, crumbled**
2	**tablespoons toasted sliced almonds**

VINAIGRETTE DRESSING:

2	**tablespoons olive oil**
2	**tablespoons lemon juice**
3	**tablespoons water**
1	**clove garlic, finely chopped**
½	**teaspoon oregano**
	Salt and freshly ground pepper

Trim ends of broccoli. Cut into florets. Peel stalks and cut into 1-inch long strips about ¼ inch wide. You should have about 6½ cups of broccoli.

In large pot of rapidly boiling water, cook broccoli for 2 minutes; drain, and refresh under cold running water to prevent further cooking and to set color; drain and dry with paper towels. (If preparing a day in advance, do not cook broccoli; use raw.)

In salad bowl, toss broccoli with onion, mushrooms, and cheese.

Vinaigrette Dressing: Combine oil, lemon juice, water, garlic, and oregano; mix well. Pour over vegetables and toss to mix. Season with salt and pepper to taste. Toss again. Sprinkle almonds over top. Serve immediately, or cover and refrigerate for up to 3 hours. Stir before serving. Makes about 8 servings (1 cup each).

Calories per 1-cup serving: 120
Grams fat per serving: 7.8
Fiber: Excellent
Calcium, phosphorus, riboflavin, and niacin: Good
Vitamins A and C: Excellent

Artichoke-Tomato Salad

Tasty chunks of artichoke heart combine with cucumbers, tomatoes, and scallions for a sensational summer salad. Serve with soup or cheese and fresh bread for lunch or supper.

2	*tablespoons red wine vinegar*
¹/₂	*teaspoon Dijon mustard*
1	*clove garlic, finely chopped*
¹/₄	*cup vegetable or olive oil*
4	*scallions, chopped*
1	*long seedless cucumber, cut in chunks*
5	*tomatoes, coarsely chopped*
1	*14-ounce can artichoke hearts, drained and quartered*
2	*hard-cooked eggs, grated or chopped*
	Salt and freshly ground pepper
	Lemon juice

In large salad bowl, mix together vinegar, mustard, and garlic. Gradually whisk in oil. Add following ingredients in layers: scallions, cucumber, tomatoes, and artichokes. Sprinkle eggs over top. Cover and refrigerate.

About 15 minutes before serving, toss salad and add salt, pepper, and lemon juice to taste. Makes 6 large servings (about 1 cup each).

Calories per serving: 134
Grams fat per serving: 10
Fiber: Good
Vitamin C: Excellent
Vitamin A: Good

For Perfect Hard-Cooked Eggs:

For tender hard-cooked eggs without a dark ring, cover eggs with cold water and bring to a boil. Remove pan from heat; cover and let stand for 20 minutes before rinsing in cold water. Hard-cooked eggs can be stored for up to 1 week in the refrigerator.

Compare:	**Per 3¹/₂ ounces Grams fiber**
Lettuce (iceberg, romaine, or Boston)	1.5
Cabbage (red, green, or Savoy)	3.4
Spinach	3.9

Tabbouleh

This Mediterranean salad is delicious as part of a salad plate for picnics or lunches, and keeps well in the refrigerator. Bulgur, or cracked wheat, adds a nutty flavor and texture, and fresh mint lends a special touch. If mint isn't in season, simply omit it.

---

1   **cup bulgur (cracked wheat)**
⅓   **cup olive oil**
⅓   **cup lemon juice**
1   **cup finely chopped scallions**
2   **cups lightly packed chopped fresh parsley**
¼   **cup chopped fresh mint**
3   **tomatoes, diced**
1   **cucumber, peeled, seeded, and chopped**
1   **teaspoon salt**
    Freshly ground pepper

Soak bulgur in enough warm water to cover for 1 hour; drain well. Toss with oil, lemon juice, scallions, parsley, mint, tomatoes, and cucumber. Cover and refrigerate for at least 1 hour or overnight. Add salt, and pepper to taste. Makes 10 servings (about ⅔ cup each).

Calories per serving: 148
Grams fat per serving: 7
Fiber: Good
Vitamins A and C: Excellent

Picnic Salad Supper

White Kidney Bean Salad
    (page 84)
Pasta Salad with Sweet Peppers
    and Dill (page 90)
Tabbouleh
Whole wheat pita bread
Fresh peaches

Bulgur and Cracked Wheat

Bulgur and cracked wheat add a new dimension in texture, a nutty flavor, good nutrients, and fiber to dishes. They are both made from wheat berries and can be used interchangeably in most recipes. Cracked wheat is basically made from wheat berries that have been cracked, then coarsely milled. Bulgur is made from wheat berries that have been crushed, then either parboiled (European) or steamed (American), then dried. When made from club wheat or hard red winter wheat, it has much more fiber than when it is made from white wheat. Three and a half ounces of bulgur made from hard red winter wheat has 7 grams of dietary fiber.

    Bulgur and cracked wheat are available in some supermarkets, but you can always find them in health food stores. Use in salads (Tabbouleh) or stuffings, or mix with other grains or vegetables. To cook, combine with twice as much water as grain and simmer bulgur for about 15 minutes, cracked wheat for about 25 minutes, or until tender but not mushy.

Danish Cucumber Salad

Danes serve this salad often, especially with chicken or as a topping for open-face sandwiches. Sprinkling the cucumbers with salt draws out the water and makes the cucumbers crisp. The dressing has virtually no fat.

2   **English cucumbers**
1   **tablespoon salt**
1   **cup granulated sugar**
1   **cup vinegar**
    Salt and freshly ground pepper
    Chopped fresh dill

Thinly slice unpeeled cucumbers and place in bowl or sieve. Sprinkle with salt and let stand for 1 hour. Pour off liquid, rinse under cold running water, and pat dry; transfer to bowl.

In a small saucepan or microwave-safe dish, combine sugar and vinegar; stir over low heat or heat in microwave until sugar is dissolved; remove from heat and let cool. Pour over cucumbers; let stand for 30 to 60 minutes. Drain cucumbers; season with salt and pepper to taste. Garnish with chopped dill. Makes 6 to 8 servings.

Calories per serving: 40
Grams fat per serving: trace
Vitamin C: Good

To Cook Beets:

Cut tops from beets, leaving at least 1 inch of greens attached; don't trim off tapering root. (If beets are trimmed too close, color and vitamins are lost in the water.) Cook beets in boiling water or steam for 1 hour or longer, until beets are tender when pierced with a fork. Drain; under cold running water, slide off skins. Serve hot or let cool and add to salads.

Beet Greens

Don't throw out the beet tops. Cooked beet greens are an excellent source of vitamin A and folic acid, and a good source of vitamin C, riboflavin, calcium, and fiber. They're delicious steamed, boiled, or used instead of collard leaves in Portuguese Collard Soup (page 62).

Beet greens are best when cooked fresh from the garden or within a day or two of picking. They are prepared and cooked like spinach, but require a longer cooking time.

To prepare and cook beet greens: Cut off and discard tough stems or blemished leaves. Either steam in covered steamer over simmering water for 10 to 15 minutes or until wilted and tender, or boil, covered, in ½ inch of water in large saucepan for 10 to 15 minutes or until tender. Drain, and season with salt, pepper, lemon juice, and a dab of butter.

Arugula and Radicchio Salad with Balsamic Vinaigrette

Arugula is a tender lettuce with a buttery-nutty flavor—it's very special and very expensive. Radicchio, a red leaf lettuce, is much like a small cabbage in appearance. Together they make an elegant salad. The flavors are wonderful, so it isn't necessary to add a lot of other ingredients.

1	**small head radicchio**
1	**bunch arugula**
1	**head Boston or Bibb lettuce**
1	**orange (optional)**
¼	**cup coarsely chopped fresh parsley**
2	**tablespoons balsamic vinegar***
2	**tablespoons olive oil**
	Salt and freshly ground pepper

Separate lettuce leaves and wash thoroughly. Spin, or pat dry on paper towels. Wrap in paper towels and refrigerate until serving time. Cut off rind and white pith from orange (if using); cut into thin slices.

Just before serving, tear lettuces into large pieces. Combine with orange slices in glass salad bowl. (Alternatively, arrange lettuce on individual salad plates. Arrange orange slices on top.) Sprinkle with parsley, vinegar, oil, salt, and pepper, and toss to mix. Makes 6 servings.

Calories per serving: 56
Grams fat per serving: 4
Vitamin C: Excellent
Vitamin A: Good

Easter Luncheon

Melon with lime
Hard-Cooked Eggs with Curry
 Sauce over Rice (page 108)
Tossed salad greens with
 Balsamic Vinaigrette
Rhubarb Crumb Pie (page 228)

*Available in some supermarkets and most specialty food stores. It has such a wonderful, mild, sweet flavor that it is well worth searching out. If not available, use rice vinegar or lemon juice.

Julienne Vegetable Salad with Lemon Vinaigrette

White or yellow turnip or tender parsnips cut into julienne, or matchstick-size, strips are attractive additions to this salad.

> 1 cup julienne strips of carrot
> 1 cup julienne strips of zucchini
> 1 cup green beans, in 1½-inch lengths
> 1 cup julienne strips of celery
> Salt and freshly ground pepper

LEMON VINAIGRETTE:
> 1 tablespoon olive or walnut oil
> ¼ cup lemon juice
> 2 tablespoons chopped fresh parsley
> 2 tablespoons chopped scallion tops or fresh
>   chives
> 1 clove garlic, finely chopped

In bowl, combine carrot, zucchini, green beans, and celery.
Lemon Vinaigrette: In small bowl, combine oil, lemon juice, parsley, scallions, and garlic; mix thoroughly. Pour over vegetables and toss to mix. Add salt and pepper to taste. Cover and refrigerate until serving time. Makes 6 servings (⅔ cup each).

Calories per serving: 45
Grams fat per serving: 2.4
Fiber: Good
Vitamins A and C: Excellent

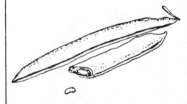

Making the Most of Salad Oils

1 tablespoon of oil contains 14 grams of fat, so use it sparingly. A heavier oil, such as olive or walnut, gives more of an oil flavor.

Coleslaw with Apple and Scallions

This is a good everyday summer salad, using new-crop, mild-flavored, crisp cabbage, and a fine winter salad when lettuce and tomatoes aren't plentiful or flavorful.

2   cups finely shredded cabbage
1   medium carrot, grated
½   green pepper, chopped
1   apple, chopped
2   scallions, chopped
    Salt and freshly ground pepper

YOGURT DRESSING: *
3   tablespoons low-fat yogurt
2   tablespoons low-fat sour cream
1   tablespoon low-fat mayonnaise
1   teaspoon lemon juice
¼   teaspoon dillweed

In serving bowl, combine cabbage, carrot, green pepper, apple, and scallions.

Yogurt Dressing: Combine yogurt, sour cream, mayonnaise, lemon juice, and dillweed; mix well. Pour over salad and toss to mix. Add salt and pepper to taste. Makes 4 servings (about ½ cup each).

Calories per serving: 60
Grams fat per serving: 1.7
Fiber: Good
Vitamin A: Excellent
Vitamin C: Good

*To reduce the fat content and to give a lighter flavor and texture, substitute low-fat yogurt for mayonnaise in salad dressing recipes, or use half yogurt and half sour cream. As your taste buds become familiar with the lighter flavor, you can work toward using all low-fat yogurt.

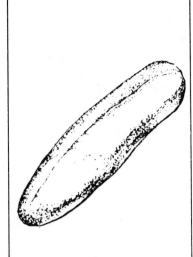

Tomato Raita

Raita is an East Indian type of salad. Delicious with curries, it adds a colorful note to the meal.

1	*medium cucumber*
1	*teaspoon salt*
2	*medium tomatoes*
1	*tablespoon finely chopped onion*
1	*cup low-fat yogurt*
1/4	*cup chopped fresh parsley*
2	*tablespoons chopped fresh coriander (cilantro)*
1	*teaspoon cumin*

Peel cucumber. Cut in half lengthwise and remove seeds. Cut into thin slices by hand or in food processor; sprinkle with salt and let stand for about 40 minutes. Drain cucumber, squeezing slightly to remove excess liquid.

Core tomatoes; cut into ½-inch cubes. Toss together tomatoes, cucumber, and onion; drain off any liquid. Combine yogurt, parsley, coriander, and cumin; pour over vegetables and mix with a spoon. Cover, and refrigerate until ready to serve. Makes 4 servings (about ¾ cup each).

Calories per serving: 59
Grams fat per serving: 0.3
Calcium: Good
Vitamin C: Excellent
Vitamin A: Good

Red Potato Salad with Sour Cream and Chives

Red-skinned potatoes add color, but any kind of new potato can be used. Be sure to leave the skin on, for additional flavor and fiber. Sour cream and yogurt combine to make a light yet creamy dressing that is much lower in fat than traditional mayonnaise.

6	medium-large red-skinned potatoes
½	cup low-fat sour cream
½	cup low-fat yogurt
¼	cup finely chopped fresh chives or scallions
1	teaspoon salt
	Freshly ground pepper

Scrub potatoes (don't peel). If large, cut in half or in quarters. Boil potatoes in their skins until fork-tender; drain. Shake pan over medium heat for a few seconds to dry potatoes. Cut into ½-inch cubes; let cool.

Combine sour cream, yogurt, and chives; toss with potatoes. Add salt, and pepper to taste. Refrigerate until serving. Makes 10 servings (½ cup each).

Calories per serving: 121
Grams fat per serving: 3
Fiber: Good
Vitamin C: Excellent

		Per ½ cup	
Compare:		*Calories*	*Grams fat*
Potato salad made with:			
mayonnaise		235	18
yogurt and sour cream		130	4

Chicken and Melon Salad

For an elegant but easy lunch, serve this main-course salad. The chicken can be cooked and all ingredients chopped a day in advance; then simply assemble the salad before serving. Instead of grapes or honeydew melon, you can substitute other melons, papaya, pineapple, mushrooms, or water chestnuts.

1	**small honeydew melon or canteloupe**
6	**cups cubed cooked skinless chicken***
2	**cups chopped celery**
2	**cups seedless green or red grapes**
1	**cup sliced water chestnuts (optional)**
½	**cup low-fat sour cream**
½	**cup low-fat yogurt**
1½	**teaspoons curry powder**
	Salt and freshly ground pepper

Cut melon in half and remove seeds. With melon baller, scoop out pulp (alternatively, cut into cubes). In large bowl, combine melon balls, chicken, celery, grapes, and water chestnuts (if using).

In small bowl, mix together sour cream, yogurt, and curry powder; stir gently into salad. Season with salt and pepper to taste. Makes 10 servings (about 1 cup each).

Calories per serving: 226
Grams fat per serving: 5
Vitamin C and niacin: Excellent
Phosphorus: Good

*For 6 cups cubed cooked chicken, use two 2½-pound roasting chickens or eight chicken breasts. To cook whole chicken in microwave oven, put chicken in microwave dish, cover dish with plastic wrap, folding back corner to vent steam. Microwave on High for about 17 minutes or until juices run clear when thigh is pierced. To cook conventionally, simmer whole chicken in water to cover for 1 hour or until tender, skimming off scum occasionally.

Melon and Bean Salad

Red kidney beans, juicy melon balls, and strips of sweet red pepper are a winning combination that will perk up any meal from cold turkey to meat loaf and sandwiches. (See color photograph.)

Summer Salad Buffet

Melon and Bean Salad
Julienne Vegetable Salad with
   Lemon Vinaigrette (page 77)
Red Potato Salad with Sour
   Cream and Chives (page 80)
Sliced tomatoes and cucumbers
Toasted French bread with
   garlic
Fresh fruit in watermelon boat

1   *cantaloupe or honeydew melon*
1   *19-ounce can red or white kidney beans,*
       drained
2   *scallions, including tops*
1   *small red pepper*
1   *clove garlic, finely chopped*
2   *tablespoons chopped fresh parsley*
2   *tablespoons lemon juice*
2   *tablespoons olive oil*
    Salt and freshly ground pepper

Cut melon in half; scoop out seeds. With melon baller, scoop out pulp (alternatively, cut into cubes). You should have at least 2 cups. Place melon balls in salad bowl and toss with kidney beans. Cut scallions and red pepper into thin strips about 1 to 1½ inches long; add scallions, peppers, garlic, and parsley to melon-kidney bean mixture; toss to mix.

Whisk together lemon juice and oil; pour over salad. Add salt and pepper to taste; toss to mix. Cover and refrigerate until serving time. (Salad may be refrigerated for up to 1 day.) Makes 8 servings (about ½ cup each).

Calories per serving: 114
Grams fat per serving: 3
Fiber: Excellent
Vitamins A and C: Excellent

Cracked Wheat with Peas and Scallions

Serve this as a salad or instead of a starchy vegetable such as potatoes. It's good with beef, chicken, and fish. Bulgur, or cracked wheat, is available at some supermarkets and most health food stores. Sesame oil, available in most supermarkets, adds a nutty flavor. If not available, use olive or safflower oil, or omit oil altogether.

¾	**cup bulgur (cracked wheat)**
2	**cups green peas (fresh or frozen)**
½	**cup chopped scallions**
3	**tablespoons lemon juice**
½	**cup chopped fresh parsley**
	Salt and freshly ground pepper
1	**tablespoon sesame oil**

Pour enough boiling water over bulgur to cover by at least 1 inch; let stand for 20 to 30 minutes or until tender and doubled in volume. Drain thoroughly, pressing out excess water. Cook peas in boiling water for 1 minute; drain.

In salad bowl, combine bulgur, peas, scallions, lemon juice, parsley, and salt and pepper to taste. Sprinkle with oil and toss to mix. Serve cold or at room temperature. Makes 8 servings (½ cup each).

Calories per serving: 125
Grams fat per serving: 2
Fiber: Excellent
Vitamin C: Excellent

White Kidney Bean Salad

Cannellini, or white kidney beans, team up well with summer garden vegetables. Add cucumber and tomato and you have a salad with a gazpacho-like flavor. If white kidney beans are not available, use red. Serve as part of a salad plate, with hamburgers or cold chicken, or toss with spinach for a substantial salad.

1 **19-ounce can white kidney beans, drained and rinsed (about 2 cups)**
⅔ **cup chopped cucumber**
⅔ **cup chopped Spanish or sweet onion**
1 **sweet green pepper, chopped**
1 **large tomato, chopped**
2 **tablespoons lemon juice**
1 **tablespoon olive oil**
  Pinch cumin
  Salt and freshly ground pepper
  Lettuce (optional)

In medium bowl, combine beans, cucumber, green pepper, tomato, lemon juice, oil, and cumin. Taste, and add more lemon juice, cumin, and salt and pepper to taste. Cover, and refrigerate until serving. Serve alone or on lettuce. Makes 6 servings (⅔ cup each).

Calories per serving: 120
Grams fat per serving: 3
Fiber: Excellent
Vitamin C: Excellent
Iron: Good

Summer Salad Plate

White Kidney Bean Salad
Deviled eggs
Spinach greens with Buttermilk
  Herb Dressing (page 92)

Jiffy White Kidney Bean Salad

Keep a can of white kidney beans on hand for a salad you can make at a moment's notice. Toss 1 19-ounce can well-drained and rinsed white kidney beans with 2 tablespoons olive oil, 2 cloves garlic, finely chopped, 1 cup chopped fresh parsley, and salt, pepper, and lemon juice to taste. Makes 4 servings.

10-Minute August Supper

Corn on the cob
Sliced tomatoes
Jiffy White Kidney Bean Salad
  (see above)
Whole wheat bread
Fresh blueberries or peaches
Milk

Spinach Supper Salad

On a hot summer night, this is a perfect light meal with French bread, cold soup and, for dessert, fresh fruit. This salad is also a natural with Oil-and-Vinegar Dressing (page 93).

---

  4 **cups torn spinach leaves (4 ounces)**
  ½ **head leaf lettuce, in bite-size pieces**
  2 **cups alfalfa sprouts**
  ¼ **pound mushrooms, sliced**
  1 **large tomato, cut in chunks**
  2 **scallions, chopped**
  ½ **cup crumbled feta cheese (2 ounces)**
  1 **hard-cooked egg, peeled and coarsely**
       chopped (optional)
  ¼ **cup Buttermilk Herb Dressing (page 92)**

In large shallow salad bowl, toss spinach, lettuce, and alfalfa sprouts, or arrange on individual salad plates. Sprinkle mushrooms, tomato, scallions, feta cheese, and egg (if using) over top. Drizzle dressing over all. Makes 2 main-course or 6 side-salad servings.

Main-course serving	Without dressing	With Buttermilk Herb Dressing
Calories per serving:	231	250
Grams fat per serving:	10.3	12

Fiber: Excellent

Calcium, phosphorus, iron, vitamins A and C, riboflavin, niacin, and thiamine: Excellent

---

Side-salad—size serving:	*Oil-and-Vinegar Herb Dressing*	*Buttermilk Herb Dressing*
Calories per serving:	92	83
Grams fat per serving:	5.6	4

Mediterranean Lentil Salad

Brown or green lentils are better than red for salads since they retain their shape after cooking and are tender but not mushy. This salad keeps well in the refrigerator and is delicious served on salad plates with sliced tomatoes, artichoke hearts, green beans, or asparagus in a vinaigrette.

1	**cup brown or green lentils**
1	**cup diced carrots**
1	**cup diced red onion**
2	**large cloves garlic, finely chopped**
1	**bay leaf**
½	**teaspoon dried thyme**
2	**tablespoons olive oil**
2	**tablespoons lemon juice**
½	**cup diced celery**
¼	**cup chopped fresh parsley**
1	**teaspoon salt**
¼	**teaspoon freshly ground pepper**

In saucepan, combine lentils, carrots, onion, garlic, bay leaf and thyme. Add enough water to cover by at least 1 inch. Bring to a boil; reduce heat and simmer, uncovered, until lentils are tender but not mushy, 15 to 20 minutes. Drain and remove bay leaf. Add oil, lemon juice, celery, parsley, salt, and pepper; toss to mix. Serve at room temperature. Makes 8 servings (½ cup each).

Calories per serving: 100
Grams fat per serving: 3
Fiber: Good
Vitamins A and C: Good

Greek Salad

This salad is wonderful made with home-grown sun-ripened tomatoes that haven't seen the inside of a refrigerator. Serve with soup or an omelet or as part of a salad plate.

3	**large ripe tomatoes, chopped**
2	**cucumbers, peeled and chopped**
1	**small red onion or 2 scallions, chopped (optional)**
¼	**cup olive oil**
4	**teaspoons lemon juice**
1½	**teaspoons crumbled dried leaf oregano**
	Salt and freshly ground pepper
1	**cup crumbled feta cheese (4 ounces)**
6	**black olives (preferably Greek), sliced**

In shallow salad bowl or on serving platter, combine tomatoes, cucumber, and onion. Sprinkle with oil, then with lemon juice, oregano, and salt and pepper to taste. Sprinkle feta cheese and olives over salad. Makes 6 servings (about ¾ cup each).

Calories per serving: 126
Grams fat per serving: 9
Vitamin C: Excellent
Vitamin A, calcium, and riboflavin: Good

Chick-Pea Salad with Red Onion and Tomato

Chick-peas, or garbanzo beans, are popular in the south of France and make a substantial salad. Serve with lettuce greens and a dark bread for a light yet high-fiber lunch or supper. This dish is ideal as part of a meatless meal—chick-peas are high in protein as well as in fiber and iron.

1	19-ounce can chick-peas, drained
2	tablespoons finely chopped red onion or scallions
2	cloves garlic, finely chopped
1	tomato diced
½	cup chopped fresh parsley
3	tablespoons olive oil
1	tablespoon lemon juice
	Salt and freshly ground pepper

In salad bowl, combine all ingredients and toss. Chill for 2 hours to blend and develop flavors before serving. Taste and adjust seasoning. Makes 4 servings (about ½ cup each).

Calories per serving: 361
Grams fat per serving: 14
Fiber: Excellent
Vitamin C and iron: Excellent
Vitamin A, niacin, thiamine, and phosphorus: Good

Summer Picnic in the Park

Broccoli Buffet Salad (page 72)
Red Potato Salad with Sour
    Cream and Chives (page 80)
Sliced cucumbers
Chick-Pea Salad with Red
    Onion and Tomato
Whole Wheat Irish Soda Bread
    (page 193)
Fresh peaches

Bermuda Bean Salad

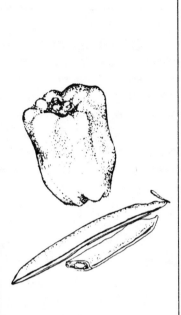

This is good with just about any meal, especially hamburgers. It keeps well in the refrigerator, and is handy at a picnic or for crowd-size entertaining. The recipe can easily be halved by using 10-ounce cans of beans and half a pound each of the fresh beans, but make the same amount of marinade. Bermuda onions—white and slightly flattened at the ends—have a wonderful sweet, mild flavor.

1	pound fresh wax beans
1	pound fresh green beans
1	19-ounce can red kidney beans, drained
1	19-ounce can lima or broad beans, drained
1	19-ounce can chick-peas, drained
1	19-ounce can pinto, romano, or white kidney beans, drained
2	sweet green peppers, chopped
2	Bermuda onions, thinly sliced into rings

MARINADE:

½	cup red wine vinegar
¼	cup vegetable oil
⅓	cup granulated sugar
⅓	cup packed brown sugar
1	teaspoon freshly ground pepper
½	teaspoon salt

Snap ends off fresh beans and cut into 1½-inch pieces. Cook beans in rapidly boiling water for 3 minutes; plunge into cold water until cool, then drain and pat dry. In large bowl, combine cooked beans, kidney beans, lima beans, chick-peas, green peppers, and onions.

Marinade: Combine vinegar, oil, both sugars, pepper, and salt; stir until sugars dissolve. Stir into bean mixture. Marinate in refrigerator overnight. Makes 20 servings (½ cup each).

Calories per serving: 248
Grams fat per serving: 4
Fiber: Excellent
Vitamin C: Excellent
Iron, thiamine, niacin, and phosphorus: Good

*If fresh dill isn't available,
substitute chopped fresh
parsley and 1 teaspoon each
dried dillweed and either basil
or oregano.

Pasta Salad with Sweet Peppers and Dill

You can add any of the usual salad ingredients to this dish except lettuce. It's terrific to have in the refrigerator for a quick and easy summer meal or a picnic. Vegetables can be crisply cooked, but you may like the crunch of them raw. To serve as a main course, add julienne strips of ham, chicken, and/or cheese.

3½   **cups rotini (corkscrew-shaped pasta) or
      ½ pound flat egg noodles**
¼   **pound snow peas or green beans**
3   **cups cauliflower, in small pieces**
1   **cup thinly sliced carrots**
2   **sweet peppers (red, yellow, green, or
      purple, or combination), chopped**
2   **scallions, chopped**
¼   **cup chopped fresh dill***

DRESSING:
2   **cloves garlic, finely chopped**
⅓   **cup red wine vinegar**
1   **tablespoon granulated sugar**
⅓   **cup vegetable oil**
3   **tablespoons water
      Salt and freshly ground pepper**

In large saucepan of boiling water, cook pasta until al dente (tender but firm—start tasting after 2 minutes for fresh pasta, 5 minutes for dry); drain, rinse under cold running water, and drain again.

Blanch snow peas or green beans in boiling water for 2 minutes. Drain; rinse under cold running water and drain again. Cut diagonally into 2-inch lengths.

In large bowl, combine cauliflower, carrots, peppers, scallions, dill, snow peas, and pasta; toss to mix.

Dressing: In food processor or bowl, combine garlic, vinegar, and sugar; mix well. While whisking or processing, gradually add oil and water; mix well. Pour over salad and toss to mix. Add salt and pepper to taste. Makes about 10 servings (1 cup each).

Calories per serving: 288
Grams fat per serving: 7.7
Vitamins A and C and thiamine: Excellent
Iron and niacin: Good
Fiber: Good, when made with whole wheat noodles (otherwise fair)

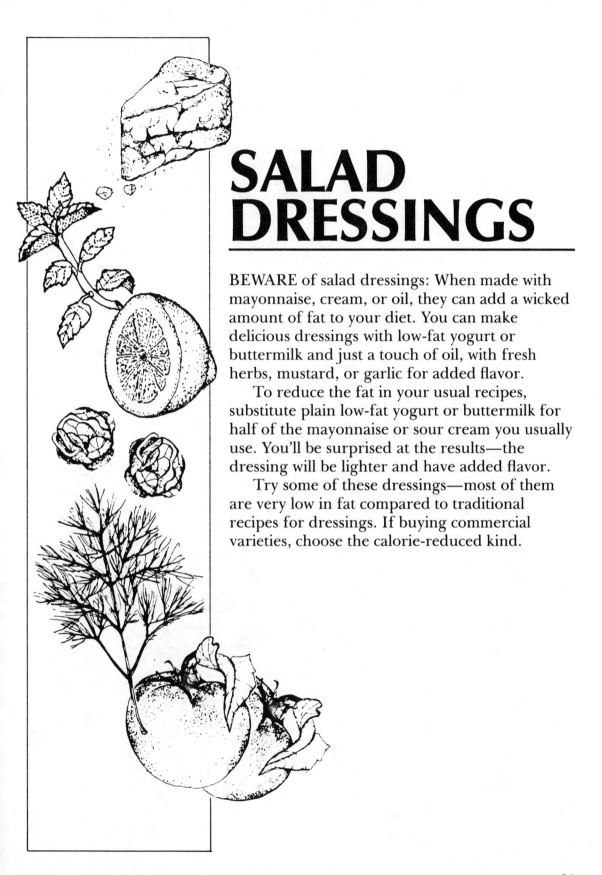

SALAD DRESSINGS

BEWARE of salad dressings: When made with mayonnaise, cream, or oil, they can add a wicked amount of fat to your diet. You can make delicious dressings with low-fat yogurt or buttermilk and just a touch of oil, with fresh herbs, mustard, or garlic for added flavor.

To reduce the fat in your usual recipes, substitute plain low-fat yogurt or buttermilk for half of the mayonnaise or sour cream you usually use. You'll be surprised at the results—the dressing will be lighter and have added flavor.

Try some of these dressings—most of them are very low in fat compared to traditional recipes for dressings. If buying commercial varieties, choose the calorie-reduced kind.

Buttermilk Herb Dressing

Buttermilk, made from low-fat milk, has only a trace of fat, yet it gives body and a wonderful flavor to this creamy salad dressing.

1 **cup buttermilk**
²/₃ **cup low-fat yogurt**
¼ **cup vegetable oil**
1 **tablespoon white vinegar**
1 **teaspoon dried dillweed or 3 tablespoons chopped fresh dill**
1 **teaspoon Dijon mustard**
½ **teaspoon salt**
1 **clove garlic, finely chopped**
   Freshly ground pepper
⅓ **cup chopped fresh parsley**

In mixing bowl or large measuring cup, combine all ingredients. Using whisk or fork, mix well. Cover and refrigerate for up to 1 week. Makes 2 cups.

Calories per 1 tablespoon: 18
Grams fat per 1 tablespoon: 1.5

Diet Hint: Reducing fat content of salad dressings

1. Instead of using mayonnaise, sour cream, or whipping cream in creamy dressings, substitute half or more of the quantity called for with low-fat yogurt, buttermilk, or cottage cheese and process in blender or food processor for a smooth texture.

2. Instead of using all the oil called for in an oil-and-vinegar dressing, use half the amount and make up the difference with water, orange juice, tomato juice, or beef stock (if the vinegar flavor is too strong, add a little sugar).

3. Use only enough dressing to lightly coat the salad ingredients. Don't let them drown!

4. When using mayonnaise and sour cream, buy light mayonnaise and light (or low-fat) sour cream.

5. Nuts are deceptively high in fat, although they are an excellent source of fiber. When the rest of the menu is high in fat, substitute water chestnuts for nuts in salads to achieve a crunchy texture.

Oil-and-Vinegar Dressing

Use this classic dressing on green salads, pasta salads, as a marinade for vegetables, or with any salad for which you want a vinaigrette dressing. It has about half the fat content of a homemade oil-and-vinegar dressing, but use it sparingly—it is still high in fat.

A classic oil-and-vinegar dressing uses 3 parts oil to 1 part vinegar (e.g., ¾ cup oil and ¼ cup vinegar), and has about 10 grams fat per 1 tablespoon. To reduce the fat content, replace half the oil with water, orange juice, or beef or chicken stock, and add a pinch of sugar.

Variation:

Herb Vinaigrette: Add ¼ teaspoon each crumbled dried thyme leaves and celery seed, and 1 tablespoon chopped fresh herbs or parsley.

2	**tablespoons vinegar**
½	**teaspoon Dijon mustard**
1	**clove garlic, finely chopped (optional)**
	Salt and freshly ground pepper
¼	**cup vegetable, olive, or walnut oil**
3	**tablespoons water**
½	**teaspoon granulated sugar (optional)**

In small bowl or food processor, combine vinegar, mustard, garlic (if using), and salt and pepper to taste, and mix well. While whisking or processing, gradually add oil. Add water; taste, and add sugar if desired. Makes about ½ cup.

Calories per 1 tablespoon: 51
Grams fat per 1 tablespoon: 6

	Per 1 tablespoon	
	Grams fat recipes in this book	**Grams fat conventional recipes or store-bought dressings**
Compare these salad dressings:		
Buttermilk Herb	1.5	6
Oil-and-Vinegar	6	10
Orange Vinaigrette	2.8	—
Blue cheese	0.8	8
Parsley Dressing	0.5	—
Yogurt-Basil	0.1	—
Tomato-French	1.4	6
Thousand Island		8
Mayonnaise		11
Half mayonnaise, half low-fat yogurt	6	—
Half light mayonnaise, half low-fat yogurt	3	—

Orange Vinaigrette

Use this citrusy oil-and-vinegar dressing with tossed salads or as a marinade for vegetables.

Spring Appetizer: Marinated Asparagus

Enjoy tender-crisp asparagus with a touch of tangy flavor. Sprinkle ½ cup Orange Vinaigrette over 1¼ pounds cooked asparagus. Makes 4 servings.

1   **clove garlic**
2   **tablespoons chopped fresh parsley**
2   **tablespoons white vinegar**
1   **teaspoon granulated sugar**
½   **teaspoon salt**
    Freshly ground pepper
¼   **cup orange juice**
2   **tablespoons vegetable oil**

In food processor or blender, chop garlic and parsley. Add vinegar, sugar, salt, and pepper to taste; process to mix. With motor running, gradually add orange juice and oil. Makes about ½ cup.

Calories per 1 tablespoon: 32
Grams fat per 1 tablespoon: 2.8

Blue Cheese Dressing

Using yogurt instead of traditional mayonnaise makes a lighter but equally good-tasting dressing that's much lower in both fat and calories. Use with green and spinach salads. (See color photograph.)

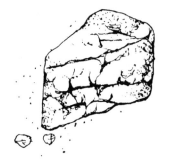

½   **cup crumbled blue cheese (about 2½**
      ounces)
1   **cup low-fat yogurt**
      1 clove garlic, finely chopped
      Pinch dry mustard
      Freshly ground pepper

In small bowl, use a fork to cream half of the cheese. Stir in yogurt, garlic, mustard, and pepper to taste; mix well. Stir in remaining cheese. Cover and store in refrigerator. Makes about 1⅓ cups.

Calories per 1 tablespoon: 16
Grams fat per 1 tablespoon: 0.8

▲ *Teriyaki Beef Rumaki (page 35); Stuffed Mushroom Croustades (page 34);*
Cherry Tomatoes Stuffed with Spinach Dip (page 37); Shrimp Wrapped with
Snow Peas (page 30); Crab-Stuffed Mini-Pitas (page 31).

▲ *Spinach and Red Cabbage Salad (page 71) with Blue Cheese Dressing (page 94).*

◀ *Crudités with Creamy Fresh Dill Dip (page 38).*

▲ *Balkan Beet Cream Soup (page 46).*

Melon and Bean Salad (page 82). ▶

▲ *Orange-Ginger Chicken with Leeks (page 103).*

▲ *Chicken Dijon (page 98); Two-Cabbage Stir-Fry (page 168); Mashed Turnips with Carrots and Orange (page 178).*

▲ *Navarin of Lamb (page 124)*.

Parsley Dressing

This thick, creamy dressing is sure to become a favorite. It's good with spinach and green salads, and can also be served as a dip for vegetables.

Variation:

Watercress Dressing: Substitute watercress leaves (stems removed because they have too strong a flavor, and also won't chop finely in food processor) for the parsley.

½	*cup chopped fresh parsley*
1	*cup low-fat cottage cheese*
1	*teaspoon Dijon mustard*
1	*egg (optional)*
1	*teaspoon lemon juice*
	Salt and freshly ground pepper

In food processor, chop parsley. Add cottage cheese, mustard, egg (if using), lemon juice, and salt and pepper to taste; process until well mixed. Cover and refrigerate until needed (will keep for a few days). Makes 1 cup.

Calories per 1 tablespoon: 16
Grams fat per 1 tablespoon: 0.5
Cottage cheese is a good course of calcium.

Yogurt-Basil Dressing

Use this low-fat dressing with green salads and cooked vegetable and pasta salads.

¼	*cup low-fat yogurt*
¼	*cup low-fat cottage cheese*
½	*teaspoon dried basil or 1 tablespoon chopped fresh*
½	*teaspoon granulated sugar*
2	*teaspoons lemon juice*
	Salt and freshly ground pepper

In a food processor or blender, combine all ingredients; blend until smooth. Makes about ½ cup.

Calories per 1 tablespoon: 9
Grams fat per 1 tablespoon: 0.1

For other salad dressing recipes, see:

Balsamic Vinaigrette (page 76)
Creamy Dill Dressing (page 38)
Lemon Vinaigrette (page 77)
Yogurt Dressing (page 78)

Tomato-French Dressing

This is one of the best low-calorie, low-fat vinaigrette dressings that we've tasted—keep it handy in your refrigerator.

½	**cup tomato juice**
1	**teaspoon cornstarch**
1	**tablespoon red wine vinegar**
1	**tablespoon olive oil**
½	**teaspoon Dijon mustard**
1	**small clove garlic, finely chopped**
½	**teaspoon dried tarragon, thyme, or basil, or chopped fresh herbs to taste**
	Salt and freshly ground pepper

In small saucepan whisk together tomato juice and cornstarch. Cook, stirring, over medium heat until mixture comes to a boil and thickens. Boil 1 minute, stirring constantly. Remove from heat and whisk in remaining ingredients. Transfer to jar with screw-top lid. Refrigerate until needed. Shake before using. Makes about ⅔ cup.

Calories per 1 tablespoon: 16
Grams fat per 1 tablespoon: 1.4

Portable Lunch Menus

Whole wheat pita bread filled with Hummus (page 40), leaf lettuce and alfalfa sprouts
Apple
Milk

Refrigerator Bran Muffins (page 188)
Raw vegetables (carrots, sweet green and red peppers, zucchini, cauliflower) with Creamy Fresh Dill Dip (page 38) or Parsley Dressing (page 95)
Banana
Milk

Green Bean Crunch (page 33) or carrot sticks
Whole wheat bagel with low-fat cream cheese
Date Meringue Squares (page 197)
Orange
Milk

Pita bread filled with Tabbouleh (page 74) or Hummus (page 40)
Cantaloupe wedge
Milk

Chicken sandwich on whole wheat bread
Fresh grapes or figs
Milk

POULTRY

FROM coq au vin to tandoori, chicken is a mainstay of cuisines around the world. Its flavor appeals to children as well as to adults and it lends itself to a wide range of seasonings and sauces.

For the health-conscious cook, chicken has the added benefit of being a low-fat source of animal protein. To keep the fat at a minimum, remove the skin and any visible fat from chicken pieces before cooking; from whole chickens cut the skin away before eating (whole chickens take longer to cook and would dry out if skin were removed before cooking). Roast chicken with skin has 53 percent fat calories, while roast chicken without skin has 31 percent fat calories.

Obviously, frying chicken adds to the fat intake; baking and broiling are far better cooking methods. Dark meat has considerably more fat than white meat. Small broilers or fryers have the least amount of fat, stewing hens the most. The larger and older the bird, the higher the fat content. When baking chicken, place pieces or whole bird on a rack so the fat drips off and the chicken doesn't roast in it. Though turkey and chicken are both low in fat, duck and goose have a much higher fat content.

Chicken Dijon

Crisp and juicy, this chicken can be prepared ahead of time and served hot, warm, or cold. (See color photograph.)

---

  6 **chicken breasts**
     Salt and freshly ground pepper
  ¼ **cup Dijon mustard**
  ⅓ **cup low-fat yogurt**
  ½ **cup fine fresh bread crumbs**
  1 **teaspoon thyme**

Remove skin from chicken. Sprinkle chicken lightly with salt and pepper. Mix mustard into yogurt. In another bowl, mix bread crumbs, thyme, ½ teaspoon salt, and ¼ teaspoon pepper.

Spread each piece of chicken with mustard mixture, then roll in bread-crumb mixture. Place chicken in single layer on lightly greased baking sheet. Bake in 350°F oven for 45 to 50 minutes for bone-in chicken, 30 to 35 minutes for boneless, or until golden brown and meat is no longer pink inside. Makes 6 servings.

Calories per serving: 190 (with skin on—241)
Grams fat per serving: 3.9 (with skin on—8.4)
Niacin: Excellent

In the Chicken Dijon the skin is removed to reduce the fat content. Because of the mustard mixture and bread-crumb coating, the chicken stays moist. Use whole wheat bread crumbs if possible. They are quick to make using a food processor.

Compare:	% fat calories
Roast chicken with skin on	53
Roast chicken without skin	31

Crispy Herbed Chicken

If you keep a small jar of herb-seasoned flour on hand you can make this chicken dish quickly. To make only enough seasoned flour for one meal, combine 2 tablespoons flour with 2 teaspoons of dried herbs, and salt and pepper.

6 chicken pieces (about 2 pounds, bone in)
2 tablespoons Herb-Seasoned Flour*
⅓ cup (approximate) warm water

Remove skin from chicken; rinse chicken under cold running water and pat dry with paper towels. Place chicken in single layer in lightly greased shallow roasting pan or baking dish. Use small sieve or spoon to sprinkle Herb-Seasoned Flour over chicken. Pour warm water down side of pan, not directly over chicken.

Bake, uncovered, in 375°F oven for 40 to 50 minutes or until chicken is no longer pink inside, basting occasionally with liquid in pan to brown top of chicken. Add more water if there's not enough liquid in pan for basting. Makes 6 servings.

Calories per serving: 200
Grams fat per serving: 3.2
Niacin: Excellent

August Dinner Menu

Fresh Tomato and Basil Soup
  (page 52)
Chicken Dijon (page 98)
Herbed Green Beans with
  Garlic (page 170)
Cracked Wheat and Basil Pilaf
  (page 183)
Melon with Blueberries (page
  214)

*Herb-Seasoned Flour

In small jar with lid, combine ½ cup all-purpose flour; 2 teaspoons each of salt, dried basil, and thyme; 1 teaspoon each of dried oregano, tarragon, and paprika; and ½ teaspoon pepper. Cover and shake to mix; store at room temperature. Makes about ⅔ cup.

Lemon Chicken Schnitzel

Serve this easy-to-make, moist and tender chicken to family and guests. You can use boneless turkey instead of chicken.

1	**pound boneless skinless chicken breasts**
	Juice of 1 lemon
1/4	**cup all-purpose flour**
1/2	**teaspoon salt**
1/2	**teaspoon thyme**
1/2	**teaspoon celery salt**
1	**egg**
1	**teaspoon water**
1/2	**cup fine dry bread crumbs**

Cut chicken horizontally into 1/4-inch-thick slices. Place between 2 pieces of waxed paper and flatten chicken, using the flat side of cleaver or bottom of bottle. Sprinkle chicken with lemon juice; let stand for 10 minutes.

In shallow dish, combine flour, salt, thyme, and celery salt; mix well. In another shallow dish, lightly beat egg with water. Dip chicken pieces into flour mixture, then into egg mixture, then into bread crumbs. Place on lightly greased baking sheet or in microwave dish. Bake in 400°F oven for 10 to 15 minutes, or microwave, uncovered, on High for 4 minutes, or until chicken is no longer pink inside. Makes 5 servings.

Calories per serving: 274
Grams fat per serving: 7.2
Niacin: Excellent
Iron: Good

1 pound of boneless chicken will usually serve four people; since the chicken in this recipe is cut into thin slices, it goes further, and you should be able to serve five people instead of four.

	per 3½ ounces
Compare:	**Grams fat**
Southern-fried chicken (1 piece)	17
Broiled chicken without skin (1 piece)	4

Sautéed Chicken with Yogurt and Mushrooms

A flavorful dish for company or guests; serve with broiled tomatoes, a green vegetable, and rice. Any kind of mushrooms can be used— domestic, wild, or dried (soak dried mushrooms for about 30 minutes). Try shiitake, cepe, oyster, or a combination.

6	**chicken pieces (about 2 pounds, bone in)**
1	**tablespoon all-purpose flour**
4	**teaspoons butter**
2	**onions, thinly sliced**
¼	**pound mushrooms, sliced**
½	**cup water (or half water and half white wine)**
½	**cup low-fat yogurt**
	Salt and freshly ground pepper

Remove skin from chicken. Sprinkle chicken lightly with flour. In large nonstick skillet, melt butter over medium-high heat; cook chicken until browned all over, about 5 minutes on each side. Reduce heat to medium or medium-low and cook for 10 minutes longer on each side or until meat is no longer pink inside. Remove from pan and keep warm.

Add onions and mushrooms to pan and cook, stirring often, until tender, 5 to 10 minutes. Stir in water and bring to a full boil, loosening any brown bits on bottom of pan to flavor sauce. Remove from heat and stir in yogurt, and salt and pepper to taste. Return chicken to pan and spoon sauce over it. Makes 6 servings.

Calories per serving: 200
Grams fat per serving: 6
Niacin: Excellent
Calcium, phosphorus, and riboflavin: Good

*Enoki mushrooms have long, thin stems and small, round heads. They add a woodsy flavor to salads, and are lovely as a garnish on cooked meats and chicken. They are available in some supermarkets and specialty vegetable stores. Eat them raw or cooked.

Breast of Chicken Florentine

Because most of the preparation can be done in advance, this recipe is ideal for a dinner party. Complete the dish just before serving, while you reheat the sauce and spinach. Serve with Two-Cabbage Stir-Fry (page 168) and brown rice.

¼ **cup all-purpose flour**
½ **teaspoon salt**
½ **teaspoon thyme**
  Pepper to taste
1 **egg, lightly beaten**
1 **tablespoon water**
½ **cup fine dry bread crumbs**
¼ **cup grated Parmesan cheese**
4 **boneless skinless chicken breasts (about 1 pound)**
  Tarragon and Mushroom Sauce (page 158)
  Enoki mushrooms for garnish (optional)*
1 **pound fresh spinach**
1 **teaspoon fresh lemon juice**
1 **teaspoon butter**
  Salt and freshly ground pepper

On plate, combine flour, salt, thyme, and pepper to taste; mix well. In shallow bowl, combine egg and water; mix well. On another plate, combine bread crumbs and cheese. Coat chicken pieces with seasoned flour; shake off excess. Dip into beaten-egg mixture, then roll in cheese-crumb mixture. Refrigerate for 20 minutes or up to 2 hours.

Prepare Tarragon and Mushroom Sauce.

On lightly greased baking sheet or microwave dish, bake chicken in 400°F oven for 15 minutes, or microwave, uncovered, on High for 4 to 5 minutes, or until chicken is no longer pink inside. If microwaving, let stand for 1 to 2 minutes (cooking time will vary, depending on thickness of chicken).

Trim stems from spinach. Wash and place in saucepan in just the water clinging to leaves. Cover and cook over medium-high heat until spinach has wilted. Drain thoroughly, and chop coarsely; toss with lemon juice, butter, and salt and pepper to taste. Place on warm plates or platter and keep warm in 200°F oven until chicken is cooked.

Place chicken on top of spinach and garnish with a few spoonfuls of Tarragon and Mushroom Sauce or raw enoki mushrooms, if desired. Makes 4 servings.

Calories per serving: 260
Grams fat per serving: 6.2
Fiber: Excellent   *Spinach is an excellent source of fiber.*
Vitamins A and C and niacin: Excellent
Iron and phosphorus: Good

Orange-Ginger Chicken with Leeks

A quickly prepared dish for guests or family. To make it special, garnish with slices of fresh mango or grapes and cooked snow peas. Serve over Chinese vermicelli or rice. (See color photograph.)

1¼	**pounds boneless skinless chicken breasts**
2	**large leeks**
1	**tablespoon butter**
2	**scallions, chopped**
¼	**cup dry white wine**
1	**tablespoon grated fresh ginger root**
1	**tomato, chopped**
½	**cup fresh orange juice**
½	**teaspoon grated orange rind**
1	**tablespoon all-purpose flour**
¼	**teaspoon granulated sugar**
1	**cup seedless green grapes**
	Salt and freshly ground pepper

Cut chicken into 1-inch cubes. Cut off and discard tough green part of leeks. Cut leeks in half and wash thoroughly under cold water. Cut into matchstick-size julienne strips.

In large, heavy skillet, melt butter. Cook chicken over high heat, for 2 to 3 minutes or until lightly browned; remove chicken to side plate. Stir in leeks and scallions and cook 1 minute, or until leeks are wilted. Stir in wine, ginger, and tomato, scraping up any brown bits from bottom of pan.

In measuring cup, combine orange juice, rind, flour, and sugar; mix until smooth. Pour into hot mixture, stirring constantly. Bring to a boil, stirring constantly, and simmer 2 to 3 minutes. (Dish may be prepared in advance to this point. Reheat sauce.) Return chicken to pan. Stir in grapes, and salt and pepper to taste. Makes 4 servings.

Calories per serving: 337
Grams fat per serving: 13
Vitamin C, niacin, and phosphorus: Excellent
Iron: Good

Chinese rice vermicelli, or rice sticks, are available in some supermarkets and Chinese grocery stores. They take only a few minutes to boil, or for a special occasion, drop a few noodles at a time into hot oil in a wok and watch them explode to six times their volume.

Stir-Frying

Almond Chicken

Stir-Frying

Stir-frying is a quick and easy way to cook meats, poultry, seafood, and vegetables. By frying in a small amount of oil over high heat and stirring continuously and vigorously, foods are seared and quickly cooked. Vegetables are crisp, and meats are very tender. You can control the temperature by moving the pan on and off the heat.

Use a wok or heavy skillet. Heat the oil before adding the ingredients; otherwise, the food will absorb the oil.

Because stir-frying is so fast, have all your food chopped and measured before you start to cook. The food should be evenly shredded, diced, or cut into thin slices so it will cook in a short time. By cutting meats and vegetables on the diagonal, meats will be tenderized, and the largest possible surface area of the food is exposed to the heat.

To add flavor and tenderize the meat, marinate it in advance; using cornstarch in the marinade helps to tenderize the meat and thicken the dish.

When using vegetables that require a longer cooking time, add a little water, chicken stock, or rice vinegar, then cover and steam for a few minutes. When preparing a large quantity of stir-fried vegetables, blanch the longer-cooking vegetables first (blanch cut vegetables in boiling water, then cool under cold running water, to prevent further cooking.)

*To toast almonds, roast on pie plate in 350°F oven for 5 minutes or until golden.

Stir-frying is a great way to make one pound of chicken serve four people and look like a lot. It's a great family dish that's pretty enough for casual entertaining. Serve over rice or noodles.

4	**teaspoons cornstarch**
2	**tablespoons soy sauce**
1	**pound boneless skinless chicken breasts, cut into strips**
½	**cup chicken stock**
2	**tablespoons vegetable oil**
2	**cups thinly sliced celery**
2	**cups diagonally cut green beans or snow peas**
1	**cup thinly sliced carrots**
1	**large onion, halved and thinly sliced**
2	**cloves garlic, finely chopped**
2	**tablespoons water**
	Salt and freshly ground pepper
2	**tablespoons toasted sliced almonds***

In medium bowl, combine 3 teaspoons of cornstarch and soy sauce; mix well. Add chicken and toss to coat; set aside. Stir remaining 1 teaspoon cornstarch into chicken stock; set aside.

Heat wok or heavy skillet over medium-high heat. When hot, add oil, then chicken, and stir-fry for 4 minutes or until chicken is opaque. Remove chicken and set aside. To wok, add celery, beans, carrots, onion, and garlic; stir-fry for 1 minute. Add water, cover, and cook for 2 minutes. Stir chicken stock mixture into pan. Return chicken to pan; cook, stirring, for another minute or until mixture boils and vegetables are tender-crisp. Season with salt and pepper to taste. Sprinkle with toasted almonds. Makes 4 servings.

Calories per serving: 340
Grams fat per serving: 13.7
Fiber: Excellent
Niacin and vitamin A: Excellent
Iron: Good

Chicken with Snow Peas

Keep this stir-fried dish in mind for when you want a special meal but have only a few minutes to prepare it.

1   **pound boneless chicken breasts**
3   **tablespoons dry sherry**
4   **teaspoons cornstarch**
2   **tablespoons low-sodium soy sauce***
1   **teaspoon granulated sugar**
2   **tablespoons vegetable oil**
4   **cloves garlic, finely chopped**
2   **teaspoons peeled and grated ginger root,**
      or ¾ teaspoon dried ginger
2   **onions, coarsely chopped**
½   **pound snow peas**
½   **cup water**

Remove skin from chicken. Cut chicken into 1-inch cubes. In bowl, combine 2 tablespoons of the sherry and 3 teaspoons of the cornstarch; mix well. Stir in chicken. Cover, and marinate in refrigerator for at least 1 hour.

In small bowl, combine soy sauce, remaining sherry, remaining cornstarch, and sugar; set aside.

In large, heavy skillet or wok, heat oil over high heat until hot but not smoking. Add chicken and stir-fry for 2 minutes. Remove chicken from pan and set aside.

Add garlic and ginger to pan; stir well, then add onions, snow peas, and water. Stir-fry for 2 minutes. Return chicken and soy-sauce mixture to pan and stir rapidly over high heat until hot. Serve with rice or noodles. Makes 4 servings.

Calories per serving: 307
Grams fat per serving: 13
Fiber: Good
Niacin: Excellent
Iron and vitamin C: Good

Step-by-Step Stir-Frying:

1. Have all ingredients cut and measured.

2. Heat wok or heavy skillet over high heat.

3. Add corn oil or vegetable oil, and when hot (but not smoking), add foods in the order listed in the recipe (or the ones requiring the longest cooking time first).

4. Use a long-handled spatula or wooden spoon to continuously stir the foods.

5. Add chopped garlic, ginger, or onions along with vegetables; soy sauce, sherry or vinegar at the end for flavor.

6. Mix 1 to 2 teaspoons cornstarch with 3 tablespoons cold water or stock and add to wok to thicken dish if desired.

Once you have tried a few recipes for stir-frying, you'll find it easy to improvise and make up your own. Stir-frying is an excellent way to stretch a small amount of meat, chicken, or seafood; and, along with the vegetables, stir-fries are ideal for low-fat main dishes.

*Soy sauce is very high in sodium. If possible, use a sodium-reduced soy sauce. If unavailable, look for naturally brewed soy sauce. The highest amount of sodium is found in chemically brewed soy sauce.

How to Microwave Whole Poultry

How to Microwave Whole Poultry

Microwaving is an easy, quick, and moist way to cook chicken or turkey when you want to remove the meat from the bone to use in salads, such as Chicken and Melon (page 81), or other dishes such as Casserole of Turkey with Melon and Curry Sauce (page 108).

- Tie wings and legs tightly to body.

- Place bird in shallow microwave dish; cover with plastic or waxed paper, folding back one corner to allow steam to escape.

- Microwave chicken on High for about 17 minutes for a 2½-pound chicken (6 to 7 minutes per pound), turning dish occasionally depending on your microwave.

- For 12-pound turkey, microwave breast side down, covered loosely with waxed paper or plastic wrap, on Medium-High for 24 minutes, draining liquid once or twice. Turn breast-side up and microwave on Medium-High for 45 minutes to 1 hour or until meat registers 190°F (older ovens may take a longer time). Drain off juices every 15 minutes.

- Pour juices from chicken into container and refrigerate or freeze—fat will rise to the surface and solidify; lift fat off and discard. Use remaining liquid for stock or for making sauces or soups.

- Let chicken stand for 10 to 15 minutes, turkey for 20 minutes, before using.

Microwave Tarragon Chicken with Julienne Vegetables and Yogurt Hollandaise

Leeks are particularly good when cooked in this way with chicken, but carrots, zucchini, celery, or a combination of these also work well. The sauce adds a rich flavor, yet it is deceptively low in fat and calories.

3	cups julienne strips of carrots, leeks, celery, or zucchini (in thin matchsticks strips)
4	chicken breasts
	Salt and freshly ground pepper
2	teaspoons butter
¼	teaspoon dried tarragon or 4 sprigs fresh tarragon or rosemary
½	cup Yogurt Hollandaise (page 159)

In baking dish just large enough to hold chicken in a single layer, sprinkle half the vegetables. Remove skin from chicken. Place chicken on top of vegetables and season lightly with salt and pepper. Top with remaining vegetables and dot with butter. Sprinkle with tarragon and pepper to taste.

Cover with plastic wrap, turning back one corner to vent; microwave on High for 6 minutes if boneless, 8 to 10 minutes bone in, or until chicken is no longer pink inside. Spoon Yogurt Hollandaise over and serve.

	Without Sauce	With Sauce
Calories per serving:	194	228
Grams fat per serving:	5.2	7

Fiber: Good
Niacin and vitamin A: Excellent
Vitamin C and phosphorus: Good

To Roast Turkey or Chicken

- Truss bird, with kitchen twine or string, tying wings and legs close to body (do not use synthetic twine).

- Place bird on rack in roasting pan. This makes it easier to remove the bird and keeps it from cooking in its own juices and fat.

- Cover turkey lightly with lid or foil (shiny side down); remove foil during last hour of roasting to brown top.

- Bird is cooked when it reaches an internal temperature of 185°F, drumstick moves easily in socket, and juices from thigh run clear when pierced.

- Remove from oven and transfer to platter; let stand for 15 minutes before carving.

- Roast turkey in 325°F oven for 4 to 5 hours for 12- to 14-pound bird (20 to 25 minutes per pound if small; 15 minutes per pound if over 18 pounds).

- Roast chicken in 350° oven for about 1½ hours for 4-pound chicken.

Diet Hint: Reducing fat content when roasting chicken or turkey

- Avoid recipes for stuffing that use oil or butter.

- Instead of stuffing poultry, slip garlic slivers, fresh herbs, and/or sliced fresh ginger root under the skin (between flesh and skin) or place in cavity.

- Stuff cavity with apple slices, onion wedges, mushrooms, and/or orange sections.

- If making a bread stuffing, use fairly fresh bread, or moisten stale bread with chicken stock; add chopped onions, celery, and apple instead of oil or butter.

- Instead of gravy, serve pan juices with fat removed, Blackberry Sauce (page 154), or cranberry sauce (you can add flavor and interest with chutney, port or brandy).

- Discard skin before serving.

Casserole of Turkey with Melon and Curry Sauce

Juicy melons, mangoes, or peaches add a festive touch and cooling flavor to this curry dish. The sauce is also good with shrimp or hard-cooked eggs. If using the sauce for shrimp, use half chicken stock and half clam juice.

3   **cups chopped cooked turkey (in large chunks)** *
2   **cups melon balls, sliced mango, or sliced peaches**

CURRY SAUCE:
1/4   **cup butter**
1   **onion, chopped**
1   **clove garlic, finely chopped**
4   **teaspoons curry powder**
1/2   **teaspoon chili powder**
1/2   **teaspoon cumin**
1/3   **cup all-purpose flour**
2   **cups chicken stock**
1/2   **teaspoon salt**
    Freshly ground pepper

Curry Sauce: In flameproof casserole or saucepan, melt butter. Stir in onion, garlic, curry powder, chili powder, and cumin; cook, stirring, over medium-low heat until onion is tender. Stir in flour and mix well. Stir in stock; bring to a boil, stirring, and simmer, uncovered, for 5 minutes. Add salt and pepper to taste.

Stir in turkey. (Casserole may be prepared in advance to this point, covered, and refrigerated for up to 2 days. Reheat gently before continuing with recipe.) Add melon and cook, stirring, until heated through, 5 to 10 minutes. Makes 6 servings.

Calories per serving: 209
Grams fat per serving: 7
Iron, niacin, and vitamin C: Excellent
Phosphorus: Good
Cantaloupe is an excellent source of vitamin A and a good source of vitamin C.

Holiday Buffet

Casserole of Turkey with Melon and Curry Sauce
Brown and wild rice
Chutney
Steamed snow peas
Tossed green salad
Orange Sponge Cake (page 225) with Sherry Orange Sauce (page 215) and Frozen Lemon Cream (page 209)

This is a lovely buffet casserole. It's easy to eat without a knife and can be prepared in advance. (Add melon just before serving.) It can be doubled or tripled for a larger number of guests. You can substitute chicken for the turkey and can also include shrimp. Plan on about ¼ pound snow peas per person or use less and serve another vegetable as well.

Hard-Cooked Eggs with Curry Sauce

Here's a delicious dish at an Easter buffet. In a large skillet, prepare Curry Sauce (page 108). Add peeled, halved, hard-cooked eggs (about 1½ eggs per person) to Curry Sauce and warm over low heat until heated through, about 5 minutes. Serve over rice.

*You can substitute chicken for the turkey. See page 106 for microwave instructions.

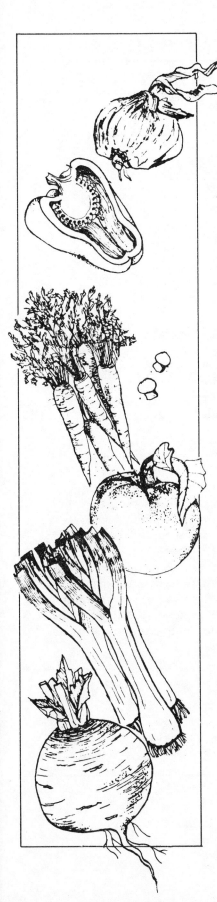

MEAT

MEAT can be a high source of fat in our diet. Two ways of reducing our intake of fat are to eat lean cuts of meat and to cut down on the amount of meat we eat. Remember: Cut down, *don't cut out.* Meat is an important source of complete protein; this means it has all the essential amino acids, the building blocks of protein. It is also an important source of iron in a form the body can easily use, as well as a good source of B vitamins and minerals. Just 3½ ounces of cooked lean beef (such as flank steak or lean hamburger) provides 30 grams of protein and nearly 4 milligrams of iron. This constitutes more than half of an adult's average daily requirement for protein and half of a male adult's average daily requirement for iron (teenagers, and women age 16 to 49, require up to 14 milligrams of iron a day).

The problem is that we don't often limit our meat portions to 3 to 4 ounces. We eat fatty marbled as well as lean meat. To help us eat more healthily, the meat industry is producing leaner beef and pork.

To keep the size of portions down, yet still make them appear satisfying, use meat in mixed dishes such as stir-fries, stews, and soups, or in sauces such as spaghetti sauce. Americans still aren't used to eating only 4-ounce portions of steak, but if you slice the steak in thin slices before serving, a 4-ounce portion will look like much more.

Stews are an ideal way to serve a 4-ounce portion of meat without it appearing skimpy. With the addition of vegetables, this not only stretches the meat but increases the fiber; add a potato (boiled with skin) per person, and the fiber content is up to 10 grams per serving.

When making any kind of stew, make it a day in advance and refrigerate. Any fat will solidify on the surface and then can easily be removed.

Diet Hint: Reducing fat content in meat and meat dishes

- Buy lean cuts of meat such as flank, sirloin tip, and lean ground beef.

- Trim all visible fat from meat.

- When browning meat or cooking ground meat, pour off all fat before adding other ingredients.

- Cook stews and simmered meat dishes a day in advance and refrigerate overnight. The next day you can easily remove hardened fat from the surface.

- Cut off any fat from cooked meat before eating.

- Processed meats such as salami, bologna, hot dogs, and sausages are usually high in fat as well as salt, nitrates, and nitrites. They should be avoided, or eaten in only small amounts.

See Table C, page 245, for fat content of various meats.

Beef and Vegetable Stew

This savory stew tastes even better the second day, when flavors have had a chance to blend. Serve with mashed or boiled potatoes or over hot noodles.

1¼	**pounds boneless stewing beef**
2	**tablespoons all-purpose flour**
1	**tablespoon vegetable oil**
2	**cups water**
3	**onions, quartered**
1	**bay leaf**
1	**teaspoon thyme**
½	**teaspoon marjoram or oregano**
1	**teaspoon salt**
¼	**teaspoon freshly ground pepper**
1	**teaspoon grated orange rind**
1	**small turnip (about 1 pound)**
5	**carrots**
1	**cup frozen peas**
¼	**cup chopped fresh parsley**
	Salt and freshly ground pepper

Cut all visible fat from beef and discard. Cut beef into about 1-inch cubes. Coat beef with flour, using up all flour.

In heavy pan, heat oil over medium-high heat. Add beef and cook, stirring, until brown on all sides.

Pour in water and bring to a boil, scraping up any brown bits on bottom of pan. Add onions, bay leaf, thyme, marjoram, salt, pepper, and orange rind. Cover, and simmer for 1½ hours.

Peel turnip and cut into ¾-inch pieces (you should have about 3 cups). Scrape carrots and cut into 1-inch pieces. Add carrots and turnip to pan; simmer, covered, for 40 minutes or until vegetables are tender. Add peas, parsley, and salt and pepper to taste. Simmer until peas are hot. Makes 6 servings.

Calories per serving: 220
Grams fat per serving: 9
Fiber: Excellent
Niacin and vitamins A and C: Excellent
Iron: Good

Marinated Flank Steak

This tender, flavorful steak is from one of the leanest cuts of beef.

1   **pound flank steak**
¼   **cup soy sauce**
¼   **cup vegetable oil**
2   **tablespoons vinegar**
2   **tablespoons sugar or honey**
1   **tablespoon peeled and grated fresh ginger root or 1 teaspoon ground ginger**

Score one side of the steak by making shallow cuts in a crisscross pattern. Place meat in a shallow dish or plastic bag. Combine soy sauce, oil, vinegar, sugar, and ginger; pour over meat. Cover, and refrigerate for 1 to 3 days, or at room temperature for up to 3 hours.

Remove meat from marinade and broil for 4 to 5 minutes on each side. Slice thinly on an angle across the grain. Serve hot or cold. Makes 4 servings.

Calories per serving: 200
Grams fat per serving: 9
Niacin: Excellent
Iron and riboflavin: Good

September Dinner

Balkan Beet Cream Soup (page 46)
Marinated Flank Steak
Tomatoes Florentine (page 163) or Tarragon Carrots (page 165)
Barley and Parsley Pilaf (page 175)
Lemon and Fresh Blueberry Tart (pages 218)

Making the Most of Pan Juices

Pan juices from roasting meats are flavorful and make a wonderful sauce. To remove fat, either use a large spoon and skim from surface, or add a tray of ice cubes to the juices (the fat will cool and harden, and can then be easily removed). Bring the juices to a boil; boil for a few minutes to evaporate extra water and reduce sauce to desired consistency. Pan juices and brown bits on the bottom of the pan after broiling or sautéing meats, chicken, and fish make a good base for a savory sauce. Simply spoon off the fat, add a large spoonful or two of wine, vinegar, or fruit juice, and bring to a boil, scraping up all brown bits from bottom of the pan. Add other flavorings, such as garlic, onions, shallots, and parsley, if desired. Remove from heat and stir in a little low-fat yogurt.

Stuffed Baby Peppers with Tomato-Basil Sauce

September Family Supper

Stuffed Baby Peppers with
   Tomato-Basil Sauce
Steamed carrots
Whole wheat bread
Peach Blueberry Crisp
   (page 219)

Stuffed peppers can be frozen. Cook frozen or thawed peppers in a microwave or in a conventional oven.

Variation:

Instead of Tomato-Basil Sauce, sprinkle stuffed peppers with grated Parmesan cheese or part skim mozzarella cheese before baking.

*Instead of tomato sauce, you can use ¼ cup each tomato paste and water (mixed), or ½ cup catsup.

Tiny sweet peppers are available in specialty grocery stores. For a truly attractive dish, use a variety of colors. If the tiny ones are not available, substitute regular-size peppers.

24	baby red, green, yellow, or purple peppers (or 12 medium)
¾	pound medium ground beef
1	onion, finely chopped
2	cups cooked rice (made from 1 cup raw)
1½	cups drained canned or chopped fresh tomatoes
½	cup tomato sauce*
1	tablespoon Worcestershire sauce
1	teaspoon salt
1½	cups Tomato-Basil Sauce (page 156)

Slice top off each pepper; chop tops and save to add to filling. Remove core, seeds, and white membranes from peppers. Blanch peppers in boiling water for 3 minutes; drain and set aside.

In large skillet or heavy saucepan, cook beef, onion, and chopped pepper until beef is browned and onions are tender. Drain off any fat. Stir in rice, tomatoes, tomato sauce, Worcestershire, and salt; simmer for 2 minutes. Spoon meat mixture into peppers. (Recipe may be prepared ahead to this point and refrigerated or frozen.) Bake in 350°F oven for 20 minutes or until hot. Serve with Tomato-Basil Sauce to spoon over. Makes 6 servings.

Calories per serving: 213
Grams fat per serving: 6
Vitamins A and C and niacin: Excellent
Iron, riboflavin, and phosphorus: Good

Tex-Mex Chili

Tex-Mex is hot and spicy Mexican food adapted to a north-of-the-border palate. You can add cooked brown beans or any other type of beans.

1	*pound lean ground beef*
2	*large onions, coarsely chopped*
2	*large cloves garlic, finely chopped*
2	*tablespoons (approximate) chili powder*
1	*teaspoon ground cumin*
1/2	*teaspoon oregano*
1/2	*teaspoon crushed red chili peppers*
1	*28-ounce can tomatoes*
4	*cups cooked red kidney beans or 2 19-ounce cans drained*
1	*teaspoon salt*
1 1/2	*cups kernel corn (canned, frozen, or fresh)*

In large, heavy saucepan or nonstick skillet, cook beef for about 5 minutes or until brown. Pour off any fat. Add onions, garlic, chili, cumin, oregano, and red pepper; cook, stirring, over low heat until onions are tender (about 5 minutes). Stir in tomatoes, kidney beans, and salt; bring to a boil, reduce heat, and simmer for 20 minutes, or until desired consistency is reached. Add corn, and cook until corn is heated through. This is a mild chili; add more chili powder and crushed red chili peppers to taste. Makes 6 servings.

Calories per serving: 349
Grams fat per serving: 8.5
Fiber: Excellent
Iron, niacin, vitamins A and C: Excellent
Thiamine: Good

Old-Fashioned Meat Loaf

Adding bran to this family favorite is an easy way to add a little fiber to your meals. Serve with baked potatoes and a green vegetable.

1	**pound lean ground beef**
1	**large onion, finely chopped**
¼	**cup natural bran**
1	**slice whole wheat bread, crumbled**
½	**teaspoon thyme**
½	**teaspoon salt**
	Dash Worcestershire sauce
	Freshly ground pepper
1	**cup tomato juice or tomato sauce**
1	**egg, lightly beaten**
1	**tablespoon chopped fresh herbs—thyme, rosemary, savory, sage (optional)**

In mixing bowl, combine beef, onion, bran, bread crumbs, thyme, salt, Worcestershire, and pepper to taste. Stir in tomato juice, egg, and herbs (if using); mix lightly. Turn into 9 × 5-inch loaf pan or baking dish. Bake in 350°F oven for 45 minutes, or until brown and firm to the touch.
Remove from oven; pour off fat. Makes 5 servings.

	Using lean ground beef	Using regular ground beef
Calories per serving:	186	267
Grams fat per serving	9.5	17
Niacin: Excellent		
Iron and phosphorus: Good		

Hamburgers au Poivre

Dress up peppery hamburgers with this shallot-yogurt sauce.

1   **pound lean ground beef**
2   **teaspoons peppercorns**
1   **tablespoon vegetable or corn oil**
1   **tablespoon finely chopped shallots***
1   **tablespoon red wine vinegar**
¼   **cup low-fat yogurt or sour cream**
1   **tablespoon finely chopped fresh parsley**

Divide meat into 4 portions and shape into hamburger patties.

Put peppercorns on large piece of waxed paper or foil. Using bottom of heavy skillet or pan, crack peppercorns coarsely. Spread out peppercorns, and place patties on top. Press patties down; turn patties over and sprinkle any remaining peppercorns over top. Press peppercorns so they stick to meat.

In large skillet, heat oil over high heat. Add patties and cook over high heat for 2 to 3 minutes or until browned; turn and cook other side for 1 to 2 minutes or until browned, and at desired degree of doneness (reduce heat if necessary to prevent burning).

Transfer patties to warm serving plate. Pour off fat in pan; add shallots and wine vinegar and cook over medium heat, scraping up brown bits from bottom of pan. Remove from heat; add yogurt and stir to mix well. Stir in parsley. Place patties on individual plates, then spoon sauce over them. Makes 4 servings.

Calories per serving: 244
Grams fat per serving: 13
Niacin: Excellent
Iron and phosphorus: Good

*If shallots are unavailable, use cooking onions.

Pot-au-Feu

This French savory classic consists of a pot roast of beef and various vegetables slowly simmered together. The heavenly broth can be served as a first course, and the meat and vegetables as the main course. Or the meat and vegetables can be served as the main course, then any leftovers added to the broth and served for dinner another night. It's best to start this a day in advance and refrigerate it overnight so the fat will solidify on top for easy removal. Serve with boiled potatoes and horseradish.

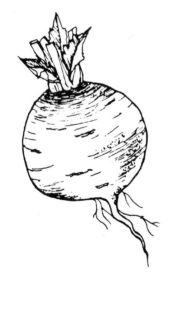

4	*pounds (approximate) boneless rib, blade, or sirloin tip roast*
8	*cups water*
3	*large carrots*
3	*large onions*
2	*small white turnips (or half a yellow rutabaga)*
2	*stalks celery*
1	*small cabbage*
	Salt and freshly ground pepper

Be sure roast is securely tied. Place in large, deep saucepan or flameproof casserole and add water. Bring to a boil over medium heat; remove any scum. Simmer for 1½ hours.

Meanwhile, peel carrots, onions, and turnips; cut into even-size chunks and add to pot with meat. Cut celery into similar-size chunks and add to stock. Cover, and simmer for another hour or until vegetables are nearly tender. Skim off fat or refrigerate overnight, then remove fat.

Reheat if necessary. Quarter cabbage and add to pot. Cook for 15 minutes or until tender. Season with salt and pepper to taste. Remove meat to platter; let stand for 10 minutes before carving. Keep vegetables warm, and serve broth as a first course (save a little to pour over meat and vegetables). Makes 10 servings.

Calories per serving (including broth): 420
Grams fat per serving: 20
Fiber: Good
Vitamins A and C, iron, and niacin: Excellent

Tomato Sauce Provençal with Veal on Pasta

Thin strips of tender veal combine with tomatoes and Provençal seasonings of garlic and parsley in this simple dish. The small amount of veal keeps the cost within reason and the fat content down.

1 **tablespoon butter**
1 **large onion, chopped**
2 **tablespoons (approximate) water**
½ **pound whole wheat noodles**
1 **28-ounce can plum tomatoes, drained**
½ **pound lean veal**
4 **cloves garlic, finely chopped**
½ **cup finely chopped fresh parsley**
Salt and freshly ground pepper

In large heavy skillet, melt butter over medium heat; cook onion until tender. Add water to prevent onion from burning (add more if necessary).

In large pot of boiling water, cook noodles until al dente (tender but firm). (Dry whole wheat noodles require a longer cooking time than regular noodles or fresh pasta; follow package directions and taste every few minutes.)

Coarsely chop tomatoes and add to onion in skillet. Cut veal into 2-inch strips about ¼ inch wide; add to skillet and cook over medium heat, stirring occasionally, until veal is cooked (about 2 minutes). Add garlic and parsley.

Drain noodles and arrange on hot dinner plates or platter. Season sauce with salt and pepper to taste; spoon over noodles. Serve immediately. Makes 4 main-course servings, 6 appetizer servings.

Calories per main-course serving: 574
Grams fat per main-course serving: 12
Fiber: Good
Iron, vitamins A and C, and niacin: Excellent
Thiamine and riboflavin: Good

Fettuccini with Clam Sauce

For a delightfully easy pasta dish, substitute 1 5-ounce can of clams, drained, for the veal in Tomato Sauce Provençal with Veal on Pasta. Toss with hot, drained fettuccine. For two people, use the same basic recipe but substitute 1 16-ounce can tomatoes for the larger can; use slightly less pasta (toss any leftover noodles with sauce and reheat the next day in microwave or saucepan).

Mexican Pork Stew

Pork cut in cubes cooks much faster than chops or a roast, making this ideal for a quick family dinner. Add dried hot chili peppers to taste and other vegetables, such as eggplant or zucchini in season. Serve with boiled potatoes or over hot noodles.

1	**pound boneless pork (shoulder or tenderloin)**
1	**teaspoon vegetable oil**
1	**large onion, coarsely chopped**
1	**clove garlic, finely chopped**
1	**16-ounce can tomatoes**
1	**small sweet green pepper, coarsely chopped**
2	**tablespoons chopped fresh parsley**
½	**teaspoon dried cumin**
½	**teaspoon dried oregano**
¼	**teaspoon dried thyme**
	Salt and freshly ground pepper

Cut off any visible fat from pork. In heavy saucepan or skillet, heat oil over medium-high heat; add pork a few pieces at a time and cook until lightly browned on all sides. (There should be enough fat in pork to prevent burning—a heavy or nonstick pan is important.) Add onion and garlic; cook, stirring, until onion is tender, about 2 minutes.

Stir in green pepper, tomatoes, parsley, cumin, oregano, thyme, and salt and pepper to taste. Bring to a boil; reduce heat and simmer, covered, for 15 minutes. Makes 4 servings.

Calories per serving: 252
Grams fat per serving: 13.6
Vitamins A and C, niacin, and thiamine: Excellent
Iron and phosphorus: Good

Shopping Tip

Boneless pork shoulders are often featured in supermarket specials. Cut the meat into cubes or strips, discarding fat, and use in stews and stir-fries or on skewers. Package them in 1-pound portions (or a size to suit your household) and freeze until needed.

Chinese Pork and Vegetables

Children will enjoy this dish because it isn't very spicy. You may want to add sherry, dried chili peppers, or perhaps more ginger to taste. Serve on a bed of hot, fluffy rice.

1	**tablespoon cooking oil**
1	**pound lean boneless pork, cut in thin strips**
2	**cloves garlic, finely chopped**
1	**onion, sliced**
5	**stalks celery, diagonally sliced**
4	**carrots, diagonally sliced**
1	**tablespoon peeled and grated fresh ginger root**
1	**cup hot chicken stock**
2	**tablespoons low-sodium soy sauce**
1/4	**teaspoon freshly ground pepper**
1	**small head cabbage**
1	**tablespoon cornstarch**
2	**tablespoons cold water**
	Lemon juice
	Salt and freshly ground pepper

In wok or large, heavy skillet, heat oil over high heat. Add pork and stir-fry until pork is no longer pink. Add garlic, onion, celery, carrots, and ginger; stir-fry until onion is tender. Add stock, soy sauce, and pepper. Cover, and simmer for 5 minutes.

Shred cabbage (you should have about 4 cups packed shredded cabbage). Stir into skillet and cook for 3 to 4 minutes longer or until vegetables are tender-crisp. Blend cornstarch with cold water; gradually add to skillet, stirring constantly, until sauce thickens. Add lemon juice, salt and pepper to taste. Makes 5 servings.

Calories per serving: 279
Grams fat per serving: 14
Fiber: Excellent
Thiamine, niacin, and vitamins A and C: Excellent
Iron, riboflavin, and phosphorus: Good

Fresh Ginger

Whenever possible, use fresh, not ground, ginger in recipes calling for fresh—the flavor is far superior. Fresh ginger can elevate an ordinary dish into something really delicious. Use it in stir-fries, with vegetables, and in stuffings, stews, and other savory dishes. This brown, knobby root is available in the vegetable section of most supermarkets and fruit and vegetable stores.

To buy:

Buy young ginger with pale brown skin. Shriveled skin is a sign of age. Avoid buying ginger with cracks, mold, or a musty smell.

To store:

Wrap ginger in a plastic bag to prevent drying out and store in a cool place or refrigerate for a few weeks. For longer storage, freeze ginger, or peel, place in a jar, and cover with sherry or vodka; seal and refrigerate.

To use:

With a vegetable peeler or knife, peel skin from portion of root you plan to use. Depending on the recipe, either grate or chop it before adding to the dish. Sometimes a slice of fresh ginger is added to a marinade or stew, then discarded before serving.

Pork Tenderloin with Rosemary and Thyme

Pork tenderloin is the leanest cut of pork with little fat. This very easy-to-prepare dish is ideal for a casual Friday night dinner party. In fall, serve with squash or sweet peppers, in summer with Tomatoes Provençal (page 163), in spring with Asparagus with Red Pepper Purée (pages 166), and in winter with Braised Red Cabbage (page 168). (See color photograph.)

> 2 **tablespoons Dijon mustard**
> 1 **teaspoon rosemary**
> ½ **teaspoon thyme**
> ¼ **teaspoon whole black peppercorns, crushed**
> 1 **pound pork tenderloin**

In small bowl, combine mustard, rosemary, thyme, and peppercorns and mix. Spread over pork. Place in roasting pan. Roast in 350°F oven for 35 to 45 minutes or until no longer pink inside. Garnish with fresh rosemary. To serve, cut in thin slices. Makes 3 servings.

Calories per serving: 248
Grams fat per serving: 14
Iron, thiamine, and niacin: Excellent
Phosphorus: Good

Compare:	4-ounce serving Grams fat
Spareribs	44
Pork chop—lean and fat	42
Pork chop—lean only, fat removed	14
Pork tenderloin	14

Sherry-Braised Ham with Curried Fruit

This dish is wonderful for entertaining a large group. If you remove the fat before cooking, there will be less salt as well. Cooking ham in liquid makes it very juicy and tender.

1	*9-pound cooked ham*
1	*large onion, sliced*
2	*carrots, sliced*
2½	*cups beef stock*
½	*cup sherry*
1	*bay leaf*
½	*teaspoon thyme*
1	*bunch watercress*
	Curried Fruit with Rice (page 181)

Remove skin and all but a very thin layer of fat covering ham. Place ham in roasting pan; arrange vegetables around it. Pour beef stock and sherry over ham; add bay leaf and thyme. Bring to a boil on top of stove. Cover and bake in 325°F oven for 2½ hours, basting 3 or 4 times during roasting. Uncover and cook for 15 minutes longer. Remove from oven; transfer to platter and let stand for at least 15 minutes before carving (discard vegetables in pan).

Slice ham into thin slices. Garnish platter with watercress and be sure to include a sprig on each person's plate. Arrange hot Curried Fruit with Rice on another plate. Makes about 18 servings.

Calories per 3-ounce serving: 186
Grams fat per 3-ounce serving: 8.1
Vitamin A, iron, niacin, and thiamine: Excellent
Riboflavin: Good

Easter Dinner

Crudités with Creamy Fresh
  Dill Dip (page 38)
Sherry-Braised Ham with
  Curried Fruit
Rice
Green beans
Lemon Charlotte with
  Strawberries (page 216)

Warning:

Because of the nitrites in most ham it should be eaten only occasionally and in moderation.

Ginger-Apricot Stuffed Lamb with Kumquats

Bright orange, grape-size kumquats are a most attractive garnish for this dish. Make it in the spring when kumquats are readily available.

1   *3-pound boneless leg or shoulder of lamb,*
       ready for stuffing (about 5 pounds, bone in)

STUFFING:
1   *teaspoon butter*
1   *small onion, chopped*
²/₃   *cup coarsely chopped dried apricots*
1   *tablespoon peeled and grated fresh ginger*
       root
1   *teaspoon grated lemon rind*
       Salt and freshly ground pepper

GLAZE:
2   *tablespoons apricot jam*
½   *teaspoon Dijon mustard*
¼   *teaspoon ground ginger*

GARNISH:
8   *apricots (fresh or canned), halved and*
       pitted
8   *sprigs fresh rosemary or watercress*
8   *small ripe kumquats (optional)*

Stuffing: In small skillet, melt butter over medium heat; add onion and cook until soft. Stir in apricots, ginger, lemon rind, and salt and pepper to taste. Place stuffing in lamb cavity and sew or tie together. Place on rack in baking pan. Roast in 325°F oven for 1½ hours.

Glaze: Combine jam, mustard, and ginger; mix well. Brush over outside of lamb and continue roasting for 15 minutes longer or until lamb is brown outside and pink inside. Transfer to serving platter and let stand for 15 minutes before carving. Arrange halved apricots, rosemary sprigs, and whole unpeeled kumquats around lamb. Makes 8 servings.

Calories per serving: 326
Grams fat per serving: 10
Fiber: Good
Vitamin A and niacin: Excellent
Iron, thiamine, phosphorus, and riboflavin: Good

Marinated Leg of Lamb with Coriander

Boneless butterflied legs of lamb are available in the frozen-food sections of many supermarkets or fresh at butcher stores. This marinade is also delicious with lamb chops and rack of lamb. An easy dish to prepare in advance, marinated leg of lamb is also easy to transport (in a plastic bag) to a weekend or beach house.

1   **boneless butterflied leg of lamb (about 3½ pounds)**
    Salt and freshly ground pepper
    Dijon mustard or Blackberry Sauce (page 154)

MARINADE:
1   **tablespoon coriander seeds**
½   **cup lemon juice**
2   **tablespoons vegetable oil**
1   **small onion, chopped**
1   **tablespoon grated fresh ginger root**
2   **cloves garlic, chopped**
1   **teaspoon black peppercorns, crushed**

Marinade: In skillet, toast coriander seeds over medium heat for 5 minutes, shaking pan occasionally. Remove from heat; let cool, then crush seeds. Combine crushed seeds, lemon juice, oil, onion, ginger, garlic, and peppercorns.

Cut off any fat from lamb and discard. If meat is not of even thickness, slash thickest section and open up, book fashion. Place lamb in glass or ceramic dish or plastic bag and coat both sides of meat with marinade. Cover and refrigerate for 48 hours, turning once. Remove lamb from refrigerator about 1 hour before cooking.

Drain lamb and wipe dry. Place on broiler rack and broil about 6 inches from heat for about 12 minutes on each side for medium-rare, 15 to 20 minutes on each side for well-done. Meat thermometer should register 140°F for rare, 160°F for medium, and 180°F for well-done. Remove from heat; let stand for 5 minutes, season with salt and pepper to taste, then slice thin across the grain. Serve with Dijon mustard or Blackberry Sauce. Makes 8 servings.

Calories per 5-ounce serving: 393
Grams fat per 5-ounce serving: 11
Iron, riboflavin, phosphorus, niacin, and thiamine: Excellent

---

Butterflied means it has been cut open but not all the way through; it will lie as flat as possible, which makes it easier to broil.

Should lamb be rare or well-done?

As with beef, this is a matter of personal taste. However, if it is too rare, it can be tough. If overcooked, it will be dry. The safest is medium-rare—it will be tender, juicy, and pink on the inside.

Navarin of Lamb

This is a beautiful dish for cold-weather entertaining. Though it may appear to be a lot of garlic, when simmered in milk it becomes sweet and mild. Fresh rosemary adds a very special flavor and is worth trying to find. Serve with wild or plain rice, noodles, or potatoes. (See color photograph.)

Start this a day in advance and refrigerate overnight. The fat will solidify on top and be easy to remove. Combining meat with vegetables in one dish allows you to get away with serving less meat.

2 pounds boneless leg of lamb
1 teaspoon granulated sugar
 Salt and freshly ground pepper
1 tablespoon vegetable oil
2 tablespoons all-purpose flour
2 cups beef or lamb stock
1 clove garlic, finely chopped
1 tablespoon tomato paste
 Bouquet garni*
1 long strip orange rind (orange part only)
1 tablespoon fresh rosemary leaves or 1 teaspoon dried

VEGETABLES:
5 carrots
3 small white turnips or 1 yellow rutabaga (about 1 pound)
10 small onions or 1 cup pearl onions

GARLIC GARNISH:
4 heads garlic
½ cup milk

*Bouquet garni:

2 sprigs fresh parsley, 1 sprig thyme, 1 bay leaf, 1 stalk celery all tied with a sprig of parsley or a piece of string, or in cheesecloth tied with string (if you don't have fresh thyme, use ½ teaspoon dried thyme).

Trim any fat from lamb; sprinkle with sugar, and salt and pepper. In large, heavy Dutch oven or nonstick pan, heat oil over medium heat until hot. Add meat a few pieces at a time and brown well.

Remove meat from pan and pour off all fat. Return meat to pan; add flour and cook over medium heat, stirring constantly, for 1 minute or until flour has browned. Add stock, garlic, tomato paste, bouquet garni, and orange rind. Bring to a boil, stirring to scrape up all the flavorful brown bits from bottom of pan. Cover and bake in 325°F oven for 1 hour. Let cool, then refrigerate overnight or until cold.

Remove fat from surface of stew; discard orange rind and bouquet garni.

Vegetables: Scrape carrots; peel turnips and onions. If using pearl onions, blanch in boiling water for 1 minute;

drain, then cut off root end and gently squeeze to remove skin. Cut carrots and turnips into ¾-inch pieces.

Garlic Garnish: Separate garlic heads into cloves. Combine garlic with milk in small saucepan. Bring to a boil and boil for 2 minutes. Reduce heat to low; cover, and simmer until garlic cloves are soft. Drain. When cool, gently squeeze cloves to remove skins. Set aside.

About 45 minutes before serving, gently reheat lamb mixture, stirring to prevent scorching. Add vegetables and simmer, covered, for 30 minutes or until vegetables are tender; add water if necessary. (For a thicker gravy, add 2 tablespoons flour mixed with ½ cup cold water or stock; bring to a boil and cook, stirring, until thickened slightly.) Add rosemary and garnish with garlic cloves. Makes 8 servings.

Calories per serving: 261
Grams fat per serving: 11
Fiber: Good
Vitamins A and C and niacin: Excellent
Iron and phosphorus: Good

Winter Dinner Party

Cream of Broccoli Soup (page 51)
Navarin of Lamb
Tiny boiled potatoes
Arugula and Radicchio Salad with Balsamic Vinaigrette (page 76)
Apple Cinnamon Sorbet (page 208) or Grapefruit Ice (page 210)
Coconut-Oatmeal Cookies (page 198)

Spring Dinner Buffet

Asparagus with Orange Vinaigrette (page 94)
Navarin of Lamb
Tiny boiled potatoes
Tossed green salad with Watercress Dressing (page 95)
Rhubarb Crumb Pie (page 228)

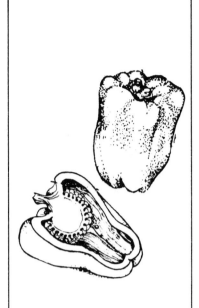

Souvlakia of Lamb

Greece is famous for its souvlakia, or skewered lamb, which the Greeks season with lemon juice and oregano. They don't usually have vegetables on the skewers, but it's more colorful when you include them—and they add extra flavor. Serve the skewers on hot rice.

1   **boneless leg of lamb**
2   **tablespoons lemon juice**
1   **teaspoon crumbled leaf oregano**
     Salt and freshly ground pepper
8   **small onions**
1   **small red pepper**
1   **small yellow or green pepper**

Cut lamb into 1-inch cubes. Place in glass dish or plate and sprinkle with lemon juice, oregano, and salt and pepper to taste. Blanch onions in boiling water for 10 to 15 minutes or until almost tender; drain. When cool enough to handle, cut off root ends of onions and squeeze off skins. Seed peppers and cut into 1½-inch pieces.

Thread lamb alternating with vegetables onto flat-bladed metal skewers or wooden skewers that have been soaked in water.

Preheat broiler. Place skewers on broiler rack and broil about 5 inches from heat, turning every 3 to 4 minutes, for 12 minutes or until meat is brown outside but still pink inside. Makes 4 servings.

Calories per serving: 224
Grams fat per serving: 7
Fiber: Good
Niacin and vitamins A and C: Excellent
Iron and phosphorus: Good

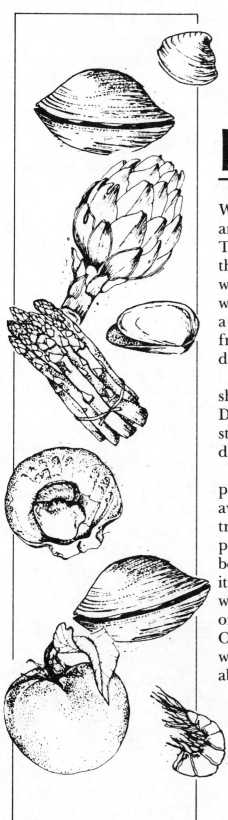

FISH

WHEN it comes to fish, Americans on the East and West coasts don't know how lucky they are. They are used to fresh fish—this means no more than a day or two out of the water. Be careful with the meaning of the word *fresh*. Sometimes we say fresh to mean not frozen, but just because a fish has not yet been frozen it's not necessarily fresh—it may have been out of the water for days.

The best test of a fresh fish is its smell. It should be very mildly fishy, nothing stronger. Don't hesitate to ask to smell the fish; a reputable store will encourage your scrutiny, and you'll discover it pays to find a store you can rely on.

If you can't get good fresh fish, don't let that prevent you from enjoying fish. Frozen fish is available right across the country. Part of the trick of cooking frozen fish is defrosting it properly. Don't put it out on the counter hours before you plan to cook it. It's important to keep it cold so the outside portions don't deteriorate while the inside is still frozen. The best method of defrosting fish is to place it in the refrigerator. Often we don't have the time, so the next best way is to immerse the package in cold water for about 1½ hours. That way the outside thawed portion stays cold while the center is still defrosting. Before cooking, separate the fish into fillets if it has been frozen in a block; it looks more appealing that way.

There is an unnecessary mystique about cooking fish—too many people are afraid to take the plunge when in fact it is one of the easiest foods to cook: the simpler the better. Most fish has a delicate flavor that you don't want to mask with strong seasonings or heavy sauces. A sprinkling of lemon juice and chopped fresh parsley is a classic, delicious preparation. Just try Sole Fillets with Lemon and Parsley (page 129).

The Canadian method of cooking fish is the best to follow and means we no longer have to guess how long to cook a piece of fish. It's very simple: Measure the thickness of the fish at the thickest part; for each 1 inch of thickness, allow 10 minutes of cooking time at 400°F; add 5 minutes if the fish is wrapped in foil, and double the time if the fish is still frozen. Perfectly cooked fish is opaque and flakes slightly. Avoid overcooking; it dries out the fish.

Best of all, fish is healthful—it's low in fat and calories and high in protein, and for cooks on the run it's one of the fastest foods around.

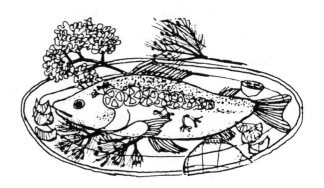

Sole Fillets with Lemon and Parsley

This is such a simple recipe, yet it's one of the very best ways to make tender, moist fish fillets. If using frozen fillets, try to thaw and separate them before cooking for best results. (See color photograph.)

Fish is an excellent source of protein and is low in fat and calories.

1	**pound sole fillets***
	Salt and freshly ground pepper
2	**teaspoons butter, melted**
2	**tablespoons chopped fresh parsley**
1	**tablespoon lemon juice**

Place fillets in lightly oiled baking dish just large enough to hold them in single layer. Sprinkle with salt and pepper to taste. Combine butter, parsley, and lemon juice. Drizzle over fish. Bake, uncovered, in 450°F oven for 8 to 10 minutes (10 minutes per inch thickness for fresh fish) or until fish is opaque and flakes easily. To microwave: Cover with plastic wrap and turn back corner to vent for steam; microwave on High for 3½ to 4½ minutes. Makes 4 servings.

Calories per serving: 117
Grams fat per serving: 7

*Cod, snapper, or Pacific perch may be substituted for the sole.

Sole Florentine

This colorful dish is a little fancier than Sole Fillets with Lemon and Parsley. You can prepare it in advance, then bake it just before serving.

1¼ **pounds sole fillets**
1 **onion, chopped**
½ **bay leaf**
2 **tablespoons lemon juice**
3 **peppercorns**
½ **teaspoon salt**
¾ **cup dry white wine**
1 **pound fresh spinach**
4 **teaspoons butter**
2 **tablespoons all-purpose flour**
½ **cup low-fat milk**
 Salt and freshly ground pepper
1 **tablespoon grated Parmesan cheese**

Roll up fillets and secure with toothpicks. Arrange rolls in skillet or pan just large enough to hold them in single layers; add onion, bay leaf, lemon juice, peppercorns, and salt. Pour in wine; bring to a boil. Cover, reduce heat, and simmer for 5 minutes. Remove fillets from liquid, reserving liquid.

Wash spinach; cook, covered, in saucepan in just the water clinging to leaves. Drain, and squeeze out excess water; chop finely.

Place spinach in shallow greased dish just large enough to hold the fish rolls. Place fish on top of spinach.

Strain reserved poaching liquid; measure 1 cup (add water if necessary). In small saucepan, melt butter; add flour and stir over low heat for 1 minute. Whisk in poaching liquid; bring to a boil, stirring constantly. Stir in milk, salt, and pepper to taste. Remove from heat. (It may be prepared ahead to this point and reheated.)

Pour sauce over fish and sprinkle with Parmesan. Bake in 375°F oven for 10 to 20 minutes or until bubbly. Makes 4 servings.

Calories per serving: 226
Grams fat per serving: 7
Fiber: Excellent
Vitamins A and C: Excellent
Iron and riboflavin: Good

Capellini with Clam Sauce and Sweet Red Peppers

Capellini (angel hair) are the thinnest of noodles, but this recipe works well with any kind of noodle; whole wheat ones are good because of their higher fiber content. Serve this extremely easy-to-make dish with steamed snow peas or tossed spinach salad. It's an emergency-shelf type of recipe: The ingredients keep well, and it's so fast to prepare—perfect for unexpected company.

2	**sweet red peppers**
2	**tablespoons butter**
3	**cloves garlic, finely chopped**
	Salt and freshly ground pepper
1	**cup dry white wine**
1	**5-ounce can clams, drained**
1	**teaspoon fresh thyme leaves or ¼ teaspoon dried**
½	**cup finely chopped fresh parsley**
½	**pound capellini (fresh or dried)**
3	**tablespoons grated Parmesan cheese**

Core and seed red peppers; cut into thin strips.

In heavy skillet, melt half the butter; add red peppers and 1 clove of finely chopped garlic. Cook over medium heat, stirring often, until peppers are tender, about 10 minutes. Season with salt and pepper to taste.

In saucepan, melt remaining butter over medium heat; add remaining garlic and cook, stirring, for 1 minute. Add wine, clams, and thyme; simmer for 5 minutes. Add parsley, and salt and pepper to taste.

Meanwhile, in large pot of boiling water, cook capellini until al dente (tender but firm); drain. Spoon capellini onto warmed dinner plates; pour sauce over. Arrange sautéed red peppers around pasta. Sprinkle pasta with Parmesan. Serve immediately. Makes 3 main-course or 6 appetizer servings.

	Main Course	Appetizer
Calories per serving:	275	138
Grams fat per serving:	9	4.5
Iron: Excellent		
Vitamins A and C and phosphorus: Good		

Mussels Sicilian Style

For a delightfully easy supper, buy fresh mussels on your way home from work and serve this dish with fresh bread and salad. If you buy cultured mussels, they take only minutes to clean, and supper can be ready in 15 minutes.

2	pounds fresh mussels (about 36)
1	teaspoon olive oil
1	small onion, finely chopped
1	large clove garlic, finely chopped
	Pinch each dried thyme and oregano
1	14-ounce can tomatoes or 2 fresh tomatoes, coarsely chopped
1/4	cup dry white wine
1/4	cup chopped fresh parsley

Scrub mussels under cold water and pull off hairy beards. In large, heavy saucepan, heat oil over medium heat; add onion and garlic and cook for 2 to 3 minutes or until tender. Stir in thyme and oregano; add tomatoes, breaking up tomatoes with back of spoon. Bring to a boil and boil for about 2 minutes to reduce liquid. Add wine and return to a boil. Add mussels; cover and cook for 5 minutes or until shells open and mussels are cooked. Discard any shells that don't open. Sprinkle with parsley.

Ladle mussels into large soup bowls, spooning tomato mixture over them. Eat with a fork and a spoon—the fork to pull the mussels out of their shells, the spoon to consume the heavenly broth. Or sop up remaining broth with bread. Makes 2 servings.

Calories per serving: 223
Grams fat per serving: 6
Fiber: Good
Vitamins A and C, iron, niacin, and phosphorus: Excellent
Calcium and thiamine: Good

How to Buy and Store Mussels

It's unbelievable that shellfish as tender and delicious as mussels are so inexpensive. Buy medium-size (about 18 to the pound) cultured mussels—they're much easier to clean and have more meat than the wild ones. Buy only those that have closed shells. The fresher the mussels, the better they taste. However, they can be kept in a bowl or paper (not plastic) bag in the refrigerator for 2 or 3 days. Serve as a first course or a main course.

Cooking Pasta

Cook pasta in a large pot of boiling water, using about 4 quarts of water for every pound of pasta. Add pasta a little at a time so the water doesn't stop boiling, and stir with a fork to make sure noodles don't stick together.

Fresh pasta cooks quickly, sometimes in as little as 2 minutes. Dried pasta takes longer, usually at least 7 minutes, sometimes 10 to 12 minutes. Begin tasting to see whether it is done before the suggested cooking time; it is cooked when it's al dente (tender but firm—not mushy) and has lost its raw starch taste. Drain in a colander, then toss immediately with sauce, butter, or oil as specified in recipe to prevent it from sticking together. Because pasta cools quickly, it's important to warm the platter or individual plates it's to be served on. For cold pasta salad, rinse pasta under cold running water to prevent sticking.

Be sure to have the sauce ready before the pasta is finished cooking (overcooked, soft, gluey pasta isn't appealing); then toss with sauce and serve immediately.

Linguine with Shrimp and Tomato

In this recipe the shrimp and tomato should be quickly cooked over high heat to preserve flavor and texture. If using fresh pasta, make sauce first, because the pasta cooks so quickly.

¼	**pound linguine or whole wheat noodles**
1	**tablespoon vegetable oil**
1	**large clove garlic, finely chopped**
2	**tablespoons finely chopped shallots**
2	**large tomatoes, coarsely chopped**
¼	**teaspoon dried basil, or fresh, chopped, to taste**
¼	**pound small or medium shrimp (raw or cooked)**
1	**or 2 scallions, chopped**
	Salt and freshly ground pepper

In a large pot of boiling water, cook linguine until al dente (tender but firm) or according to package directions; drain.

Meanwhile, in heavy skillet, heat oil over high heat. Add garlic and shallots; cook, stirring, for about 30 seconds. Add tomatoes and basil; cook, stirring, for about 1 minute. Add shrimp and cook, stirring, until shrimp are hot and, if using raw, turn pink. Sprinkle with scallions and season with salt and pepper to taste. Spoon over hot linguine. Makes 2 servings.

Calories per serving: 395
Grams fat per serving: 8
Fiber: Good
Iron, thiamine, niacin, and vitamin C: Excellent
Vitamin A and phosphorus: Good

Be very careful not to overcook scallops. They cook very fast and in just a minute can change from tender to tough and rubbery. They're cooked when they become opaque.

Although shrimp are low in fat, they're high in cholesterol. Therefore, they shouldn't be eaten too often.

½ cup whipping cream in the sauce is scrumptious but adds 8 grams fat per serving.

Special Spring Dinner

Asparagus with Red Pepper
 Purée (pages 166)
Scallops and Shrimp in Wine
 Bouillon with Julienne
 Vegetables or Sole Florentine
 (page 130)
Strawberries with Raspberry-
 Rhubarb Sauce (page 232)

Scallops and Shrimp in Wine Bouillon with Julienne Vegetables

Serve this elegant dish for a special dinner. It's the only recipe in the book with whipping cream; the cream is optional, but adds smoothness and rich flavor. Luckily, the rest of the ingredients are low in fat. (See color photograph.)

¾	*pound large raw shrimp*
16	*mussels (optional)*
2	*medium carrots*
1	*sweet red pepper*
2	*leeks (white part only)*
1	*small zucchini*
4	*teaspoons butter*
3	*shallots, finely chopped*
2	*large cloves garlic, finely chopped*
½	*cup white wine*
½	*pound scallops*
1	*cup finely chopped fresh parsley*
½	*cup whipping cream (optional)*
	Salt and freshly ground pepper
3	*cups hot cooked rice*

Shell shrimp and remove intestinal tract running down back. Scrub mussels and pull off hairy beards. Peel carrots. Seed pepper. Cut leek lengthwise halfway, then wash under cold running water. Cut ends from zucchini. Cut all vegetables into julienne strips (like matchsticks). Blanch vegetables in boiling water for 2 minutes; drain. Plunge into a bowl of ice water to cool; drain.

In large, heavy saucepan or flameproof casserole, melt the butter; stir in shallots and garlic and cook over medium-low heat, stirring, for 3 to 5 minutes or until tender. Add wine; bring to a boil. Add shrimp, mussels, scallops, and parsley; cover, and simmer for about 3 minutes or until shrimp turn pink and scallops are opaque. Discard any mussels that do not open. Be careful not to overcook or seafood will be tough. Pour in cream (if using) and vegetables and cook until hot.

Taste liquid in pan and add salt and pepper. If liquid is too thin, thicken it by adding 2 teaspoons cornstarch mixed with 2 tablespoons water; stir and bring to a boil.

Serve in bowls over rice or noodles. Makes 4 servings.

	Without cream	With cream
Calories per serving:	415	515
Grams fat per serving:	6.5	14.5
Vitamin A, niacin, and iron: Excellent		
Thiamine and calcium: Good		

Baked Salmon with Herbs

A popular dinner party dish, baked whole salmon is about the easiest main-course dish to prepare. When serving four to six people, arrange hot cooked vegetables such as green beans or snow peas on a platter alongside the salmon. It will look like a sumptuous feast.

Plan on about ½ pound per person for a salmon under 4 pounds; or about ⅓ pound per person for a salmon over 4 pounds or a chunk piece. Of the various types of Pacific salmon, chum has the lowest fat content, spring salmon the highest. Sockeye salmon is the reddest in color, and thus best for mousse recipes.

When buying a whole fish, ask the fish dealer to clean and scale it. If you don't want the head left on, ask him to cut it off. If you want fillets, the fish dealer will usually fillet the fish for you, and sometimes will even remove the backbone but leave the fish whole. (Fillets are boneless pieces of fish cut from either side of the backbone; steaks are cut crosswise and include some bone.)

NOTE: Although salmon is a high-fat fish, it is not any higher in fat than most lean cuts of meat or chicken. It contains omega-3 fatty acids, which current research indicates have a beneficial effect in relation to heart disease.

Dinner Party for Six

Fresh Tomato-Dill Bisque
   (page 48)
Baked Salmon with Herbs
Rice or tiny potatoes in skins
Herbed Green Beans with
   Garlic (page 170)
Frozen Lemon Cream (page
   209) with Raspberry Purée
   (page 207)

1   whole salmon or piece about 2½ pounds
½   cup chopped fresh parsley
2   tablespoons combination of chopped fresh
      herbs—dill, chives, chervil, basil, sage
      (optional)
      Salt and freshly ground pepper
1   tablespoon water
1   tablespoon lemon juice

GARNISH (OPTIONAL):
   Cucumber slices, parsley, dill, or
      watercress

Place salmon on foil; measure thickness at thickest part. Sprinkle parsley, herbs, and salt and pepper to taste inside cavity. Mix water with lemon juice and sprinkle over outside of salmon. Fold foil over and seal.

Place wrapped salmon on baking sheet and bake in 450°F oven for 10 minutes for every 1 inch thickness of fish, plus an additional 10 minutes cooking time because it's wrapped in foil (35 to 40 minutes total cooking time), or until salmon is opaque. Unwrap and discard skin; most of it should stick to foil. Place salmon on warmed platter. Garnish with cucumber, parsley, dill, or watercress (if using). Alternatively, arrange cooked vegetables on platter with salmon.

Serve warm with Yogurt Hollandaise (page 159), Creamy Fresh Dill Dip (page 38), or lemon wedges.

To serve cold: While salmon is still warm, discard skin and scrape off any dark fat. Brush salmon lightly with oil and cover with foil. Refrigerate until serving time. Makes about 4 servings.

Calories per serving: 391
Grams fat per serving: 16
Vitamin C, niacin, and phosphorus: Excellent
Thiamine, calcium, iron, and vitamin A: Good
These are large-size servings: 3 ounces of cooked (steamed or baked) salmon has 7 grams fat.

Sole Poached with Tomatoes, Artichokes, and Mushrooms

You can use any type of white fish fillets or steaks, such as cod, halibut, or haddock, in this moist and savory fish dish. Serve over pasta or rice.

1	**tablespoon butter**
1½	**cups thickly sliced mushrooms**
1	**clove garlic, finely chopped**
3	**tomatoes, cut in chunks**
½	**teaspoon basil**
	Pinch thyme
1	**pound sole fillets**
1	**14-ounce can artichoke hearts, drained and halved**
	Salt and freshly ground pepper
	Granulated sugar (optional)

In heavy saucepan or skillet, melt butter; cook mushrooms and garlic over medium-high heat, shaking pan or stirring, until mushrooms are tender.

Add tomatoes, basil, and thyme; bring to a simmer. Add sole and artichokes; cover and simmer for 3 minutes. Uncover and cook for 5 minutes longer or until fish is opaque. Season with salt and pepper to taste (add pinch of sugar if tomatoes are too acidic). Makes 4 servings.

Calories per serving: 141
Grams fat per serving: 5
Vitamin C: Excellent
Vitamin A: Good

Microwave Fillets Provençal

Use any lean fish fillets—red snapper, rockfish, perch, sole, cod, flounder, haddock, or monkfish. It's best to use fresh fillets if available, but you can use frozen.

1   **16-ounce can tomatoes**
1   **pound fish fillets**
    Salt and freshly ground pepper
¼   **cup chopped fresh parsley**
¼   **cup fine fresh bread crumbs**
2   **tablespoons finely chopped scallions**
        (including tops)
1   **tablespoon butter, melted**
2   **cloves garlic, finely chopped**

Drain and coarsely chop tomatoes. In microwave dish just large enough to hold fillets in single layer, spoon half the tomatoes. Arrange fillets on top and sprinkle with salt and pepper to taste. Top with remaining tomatoes.

In small bowl, combine parsley, bread crumbs, scallions, butter, and garlic; sprinkle over tomatoes. Partially cover and microwave on High for 9 to 12 minutes or until fish is opaque. Let stand for 3 minutes before serving. Makes 4 servings.

Note: To cook in conventional oven, bake in 450°F oven for 20 minutes for fresh fillets, 40 minutes for frozen, or until fish is opaque.

Calories per serving: 244
Grams fat per serving: 9
Vitamins A and C, niacin, and phosphorus: Excellent

Brochettes of Salmon and Shrimp

Serve these skewers of salmon and shrimp over a bed of rice. Either add the vegetables to the skewers or arrange them artistically around the plate. Creamy Fresh Dill Dip (page 38) goes well with this.

1½ **pounds salmon, skin removed, cut in ¾-inch cubes**
16 **raw shrimp (about 1 pound) or scallops**
8 **stalks asparagus or 16 cherry tomatoes**
16 **large mushrooms**
16 **large seedless green grapes**
3 **tablespoons vegetable oil**
1 **tablespoon lime juice**
1 **clove garlic, finely chopped**
    Salt and freshly ground pepper

Snap off tough ends of asparagus. Peel stalks if desired. Blanch in boiling water for 3 minutes; drain. Cut into 1½-inch lengths. On thin (preferably wooden) skewers, thread pieces of salmon and shrimp, alternating with asparagus, mushrooms, and grapes.

Combine oil, lime juice, garlic, and salt and pepper to taste; brush over skewers. Broil for about 10 to 15 minutes or until fish is opaque. (Alternatively, place skewers on wire rack set over boiling water in broiling pan; cover with foil and steam for 10 to 15 minutes or until fish is opaque.) Sprinkle with salt and pepper. Makes 6 main-course or 8 appetizer servings.

Calories per main-course serving: 233
Grams fat per main-course serving: 9.3
Niacin: Excellent
Iron, phosphorus, and calcium: Good

For other fish dishes, see:

Fish Chowder, Family Style
(page 63)
Nova Scotia Seafood Chowder
(page 60)
Fettuccine with Clam Sauce
(page 117)

Types of Fish

Lean fish

—red snapper
—rockfish (silver gray, canary)
—perch (ocean, yellow)
—sole
—lingcod, cod
—pike
—lake flounder
—haddock
—smelt
—monkfish
—pickerel

Medium-fat fish

—halibut
—shark
—black cod
—tuna
—skate
—trout

Fat fish

—herring
—bluefish
—shad
—swordfish
—salmon
—mackerel
—catfish

Buying Fresh Fish

When possible, buy fish the day you want to cook it. The best test for freshness is to use your nose—the fish should have a mild fishy or seawater odor. Anything stronger means the fish has been out of the water for too long.

Look for:

• mild smell

• glistening, firm flesh that springs back when touched

• very firmly attached scales

• clear, bright, convex eyes (not sunken)

Buying Frozen Fish

Look for:

• glazed fish coated with ice

• shiny, solidly frozen flesh with no signs of drying or freezer burn (white spots)

• tightly wrapped package with no sign of frost or ice crystals inside

Storing Fresh Fish

• If not cleaned, clean as soon as possible.

• Wipe with a damp cloth, wrap in waxed paper, and place in covered container.

• Store in coldest part of the refrigerator.

• Cook as soon as possible (same day for store-bought, within 4 days of freshly caught).

Storing Frozen Fish

• Keep fish at 0°F or lower for ideal storage.

• Store fat fish (salmon, mackerel, lake trout) for a maximum of 2 months.

• Store lean fish (cod, haddock, perch, pike) for a maximum of 6 months.

How to Cook Fish

• Measure fish at the thickest part (stuffed or not).

• Allow 10 minutes' cooking time per inch thickness for fresh fish; double the time if fish is frozen. If wrapped in foil, add 5 minutes for fresh, 10 minutes for frozen. This applies to all fish and all cooking methods (if in oven, cook at 450°F).

Methods of Cooking Fish

Steaming (top of stove)

Pour 2 inches of water in a steamer and bring to a boil. Season and wrap fish securely in cheesecloth. Place on a rack over boiling water. Cover and begin timing (see above).

Oven steaming

Preheat oven to 450°F. Place fresh or frozen fish on lightly greased foil. Season to taste with salt, pepper, and herbs (parsley, dill, chives, or basil). Sprinkle with lemon juice or white wine. Wrap securely. Place on a baking sheet and bake for required cooking time (see above), adding 5 minutes for fresh and 10 minutes for frozen fish because of being wrapped in foil.

Poaching

Place fish on greased heavy-duty foil. Season with salt and pepper and add chopped onion and celery. Wrap, using double folds to make package watertight. Place in rapidly boiling water. Cover pan and return to boil; reduce heat and simmer for required cooking time (see above). Fish may also be wrapped in cheesecloth and poached in court bouillon or fish stock.

To microwave fish

Place fish in glass dish. Season with pepper to taste. Cover with plastic wrap and turn back corner to allow steam to escape. Estimate cooking time at 3 to 4 minutes per pound, plus 2 to 3 minutes standing time. Microwave on High or according to appliance manual.

Fish is cooked

when it flakes and separates into solid moist sections when firmly prodded with a fork, and flesh is opaque.

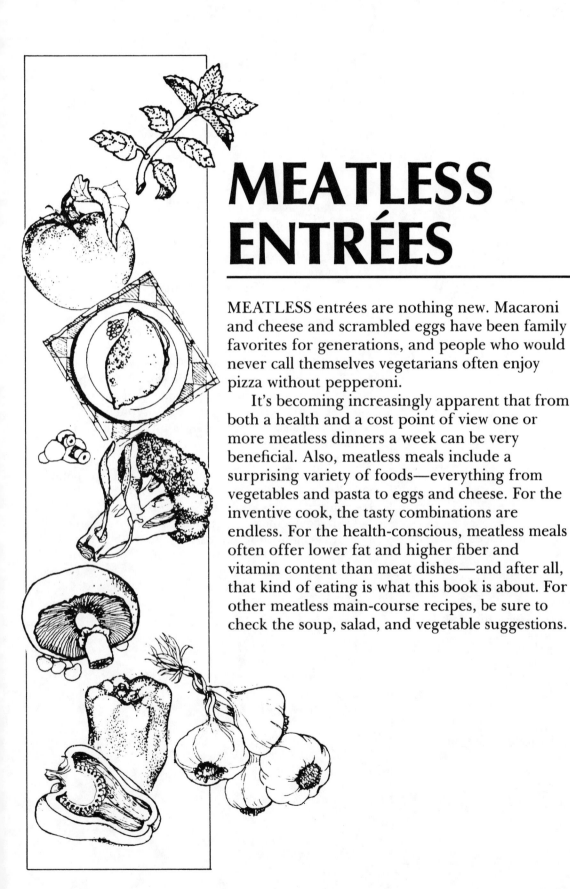

MEATLESS ENTRÉES

MEATLESS entrées are nothing new. Macaroni and cheese and scrambled eggs have been family favorites for generations, and people who would never call themselves vegetarians often enjoy pizza without pepperoni.

It's becoming increasingly apparent that from both a health and a cost point of view one or more meatless dinners a week can be very beneficial. Also, meatless meals include a surprising variety of foods—everything from vegetables and pasta to eggs and cheese. For the inventive cook, the tasty combinations are endless. For the health-conscious, meatless meals often offer lower fat and higher fiber and vitamin content than meat dishes—and after all, that kind of eating is what this book is about. For other meatless main-course recipes, be sure to check the soup, salad, and vegetable suggestions.

Broccoli Frittata

This Italian open-face omelet is delicious for supper or brunch. Unlike a French omelet, which is cooked quickly over high heat and is creamy in the center, a frittata is cooked slowly and is set, or firm, in the center.

1	**bunch broccoli**
1	**tablespoon vegetable oil**
1	**cup sliced onions**
2	**cloves garlic, finely chopped**
6	**eggs, lightly beaten**
1	**teaspoon salt**
	Pinch each nutmeg and freshly ground pepper
½	**cup grated part skim mozzarella cheese**

Trim tough ends from broccoli and peel stems. Cut stems and florets into ¾-inch pieces (you should have about 4 cups). Steam or cook broccoli in boiling water for 3 to 5 minutes or until crisp-tender; drain thoroughly.

In 10-inch skillet, preferably nonstick, heat oil; add onion and garlic and cook over medium heat until onion is tender. Stir in broccoli.

Beat together eggs, salt, nutmeg, and pepper; pour over broccoli mixture and sprinkle with cheese. Cover, and cook over medium-low heat for 5 to 10 minutes or until set but still slightly moist on top. Place under broiler for 2 to 3 minutes to lightly brown top. (If the skillet handle isn't ovenproof, wrap in foil; since the oven door is open, most of the handle will not be directly under the heat.) Loosen edges of frittata and cut into pie-shape wedges. Makes 4 servings.

Calories per serving: 172
Grams fat per serving: 9
Fiber: Excellent
Vitamins A and C: Excellent
Riboflavin and niacin: Good

Light Supper for a Winter's Day

Broccoli Frittata
Danish Cucumber Salad (page 75)
Whole Wheat Irish Soda Bread (page 193)
Baked apples

Broccoli is an excellent source of vitamins A and C and is associated with reduced risk of cancer of the colon.

Eggs Florentine

This delicious dish is perfect for brunch, lunch, or a light supper. The eggs can be poached in advance, cooled in ice water to prevent further cooking, and refrigerated in a bowl of water. Reheat them by placing in a pan of simmering water for about 30 seconds. The spinach and sauce can also be prepared in advance and gently reheated.

¾	**cup Yogurt Hollandaise (page 159)**
2	**10-ounce packages fresh spinach**
1	**teaspoon butter**
	Salt, freshly ground pepper, and freshly grated nutmeg
2	**tablespoons white vinegar**
6	**eggs**

Prepare Yogurt Hollandaise as directed and keep warm.

Wash spinach and discard stems; place leaves in saucepan. Cover and cook in just the water clinging to leaves over medium-high heat until spinach is wilted. Drain thoroughly and chop spinach coarsely; toss with butter, and salt, pepper, and nutmeg to taste. Return to saucepan, cover, and keep warm. (If preparing in advance, drain, then cool under cold running water, and drain again; reheat over low heat.)

Nearly fill a large shallow pan or skillet with water and bring to a boil; add vinegar. Break eggs over pan and gently drop into water; reduce heat until water is barely simmering and cook eggs for 3 to 5 minutes or until whites are firm and yellows are still soft; spoon water over top of yolk occasionally to cook it slightly.

Spoon spinach onto warmed plates or serving dish. Remove eggs from water with slotted spoon. Place 1 egg over each portion of spinach. Spoon about 2 tablespoons of sauce over each egg and serve immediately. Makes 6 servings.

Calories per serving: 130
Grams fat per serving: 9
Fiber: Excellent
Vitamins A and C: Excellent
Iron and niacin: Good

Brunch or Lunch Menu

Grapefruit Juice Spritzer (see below)
Eggs Florentine
Tomatoes Provençal (page 163)
Tossed green salad
Toasted English muffins
Raspberry Meringue Torte (page 220) or Pear Crisp with Rolled Oats Topping (page 222)

Grapefruit Juice Spritzer

For a refreshing nonalcoholic drink that's perfect before lunch or brunch, combine equal parts of grapefruit juice and soda water. Serve over ice cubes and garnish with thin slices of lime.

Asparagus with Poached Eggs

In spring, substitute cooked drained asparagus for the spinach in Eggs Florentine. Arrange hot asparagus spears on warmed individual plates or serving dish; sprinkle with lemon juice, salt, and pepper. Top with a poached egg and grated Parmesan cheese or Yogurt Hollandaise. If desired, place under broiler for a minute to brown.

Because egg yolks are high in cholesterol, people on low-cholesterol diets may want to skip this dish. This particular recipe is much healthier than the popular Eggs Benedict; here, the hollandaise sauce is made with yogurt instead of butter, and spinach, which is high in vitamins A and C, is used instead of ham.

A 2-egg omelet is easier to make than a 4-egg or larger omelet. Also, it's important to use the correct size of pan. For a 2- to 3-egg omelet, use an omelet pan 7 inches in diameter at the bottom; for a 4-egg omelet, use an 8- to 9-inch pan.

Egg yolks are high in cholesterol—limit your diet to about 3 eggs per week.

Omelet à la Jardinière

This is perfect for a quick dinner, lunch, or breakfast. Serve with toasted whole wheat bread and a spinach salad. (See color photograph.)

1	teaspoon vegetable oil
1	small onion, finely chopped
1	clove garlic, finely chopped
⅓	cup grated carrot
¼	cup chopped green pepper
	Salt and freshly ground pepper
4	eggs
1	tablespoon water
1	teaspoon butter
½	cup alfalfa sprouts

In skillet, heat oil; sauté onion and garlic over medium heat, stirring, until tender. Stir in carrot and green pepper and stir-fry for about 3 minutes or until carrot has wilted. Season with salt and pepper to taste.

Beat eggs with water and a large pinch of salt and pepper until whites and yolks are thoroughly blended. Heat an 8- to 9-inch nonstick omelet pan or skillet over very high heat until pan is hot. Add butter to pan. When it sizzles but just before it starts to brown, pour in beaten eggs. Continuously shake the pan back and forth, and at the same time stir eggs quickly with a fork to spread them evenly over bottom of pan as they thicken. When eggs have thickened and are almost set, spoon carrot mixture and alfalfa sprouts over eggs.

Tilt pan and roll up edges of omelet, or simply fold omelet in half. Slide onto serving plate. (This whole procedure should take about 1 minute.) Serve immediately. Makes 2 servings.

Calories per serving: 147
Grams fat per serving: 11
Vitamin A: Good
Niacin: Good

Bulgur Wheat, Tofu, and Sweet Peppers

This main-course vegetarian dish is a good source of protein and fiber. If possible, use bulgur instead of cracked wheat; it has a nuttier, richer flavor and takes less time to cook.

1	**cup coarse or medium bulgur or cracked wheat***
2	**tablespoons butter**
3	**cloves garlic, finely chopped**
2	**teaspoons ground cumin**
2	**sweet red peppers, seeded and cut in strips**
3	**tablespoons vinegar**
1/3	**cup water**
1	**10-ounce package fresh spinach, washed, stemmed, and cut in strips**
	Salt
	Freshly ground pepper
3/4	**pound firm-style tofu (bean curd), cut in cubes**

Rinse bulgur under cold water. Place in bowl and add enough cold water to cover by 2 inches; soak for 1 hour. Drain thoroughly in sieve.

In large skillet, melt butter over medium heat, add garlic, and cook for a few seconds. Stir in cumin, then peppers. Cover and cook for 5 minutes.

Add bulgur, vinegar, and water; cook, uncovered, for 5 minutes or until bulgur is nearly tender, stirring often (cracked wheat will take about 15 minutes longer; add more water as necessary). Add spinach; stir until mixed and spinach is slightly wilted. Season with salt and pepper to taste. Add tofu; cover and simmer for 5 minutes or until heated through and flavors are blended. Makes 6 main-course servings.

Calories per serving: 252
Grams fat per serving: 7
Fiber: Excellent
Vitamins A and C and iron: Excellent
Niacin and phosphorus: Good

Tofu

It's cheap, nutritious, low in calories and fat. Tofu, or soybean curd, is one of the best sources of nonanimal protein you can find, as well as being rich in calcium, phosphorus, and iron. (The amount of calcium varies depending on the method of precipitation used. Check labels before buying.)

Tofu is usually sold in a custardlike cake form, covered in water, packed either in 1-pound plastic tubs or vacuum-packs. Check the "best before" date to make sure it is fresh.

Store tofu in the refrigerator and change the water it is packaged in every day. It will stay fresh for up to 7 days.

Tofu has a mild taste and can be used in everything from appetizers to desserts. Cut it into cubes and add it to soups or salads. Mash it and season with fresh herbs or spices, mustard, or garlic; add a little low-fat yogurt or sour cream and serve as a dip or sauce.

*See page 74 for information on bulgur wheat.

Fettuccine with Fresh Tomatoes and Basil

Make this dish in late summer or fall when tomatoes are at their best. For the most fiber, try to buy whole wheat noodles.

6   *ounces fettuccine noodles or 2 cups dried medium egg noodles*
2   *tablespoons olive oil*
2   *cloves garlic, finely chopped*
4   *tomatoes, diced*
½   *teaspoon dried basil or 2 tablespoons chopped fresh*
    Pinch granulated sugar
¼   *cup chopped fresh parsley*
    Salt and freshly ground pepper
2   *tablespoons grated Parmesan cheese*

In large pot of boiling water, cook noodles until al dente (tender but firm). Meanwhile, in heavy skillet, heat oil over medium heat; stir in garlic, tomatoes, basil, and sugar and cook for 5 minutes, stirring occasionally. Add parsley, and salt and pepper to taste.

Drain noodles. Toss with tomato mixture and Parmesan. (If sauce is too thick, add a few spoonfuls of pasta cooking liquid.) Pass extra Parmesan. Makes 2 main-course servings, 4 appetizer or side-dish servings.

Calories per main-course serving: 425
Grams fat per main-course serving: 14
Fiber: Good
Vitamins A and C, thiamine, and niacin: Excellent
Calcium, riboflavin, phosphorus, and iron: Good

Easy Summer Supper

Fettuccine with Fresh Tomatoes
   and Basil
Tossed green salad with Blue
   Cheese Dressing (page 94)
Sliced fresh peaches

Creamy Pasta with Broccoli, Cauliflower, and Mushrooms

Here's a hearty pasta dish your family will love. The variety of vegetables you can use is limitless—try adding carrots, snow peas, celery, or green beans.

1	small head cauliflower, trimmed and cut in florets
1	small bunch broccoli, trimmed and cut in florets
2	tablespoons olive oil or vegetable oil
3	cloves garlic, finely chopped
2½	cups thickly sliced mushrooms
2½	cups whole wheat noodles, egg noodles, or spaghetti (about 4 ounces)
1	cup low-fat small-curd cottage cheese
½	cup low-fat milk
¼	cup low-fat sour cream
¼	cup grated Parmesan cheese
	Salt and cayenne pepper

In large pot of boiling water, cook cauliflower and broccoli until tender-crisp, about 5 minutes. With slotted spoon, remove vegetables and save the liquid for cooking the pasta.

In large skillet, heat oil; sauté garlic for 2 minutes over medium heat; add mushrooms and sauté for about 5 minutes. Stir in broccoli and cauliflower; sauté for 2 to 3 minutes longer. Set aside.

Meanwhile, in reserved boiling vegetable liquid, cook pasta, adding water if necessary, until al dente (tender but firm), about 8 to 10 minutes; drain.

In food processor, combine cottage cheese, milk, sour cream, and Parmesan. Pour over broccoli mixture; add drained pasta and toss until mixed. Season with salt and cayenne pepper to taste. Serve immediately. Makes about 8 servings.

Calories per serving: 301
Grams fat per serving: 5
Fiber: Excellent
Vitamins A and C: Excellent
Thiamine, niacin, phosphorus, and iron: Good

Deep-Dish Vegetable Pizza

This scrumptious pizza is very filling. Two slices are plenty for dinner along with a salad. (See color photograph.)

Whole Wheat Pizza Dough (page 190)
1 **cup tomato sauce**
1 **tablespoon finely chopped fresh garlic**
1 **teaspoon each oregano and basil**
1 **teaspoon olive oil or vegetable oil**
3 **onions, sliced**
2 **cups sliced mushrooms**
Salt and freshly ground pepper
6 **cups broccoli, cut in 1-inch pieces**
3 **cups grated part skim mozzarella cheese**
(1 pound)

Prepare pizza dough. Divide into 2 pieces.* Roll out each piece to fit an 8- to 9-inch round quiche or cake pan that's at least 1½ inches deep.

In small bowl, combine tomato sauce, garlic, oregano, and basil; stir to mix.

In heavy skillet, heat oil over medium heat; add onions and cook over medium to low heat, stirring until tender, 5 to 10 minutes.

Add mushrooms and cook over medium heat, stirring or shaking pan until mushrooms are lightly browned and liquid has evaporated. Sprinkle with salt and pepper to taste and set aside.

In large pot of boiling water, cook broccoli for 2 minutes or until bright green; drain and cool under cold running water to prevent any further cooking. Drain again and set aside.

Spread tomato mixture over dough in pans. Cover with broccoli, then with mushrooms-onion mixture. Sprinkle with grated cheese. Bake in 425°F oven for 30 to 40 minutes or until crust is browned and top is bubbly. Makes 2 pizzas.

Calories per ¼ pizza: 293
Grams fat per ¼ pizza: 14
Fiber: Excellent
Vitamins A and C, riboflavin, niacin, phosphorus, thiamine, and calcium: Excellent
Iron: Good

Children's Party

Deep-Dish Vegetable Pizza
Crudités with Creamy Fresh Dill Dip (page 38)
Date Squares (page 195)
Coconut-Oatmeal Cookies (page 198)
Chocolate milk

*This method makes a thick crust. If you want a thin crust, divide dough into 3 portions and use the extra dough to make another pizza base. Dough can be frozen.

Triple-Cheese Lasagne

If making this for a special occasion, add sliced mushrooms and chopped sweet green or red pepper to the tomato sauce. No one will notice it doesn't have meat.

1	16-ounce can tomatoes, undrained
1	14-ounce can tomato sauce
2	onions, chopped
2	cloves garlic, finely chopped
1	tablespoon chopped parsley
2	teaspoons granulated sugar
1	teaspoon dried basil leaves
1	teaspoon dried thyme
2	teaspoons salt
	Freshly ground pepper
½	pound lasagne noodles
⅔	cup grated Parmesan cheese
2	cups low-fat cottage cheese
1	egg, lightly beaten
1	teaspoon oregano
2	cups grated part skim mozzarella (½ pound)

In saucepan, combine tomatoes, tomato sauce, onions, garlic, parsley, sugar, basil, thyme, ½ teaspoon of the salt, and pepper to taste. Bring to a boil. Reduce heat and simmer, uncovered, stirring occasionally, for 30 minutes or until mixture has a spaghetti-sauce consistency.

In large pot of boiling water, cook lasagne noodles until al dente (tender but firm). Drain and rinse under cold running water; drain well.

Reserve 3 tablespoons of the Parmesan for topping. In bowl, combine remaining Parmesan, cottage cheese, egg, oregano, ½ teaspoon salt, and pepper to taste. Mix well and set aside.

Reserve ½ cup of the tomato sauce for topping. In 13 × 9-inch baking dish, spoon just enough of the tomato sauce to cover bottom sparingly; top with a layer of lasagne noodles. Cover with ⅓ of the cottage cheese mixture, then ⅓ of the mozzarella cheese. Repeat with remaining sauce, noodles, and cheeses to make 3 layers of each. Top with reserved tomato sauce and sprinkle with reserved Parmesan. Bake, uncovered, in 350°F oven for 45 minutes or until hot and bubbly. Remove from oven and let cool slightly before serving. Makes 8 servings.

Calories per serving: 210
Grams fat per serving: 6
Niacin: Excellent
Vitamins A and C, calcium, and phosphorus: Good

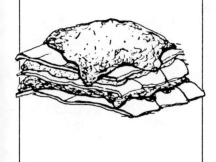

Winter Vegetable Stew

Other vegetables can be added to or substituted for the vegetables suggested here. Broccoli, green beans, asparagus in season, snow peas, or other quick-cooking vegetables can be added to the stew when you add the zucchini.

2   tablespoons vegetable oil
4   onions, coarsely chopped
4   large cloves garlic, finely chopped
1   bunch leeks (3 or 4)
4   potatoes
4   carrots
1/2 small rutabaga (yellow turnip)
1   sweet potato or small acorn squash
      (optional)
5   cups water (preferably vegetable cooking
      water) or chicken stock
2   teaspoons crumbled dried oregano leaves
2   teaspoons crumbled dried thyme leaves
2   small unpeeled zucchini, cut in chunks
      Salt and freshly ground pepper
      Chopped fresh parsley
      Grated Parmesan cheese

In large, heavy saucepan or Dutch oven, heat oil over medium heat. Add onions and garlic; cook until tender.

Discard tough green parts of leeks; cut leeks in half lengthwise and wash under cold running water. Cut into ¾-inch pieces. Peel potatoes, carrots, rutabaga, and sweet potato; cut into 1-inch cubes.

Add vegetables except zucchini to saucepan as they are prepared. Stir in water, oregano, and thyme; bring to a boil. Cover and simmer until vegetables are tender, about 30 minutes. Stir in zucchini, and salt and pepper to taste; simmer for 5 minutes or until all vegetables are tender, adding more water if desired.

Ladle stew into bowls and sprinkle with parsley. Pass Parmesan separately to sprinkle over stew. Makes 6 main-course servings.

Calories per serving without Parmesan: 205
Grams fat per serving without Parmesan: 4.8
Calories including 1 tablespoon Parmesan per serving: 237
Grams fat including 1 tablespoon Parmesan per serving: 6.3
Fiber: Excellent
Vitamins A and C, and niacin: Excellent
Phosphorus: Good

Baked Zucchini Omelet

Similar to a crustless zucchini and spinach quiche or a frittata, this is ideal with toast and salad or sliced tomatoes for brunch, lunch, or dinner.

1	**teaspoon butter**
1	**onion, chopped**
1	**clove garlic, finely chopped**
2	**cups thinly sliced unpeeled zucchini**
½	**cup grated skim-milk cheese**
2	**tablespoons chopped fresh parsley**
5	**eggs, lightly beaten**
1	**10-ounce package frozen chopped spinach, thawed and drained**
½	**teaspoon salt**
	Freshly ground pepper

In heavy skillet, melt butter over medium heat; cook onion and garlic until onion is tender. Add zucchini and cook, stirring, for 5 minutes.

In bowl, combine parsley, cheese, eggs, spinach, salt, and pepper to taste; mix well. Stir in zucchini mixture. Spoon into lightly oiled 9-inch pie plate. Bake in 325°F oven for 35 to 45 minutes or until set but still moist. Serve hot or cold. Makes 4 main-course servings.

Calories per serving: 154
Grams fat per serving: 9
Fiber: Excellent
Vitamins A and C: Excellent
Iron and niacin: Good

Tuscan White Kidney Bean and Tomato Casserole

You'll want to have a little of this left over—it's just as tasty cold. Good as a main course with a green salad and whole wheat pita bread, it's a high-fiber dinner that's easy to make.

1	tablespoon vegetable oil
1	onion, thinly sliced
1	clove garlic, finely chopped
1	large tomato, coarsely chopped
1	small sweet green pepper, diced
¼	teaspoon basil
	Pinch oregano
1	19-ounce can white kidney beans, drained
	Salt and freshly ground pepper
½	cup chopped fresh parsley

In small, heavy saucepan or flameproof casserole, heat oil over medium heat. Add onion and cook until tender. Stir in garlic, tomato, and green pepper; cook for 1 minute. Stir in basil, oregano, kidney beans, and salt and pepper to taste. Simmer over low heat for 5 minutes or until heated through and flavors are blended. Stir in parsley. Makes 2 main-course servings.

Calories per serving: 243
Grams fat per serving: 7
Fiber: Excellent
Iron and vitamins A and C: Excellent
Phosphorus, thiamine, and niacin: Good

Tomato Consommé

In large saucepan, combine 1½ cups tomato juice, 1 10-ounce can consommé or beef bouillon, 1 cup water, ½ teaspoon basil, and 1 tablespoon lemon juice. Bring to a boil. Reduce heat and simmer 1 to 2 minutes. Remove from heat and add 2 tablespoons sherry or white wine (or to taste) and some freshly ground pepper. Ladle into mugs and garnish with thinly sliced lemon. Serve hot. Makes 5 servings (¾ cup each).

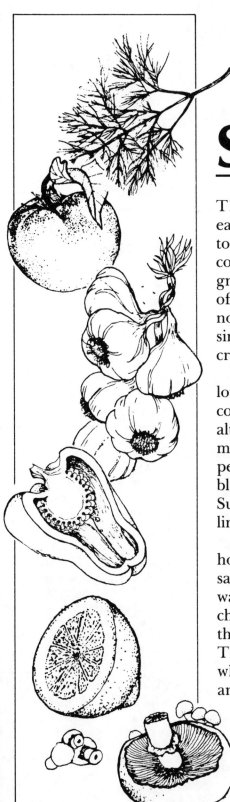

SAUCES

THE real test for chefs is in the sauce. They can easily cook meat to perfection, and garnish plates to look like a painting. But in any chefs' culinary competition sauces are tasted and discussed at great length. They have to be silky smooth, full of flavor but not overpowering, not too thick but not watery either. Often they are made with long-simmering stocks and enriched with butter and cream.

Now health-conscious diners are demanding lower-calorie sauces, and as a result a whole new collection of sauces is in vogue. Spa, light-lean, or alternative cuisines are part of many restaurant menus with exciting, innovative dishes. Red peppers are slowly roasted, then puréed to blanket a plate of tender, juicy chicken breasts. Sun-ripened mangoes, puréed with lemon or lime juice, complement perfectly cooked fish.

Most home cooks don't have wonderful homemade stock bases on hand. We want tasty sauces we can make in five to ten minutes. We want light sauces that aren't loaded with calories, cholesterol, and fat. Here is a selection of sauces that will fool even the most serious diners. They're full of flavor, yet low in fat, especially when compared to traditional sauces. And most are very quick to prepare.

Blackberry Sauce

This is delicious with turkey, chicken, and ham. Conventional gravy is much higher in fat than this sweet, yet tart, sauce. Currant jelly can be used instead of blackberry.

1   cup blackberry jelly
1/3   cup frozen orange juice concentrate
1/3   cup brandy
1/4   cup red wine vinegar or balsamic vinegar

In small saucepan, combine jelly, orange juice, brandy, and vinegar. Heat over low heat until jelly is melted; stir well. Makes 2 cups sauce.

Calories per 1 tablespoon: 30
Grams fat per 1 tablespoon: 0

Holiday Turkey Dinner

Roast turkey with Blackberry Sauce
Glazed Brussels Sprouts with Pecans (page 164)
Baked Squash with Ginger (page 174) or Turnips Paysanne (page 179)
Orange Sponge Cake (page 225) with Sherry Orange Sauce (page 215) and fruit sorbets (pages 206–208)

Diet Hint: Reducing fat content in sauces

- To remove fat from pan juices, skim surface fat or throw in ice cubes. Fat will adhere to the ice and can be easily removed. Or pour juices into a container and put in freezer. Remove solid fat from the surface. To thicken cold juices, add 2 tablespoons flour per cup of juice and heat, stirring, until thickened and smooth.

- Boil down pan juices if they're too thin and serve as a sauce.

- If using canned beef or chicken stock, refrigerate or freeze just before using. The fat will solidify on top and lift off easily.

- Use low-fat yogurt or puréed cottage cheese as a base for cold, cream-type sauces, instead of cream or mayonnaise.

- Instead of whipped cream, use fruits such as strawberries or raspberries puréed in a food processor or blender. These make delicious sauces to serve with other fruits, ice creams, sherbets, or cakes, and they're low in fat and calories.

- Many desserts are too sweet and need whipped cream or crème fraîche to tone down the sweetness. You won't need the whipped cream if you reduce the amount of sugar in puddings, pies, and fruit desserts instead.

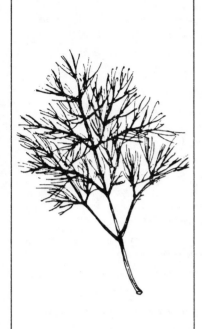

Dill Mustard Sauce

Serve with hot or cold fish dishes and seafood, as a dressing for salads, with chicken or turkey, or toss with cold cooked pasta.

$1/3$ **cup low-fat yogurt**
$1/3$ **cup low-fat cottage cheese**
2 **tablespoons chopped fresh dill***
$1/2$ **teaspoons Dijon mustard**

In food processor or blender, combine yogurt, cottage cheese, dill, and mustard; process until smooth. Alternatively, pass cottage cheese through a sieve, then mix with remaining ingredients. Makes ⅔ cup sauce.

Calories per 1 tablespoon: 11
Grams fat per 1 tablespoon: 0.1

Creamy Herb Sauce

Fresh herbs add wonderful flavor to sauces. Creamy Fresh Dill Dip (page 38) is delicious as a sauce and low in fat as well. Instead of fresh dill, substitute 1 to 2 tablespoons of chopped fresh tarragon, basil, or a combination of whatever fresh herbs you have on hand.

Calories per 1 tablespoon: 12
Grams fat per 1 tablespoon: 0.3

*Fresh dill gives this sauce excellent flavor; if not available, substitute 2 tablespoons chopped fresh parsley and 1 teaspoon dried dillweed. You can also make it using all yogurt or all cottage cheese.

Tomato Salsa

Serve this Mexican staple on lettuce, or as a topping for tacos or tostados, over cottage cheese, as a dip with Belgian endive wedges, as a filling for pita bread, or as an accompaniment to meats.

 4 **large tomatoes, diced**
 1 **large sweet green pepper, seeded and diced**
 1 **fresh hot chili pepper, 1 pickled jalapeño pepper, or 1 or 2 canned green chili peppers, seeded and diced**
 1 **tablespoon grated onion**
 1 **small clove garlic, crushed**
 2 **tablespoons chopped coriander leaves (also called cilantro or Chinese parsley)**
 1 **teaspoon crumbled leaf oregano Salt and freshly ground pepper**

In bowl, combine tomatoes, green pepper, chili pepper, onion, garlic, cilantro, and oregano; mix well. Season with salt and pepper to taste. Cover and refrigerate until needed. Makes 8 servings (½ cup each).

Calories per serving: 27
Grams fat per serving: 0.2
Vitamins A and C: Excellent

Tomato-Basil Sauce

Use this sauce over spaghetti, macaroni, or other pasta, as a base for pizza, or with cooked vegetables such as zucchini or green beans. Use the dried leaf form of basil and oregano, not ground; crush the herbs by rubbing them between the palms of your hands before adding to the sauce.

 2 **28-ounce cans plum tomatoes, undrained**
 1 **5½-ounce can tomato paste**
 2 **onions, finely chopped**
 2 **cloves garlic, finely chopped**
 1 **large bay leaf**
 2 **tablespoons crumbled basil**
 2 **teaspoons crumbled leaf oregano**
 1 **teaspoon salt Freshly ground pepper, sugar**

(continued)

In food processor, purée tomatoes or drain liquid into saucepan and chop tomatoes by hand. Pour into large, heavy saucepan and add tomato paste, onions, garlic, bay leaf, basil, and oregano. Simmer, uncovered, for 20 to 30 minutes or until sauce has thickened slightly and onions are tender. (If sauce thickens too quickly, cover for remaining cooking time.) Add salt, and pepper and sugar to taste. Makes about 6 cups sauce. (May be frozen.)

Calories per ½ cup: 38
Grams fat per ½ cup: 0.3
Vitamins A and C: Excellent

Ways to Cut Fat

Sauce for	Instead of	Grams fat per 2 tablespoons	Choose	Grams fat per 2 tablespoons
Asparagus, broccoli Fish and eggs Benedict	Conventional Hollandaise	7.8+	Yogurt Hollandaise (page 159)	1.8
Pork	Homemade gravy	5.9	Cinnamon Applesauce (page 231)	0.2
			Red Pepper Purée (page 166)	1.5
Beef	Homemade gravy	5.9	Pan juices (fat removed)	0.15
Steak	Béarnaise sauce	7.2+	Tarragon and Mushroom Sauce (page 158)	1.4
Chicken and turkey	Homemade gravy	5.9	Pan juices (fat removed)	0.15
			Cranberry sauce or Blackberry Sauce (page 154)	0.5
Hot or cold poached salmon and other fish	Cream sauces: thick (white sauce) medium thin	3.6 3.1 2.6	Creamy Herb Sauce (page 155)	0.5
	Mayonnaise	24.0	Dill Mustard Sauce (page 155)	0.2
Pasta	Butter- and cream-based sauces	10 +	Tomato-Basil Sauce (page 156)	0
	Conventional pesto recipe	7	Pesto (page 56)	3

Tarragon and Mushroom Sauce

Similar in taste to a Béarnaise sauce but with much less butter, this can be served warm with steak, meatballs, burgers, and other meats.

1   **tablespoon butter or margarine**
1   **cup chopped fresh mushrooms (about ¼ pound)**
2   **tablespoons chopped scallions**
4   **teaspoons all-purpose flour**
½   **teaspoon dried tarragon**
2   **cups beef stock**

In small saucepan, melt butter over medium heat. Add mushrooms and scallions and cook, stirring occasionally, until tender and most of the liquid has evaporated. Sprinkle with flour and tarragon; cook, stirring, for 2 minutes.

Bring stock to a boil; gradually pour into mushroom mixture while whisking constantly. Cook, stirring constantly, until mixture thickens slightly and boils. Simmer, uncovered, for 10 to 20 minutes or until sauce is reduced to about 1 cup. Serve hot. Makes 1 cup.

Calories per 1 tablespoon: 10
Grams fat per 1 tablespoon: 0.7

Yogurt Hollandaise

Use this sauce with vegetables or fish. It tastes like a Hollandaise but is made with yogurt instead of butter.

1	**cup low-fat yogurt**
2	**teaspoons lemon juice**
3	**egg yolks**
½	**teaspoon salt**
½	**teaspoon Dijon mustard**
	Pinch freshly ground pepper
1	**tablespoon chopped fresh dill or parsley (optional)**

In top of nonaluminum double boiler or saucepan,* beat yogurt, lemon juice, and egg yolks. Heat over simmering water, stirring frequently, until sauce has thickened, about 15 minutes. (Sauce will become thinner after about 10 minutes of cooking, then will thicken again.) Remove from heat and stir in salt, mustard, pepper, and dill (if using). Serve warm. (Sauce can be prepared in advance, refrigerated for up to 1 week, then reheated over hot, not simmering, water.) Makes about 1¼ cups.

Calories per 1 tablespoon: 17
Grams fat per 1 tablespoon: 0.9

For other sauce recipes, see:

Red Pepper Purée (page 166)
Curry Sauce (page 108)
Pesto (page 56)

For dessert sauces,

see pages 215, 232–233.

*Egg-yolk mixtures cooked in an aluminum pan will discolor.

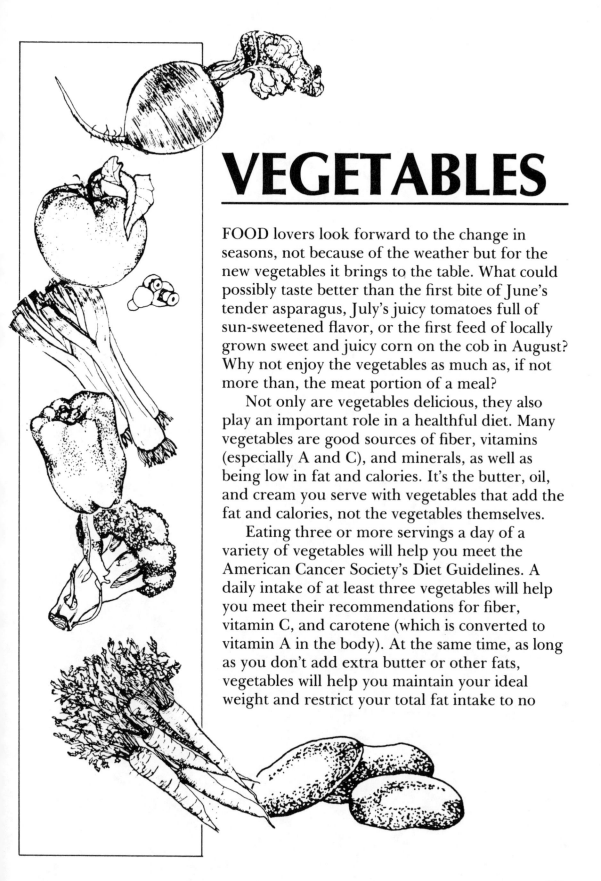

VEGETABLES

FOOD lovers look forward to the change in seasons, not because of the weather but for the new vegetables it brings to the table. What could possibly taste better than the first bite of June's tender asparagus, July's juicy tomatoes full of sun-sweetened flavor, or the first feed of locally grown sweet and juicy corn on the cob in August? Why not enjoy the vegetables as much as, if not more than, the meat portion of a meal?

Not only are vegetables delicious, they also play an important role in a healthful diet. Many vegetables are good sources of fiber, vitamins (especially A and C), and minerals, as well as being low in fat and calories. It's the butter, oil, and cream you serve with vegetables that add the fat and calories, not the vegetables themselves.

Eating three or more servings a day of a variety of vegetables will help you meet the American Cancer Society's Diet Guidelines. A daily intake of at least three vegetables will help you meet their recommendations for fiber, vitamin C, and carotene (which is converted to vitamin A in the body). At the same time, as long as you don't add extra butter or other fats, vegetables will help you maintain your ideal weight and restrict your total fat intake to no more than 30 percent of your daily calorie intake.

When planning meals, include both fresh and raw vegetables. (Raw contain more fiber and vitamin C.) Make sure you have a pleasing combination of colors, flavors, and textures. For instance, don't serve turnip, cauliflower, and parsnip at the same meal. They're all strongly flavored, similar in texture, and lacking in color contrast. Include bright green, deep yellow, and orange vegetables as much as possible, not only for their visual appeal but for their nutrients. Refer to Table G (page 251) to see which vegetables have the most fiber.

For the most fiber and vitamins:

- Don't peel vegetables if the skins are edible (e.g., potatoes, zucchini, cucumber). They contain fiber as well as nutrients.
- Don't discard the seeds if they're edible (e.g., those in tomatoes and cucumbers). They are excellent sources of fiber.
- Don't overcook vegetables.
- Eat vegetables raw as often as possible.

Tomatoes Florentine

This is an attractive make-ahead addition to a buffet table or dinner.

Variation:

Tomatoes Provençal: Cut 6 tomatoes in half crosswise. Combine ½ cup fine bread crumbs, 1 large clove finely chopped garlic, ¼ cup chopped parsley, and 1 tablespoon olive oil. Sprinkle crumb mixture over tomato halves and place on baking sheet. Bake in 400°F oven for 15 minutes or until heated through. Makes 6 servings.

6   *tomatoes*
2   *teaspoons butter*
1   *small onion, finely chopped*
1   *clove garlic, finely chopped*
1   *12-ounce package frozen chopped
     spinach, thawed and drained*
⅓   *cup low-fat milk*
      Salt and freshly ground pepper

TOPPING:

2   *tablespoons fine dry bread crumbs*
2   *tablespoons chopped fresh parsley*
2   *teaspoons grated Parmesan cheese*

Cut a slice from top of each tomato. Scoop out pulp to halfway down tomato and save for sauce or soup.

In skillet, melt butter. Stir in onion and garlic; cook over medium heat until tender. Stir in spinach, milk, and salt and pepper to taste. Spoon mixture into tomatoes and arrange in ovenproof serving dish or on baking sheet.

Topping: Combine bread crumbs, parsley, and Parmesan; sprinkle over top of tomatoes. Bake in 400°F oven for 20 minutes or until heated through. Makes 6 servings.

Calories per serving: 70
Grams fat per serving: 2
Fiber: Excellent
Vitamins A and C: Excellent
Folacin: Good

Brussels sprouts belong to the brassica genus of the cruciferous family of vegetables. People whose diets frequently include these vegetables have a lower risk of colon cancer.

Add butter at the end of the cooking of vegetables to get maximum flavor with minimum fat.

Glazed Brussels Sprouts with Pecans

Traditional with a turkey dinner, this recipe can be easily doubled or tripled. Walnuts can be used instead of pecans; just make sure they are fresh.

2 cups small Brussels sprouts
2 teaspoons butter or margarine
2 teaspoons granulated sugar
2 tablespoons coarsely chopped pecans
   Salt and freshly ground pepper

Trim base of sprouts and outside leaves. Steam sprouts over boiling water for about 10 minutes or until tender. Drain thoroughly.

   In skillet, melt butter over medium heat; add sugar and stir until melted. Add sprouts and pecans; stir to coat well and cook for 1 to 2 minutes. Season with salt and pepper to taste. Makes 4 servings.

Calories per serving: 81
Grams fat per serving: 5
Fiber: Good
Vitamin C: Excellent

Excellent Sources of Fiber
(more than 4 grams of fiber per serving):

½ cup kidney beans	½ cup pinto beans
½ cup green peas	⅔ cup broccoli
1 cup white beans	½ cup spinach

Good Sources of Fiber
(2 to 3.9 grams fiber per serving):

2 beets	1 carrot
4 Brussels sprouts	½ cup lentils
¾ cup raw cabbage	½ cup turnip
½ cup parsnips	½ cup lima beans

(Measurements are for cooked vegetables, except cabbage.)

Tarragon Carrots

Onion and tarragon add extra flavor and color to carrots. Cook them in the oven or microwave to retain the vitamins, and save time by slicing the carrots and onions in the food processor.

4   **large carrots, thinly sliced (2 cups)**
2   **small onions, thinly sliced**
1   **teaspoon tarragon**
2   **tablespoons water**
    Salt and freshly ground pepper
2   **teaspoons butter**

Lightly oil a large sheet of foil or a 6-cup microwave dish. On foil or in dish, place carrots and onion; sprinkle with tarragon, water, and pepper to taste. Wrap tightly or cover. Cook in 350°F oven for 30 minutes, or microwave on High for 10 to 12 minutes, or until tender. Stir in butter and salt to taste. Makes 4 servings.

Calories per serving: 37
Grams fat per serving: 2
Fiber: Good
Vitamin A: Excellent

Lemon-Ginger Carrots

Combine 1 tablespoon each butter, granulated sugar, and lemon juice with 1 teaspoon each grated lemon rind and grated fresh ginger root; cook until sugar dissolves. Toss with 2 to 3 cups hot cooked carrots.

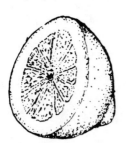

Asparagus with Red Pepper Purée

Serve this colorful dish as a first course in asparagus season. (See color photograph.)

2	**large sweet red peppers**
2	**teaspoons olive oil**
1/4	**teaspoon dried thyme**
	Freshly ground pepper
2	**pounds asparagus**

Roast peppers on a baking sheet in 375°F oven for 18 minutes. Turn and roast on other side for 18 minutes longer or until peppers are blistered and soft. Remove from oven and place in a heavy paper or plastic bag. Close bag and let peppers steam for 10 to 15 minutes. Using fingers and a small knife, peel skin from peppers (it should come off easily); seed and cut into strips.

In skillet, heat oil over medium heat; when hot, add roasted peppers and thyme. Sauté for 2 minutes; season with pepper to taste. Purée in food processor. (Purée can be prepared in advance, covered, and refrigerated for up to 1 week; reheat gently over low heat before continuing with recipe.)

Wash and break tough ends off asparagus; cook in large pot of boiling water for 5 to 8 minutes or until tender; drain thoroughly.

Spoon hot pepper purée over individual plates. Arrange hot asparagus on top. Makes 6 servings.

Calories per serving: 56
Grams fat per serving: 2.6
Fiber: Good
Vitamins A and C: Excellent

Roasted red peppers have a wonderful, rich flavor. They're usually quickly roasted under a broiler, over a flame, or on the barbecue until they char and blacken. We recommend roasting them slowly just until they blister, not until they char, since charred or barbecued foods may contain carcinogenic substances.

Spring Dinner Party Menu

Asparagus with Red Pepper Purée
Marinated Leg of Lamb with Coriander (page 123)
Cracked Wheat and Basil Pilaf (page 183)
Steamed cherry tomatoes and snow peas or Sautéed Zucchini with Yogurt and Herbs (page 173) or Stir-Fried Vegetables with Ginger and Garlic (page 176)
Fresh Strawberry Sorbet (page 207)

Broccoli and Sweet Pepper Stir-Fry

This red, yellow, and green vegetable dish tastes as good as it looks.

1	bunch broccoli (about 1 pound)
1	sweet red pepper
1	sweet yellow pepper
1	tablespoon vegetable oil
1	onion, chopped
1	teaspoon grated fresh ginger root
¼	cup chicken stock
2	teaspoons soy sauce

Peel tough broccoli stems. Cut stems and florets into pieces about 1½ inches long. Blanch in large pot of boiling water for 2 to 3 minutes or until bright green and tender-crisp; drain, cool under cold running water, and dry on paper towels. Seed peppers and cut into thin strips. (This can be done in advance.)

In large, heavy skillet or wok, heat oil over medium heat. Add onion and ginger; stir-fry for 1 minute. Add peppers and stir-fry for 2 to 3 minutes, adding chicken stock when necessary to prevent sticking or scorching. Add broccoli; stir-fry until heated through; sprinkle with soy sauce. Serve immediately. Makes 8 servings.

Calories per serving: 40
Grams fat per serving: 2
Fiber: Good
Vitamins A and C: Excellent

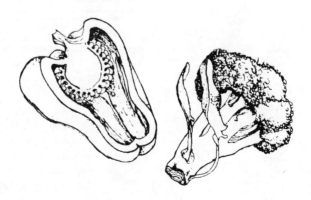

Fall Dinner Menu:

Pork Tenderloin with Rosemary and Thyme (page 120)
Two-Cabbage Stir-Fry
Mashed Potatoes with Onions (page 180) and/or green peas
Peach Blueberry Crisp (page 219)

Two-Cabbage Stir-Fry

Red and green cabbage stir-fried with ginger and onion is especially good with pork and turkey. Rice vinegar is a mild, sweet vinegar, available in the Chinese food section of many supermarkets. (Recipe can be doubled.) (See color photograph.)

1	tablespoon rice vinegar
1	tablespoon water
1	teaspoon soy sauce
1	teaspoon cornstarch
1	tablespoon vegetable oil
1	teaspoon chopped fresh ginger root
1	small onion, chopped
1	cup thinly sliced red cabbage
1	cup thinly sliced green cabbage

In small dish, mix together vinegar, water, soy sauce, and cornstarch; set aside.

In wok or heavy skillet, heat oil over medium heat. Add ginger and onion; stir-fry for 1 minute. Add both kinds of cabbage and stir-fry until tender, 3 to 5 minutes.

Pour in soy sauce mixture and stir-fry until liquid comes to a boil, about 1 minute. Serve hot. Makes 3 servings.

Calories per serving: 75
Grams fat per serving: 5
Fiber: Good
Vitamin C: Excellent

Braised Red Cabbage

Here's a flavorful vegetable that's especially good with pork or poultry. You can make this a day or two in advance and reheat it. To retain a bright red color when cooking red cabbage, include an acid such as vinegar or lemon juice in the cooking liquid.

½	medium red cabbage
1	cooking apple
⅓	cup water
¼	cup white wine vinegar
	Salt and freshly ground pepper
2	tablespoons (approximate) honey or granulated sugar

(continued)

Remove outer leaves and center core of cabbage. Slice thinly. Peel, core, and slice apple. In large skillet or heavy pan, combine cabbage, apple, water, and vinegar. Stir and bring to a boil. Reduce heat and simmer, covered, stirring occasionally, for 1 hour or until cabbage is very tender.

Stir in salt, pepper, and honey to taste. The flavor should be sweet and sour. Adjust seasonings if necessary. Makes 4 servings.

Calories per serving: 55
Grams fat per serving: 0.3
Fiber: Good
Vitamin C: Excellent

Scalloped Cabbage au Gratin

Here's a good way to serve cabbage. It's a delicious dish that adds some protein to a meatless meal, and also goes well with hot or cold beef, pork, and lamb. It can be prepared in advance and baked just before serving.

4	**cups coarsely shredded cabbage**
1	**14½-ounce can tomatoes, undrained**
2	**teaspoons granulated sugar**
¼	**teaspoon paprika**
1	**teaspoon salt**
1	**teaspoon oregano**
	Salt and freshly ground pepper
½	**cup grated cheddar cheese**
1	**cup fine fresh bread crumbs**

Cook cabbage in boiling water until wilted, about 6 minutes; drain well. Combine tomatoes, sugar, paprika, salt, and oregano, breaking up tomatoes with back of spoon. In greased 6-cup baking dish, place cabbage. Sprinkle with salt and pepper to taste. Cover with tomato mixture, then cheese. Top with crumbs. Bake, uncovered, in 350°F oven for 30 minutes or until heated through. Makes 6 servings.

Calories per serving: 98
Grams fat per serving: 3
Fiber: Good
Vitamin C: Excellent
Vitamin A: Good

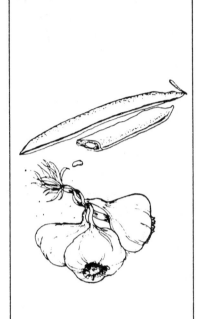

Herbed Green Beans with Garlic

Herbs, onion, and garlic enhance the flavor of beans without adding calories or fat. (See color photograph.)

1 **pound green beans**
2 **teaspoons butter or oil**
1 **small onion, thinly sliced**
1 **clove garlic, finely chopped**
1 **tablespoon chopped fresh thyme or oregano or ½ teaspoon dried**
Salt and freshly ground pepper

Trim beans and cook in rapidly boiling water for 4 to 5 minutes or until tender-crisp; drain.

In heavy skillet or saucepan, melt butter; add onion and garlic and cook over medium-low heat, stirring occasionally, until onion is tender. Stir in beans, thyme, and salt and pepper to taste. Cook until heated. Makes 4 servings.

Calories per serving: 42
Grams fat per serving: 2
Fiber: Good

October-November Friday Night Dinner Menu

Lemon Chicken Schnitzel (page 100)
Baked Leeks au Gratin
Baked Squash with Ginger (page 174)
Tossed green salad
Deep-Dish Plum Pie (page 230)

Baked Leeks au Gratin

Though leeks are available nearly all year round, they're in season and most reasonably priced during the fall. They're delicious with any cut of meat or poultry, or as part of an all-vegetable dinner.

4 **large leeks**
2 **teaspoons butter**
Salt and freshly ground pepper
4 **teaspoons grated Parmesan cheese**
1 **teaspoon water**

Trim base and tough green leaves from leeks, leaving tender green and white parts. Cut in half lengthwise; wash under cold running water and drain. Place, cut side up, in single layer in microwave dish or on lightly oiled foil. Dot with butter and season with salt and pepper to taste.

(continued)

Sprinkle Parmesan on top. Add 1 teaspoon water to side of leeks. Cover dish or wrap in foil. Microwave on High for 5 to 7 minutes, or bake in 350°F oven for 25 minutes or until tender. Makes 4 servings.

Calories per serving: 53
Grams fat per serving: 2.6
Fiber: Good
Vitamin C: Good

Braised Red Pepper and Leeks

This dish goes well with lamb, pork, or beef, but don't use more red pepper than called for—it could overpower the subtle flavor of the leeks.

   6 leeks
   1 large sweet red pepper
  ½ cup water or chicken stock
   1 tablespoon butter
     Salt and freshly ground pepper

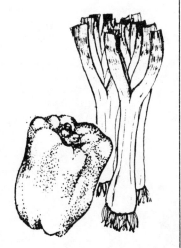

Cut dark green part and base from leeks and discard. Cut leeks in half lengthwise and wash thoroughly under cold running water. Cut into ½-inch thick slices. (You should have about 4 cups.) Remove core and seeds from red pepper; cut into thin 1-inch long strips.

In saucepan, combine chicken stock and leeks; cover and simmer for 5 to 10 minutes or until leeks are almost tender. Add red pepper strips, cover, and simmer for another 5 to 10 minutes or until tender. If too much liquid, uncover and cook for 1 to 2 minutes. Add butter, and salt and pepper to taste. Makes 4 servings.

Calories per serving: 84
Grams fat per serving: 3
Fiber: Good
Vitamins A and C: Excellent

Steam Cooking

To steam food means to cook over, not in, boiling water or other liquid. Foods wrapped in foil, then baked or barbecued, steam in their own liquids. Herbs, salt, sugar, or spices can be added to the foods or to the liquid before steaming. The advantage of steaming is that vegetables retain their flavor, color, and vitamins, and fish is moist and flavorful. Food can be steamed in the oven, on top of the stove, or on the barbecue.

Equipment for steaming

There are a number of steamers on the market, but you don't have to have special equipment.

- Wrap foods in foil, then cook in the oven or on the barbecue.

- In top-of-stove cooking, you can use a deep pot with a tight-fitting lid and something to keep the food above the liquid. This could be a steamer with perforated petals and short legs, a flat-bottomed metal colander or one with feet, or a metal strainer. Large foods such as chicken or pudding can be placed on an inverted heatproof plate or bowl, or on custard cups or a wire rack. A wok with a rack inside, and covered with a lid (or foil if the lid isn't tight-fitting), can also be used.

- To oven-steam, use a roasting pan with a trivet, wire rack, or anything that is heatproof to keep the food above the liquid.

- Steam-cook in a deep-fryer with basket set over water instead of oil.

- Use a clay baker.

Foil-Steamed Spring Vegetables

These vegetables go well with fish or chicken. In winter, use parsnips, snow peas, or beans instead of asparagus and cut the carrots into ½-inch pieces. White pearl onions, which are the size of small grapes, are sold in pint boxes. They keep for a month or two in a cool, dry place.

½	**pound fresh pearl onions**
¾	**pound fresh baby carrots**
½	**pound asparagus**
2	**tablespoons water**
1	**tablespoon butter**
1	**bay leaf**
½	**teaspoon salt**
	Pinch white pepper

In large pot of boiling water, blanch pearl onions for 2 minutes; drain. Cut off root end and gently squeeze to remove skin. In another large pot of boiling water, blanch carrots for 2 minutes; drain, rinse under cold running water, and drain again. Snap tough ends from asparagus.

On large piece of heavy-duty foil, arrange vegetables in a single layer. Sprinkle with water, dot with butter, and add bay leaf, salt, and pepper. Fold foil over vegetables and seal. Bake in 375°F oven for 20 to 30 minutes or until vegetables are tender. Makes 6 servings.

Calories per serving: 65
Grams fat per serving: 3
Fiber: Good
Vitamin A: Excellent
Vitamin C: Good

Sautéed Zucchini with Yogurt and Herbs

Sautéed zucchini dressed with yogurt or sour cream is a delicious, quick vegetable recipe; because sour cream is higher in fat content, it is healthier to substitute low-fat yogurt.

1 *pound zucchini (about 3 small)*
2 *teaspoons butter*
1 *small onion, sliced and separated into rings*
6 *tablespoons low-fat yogurt or sour cream*
2 *tablespoons chopped fresh parsley*
½ *teaspoon crumbled leaf oregano or 2 teaspoons chopped fresh*
   Salt and freshly ground pepper

Trim ends from zucchini. In food procesor or by hand, slice zucchini thin.

In heavy skillet, melt butter over medium heat; add onion and cook, stirring, until tender. Add zucchini and cook, stirring often, just until barely tender, about 5 minutes.

Remove from heat and stir in yogurt, parsley, oregano, and salt and pepper to taste. Stir to coat well and serve immediately. Makes 6 servings.

Calories per serving: 34
Grams fat per serving: 1.4
Vitamin C: Good

30-Minute Summer Dinner

Sole Fillets with Lemon and Parsley (page 129)
Sautéed Zucchini with Yogurt and Herbs
Tomatoes Provençal (page 163)
Tiny boiled potatoes in skins
Fresh strawberries or cantaloupe

Puréed vegetables, because of their creamy texture, can be served instead of a vegetable with a cream sauce. Puréed parsnips team well with green beans, broccoli, or other green vegetables that have been steamed or boiled. Serve with any meats or poultry. For a slightly milder flavor, combine puréed parsnips or turnips with mashed potatoes.

Parsnip Purée

You can use carrots, turnips, or squash instead of parsnips in this recipe. When buying parsnips, remember that the small ones are more tender and sweet than the older, fat ones.

2	**pounds parsnips**
1	**tablespoon butter**
¼	**cup low-fat milk**
1	**tablespoon sherry (optional)**
¼	**teaspoon freshly ground nutmeg**
	Salt and freshly ground pepper

Peel parsnips and cut into chunks. Cook in boiling water until tender; drain and purée in a food processor, blender, or food mill. Add butter, milk, sherry (if using), nutmeg, and salt and pepper to taste; process or stir until mixed. Return to saucepan to reheat or spoon into serving dish; cover and keep warm. (Purée can be prepared in advance and gently reheated before serving.) Makes 8 servings.

Calories per serving: 93
Grams fat per serving: 2
Fiber: Good
Vitamin C: Good

Baked Squash with Ginger

Ginger goes particularly well with squash. Grated orange rind also heightens the flavor and can be used instead of ginger.

2¼	**pounds squash (Hubbard, butternut, or acorn)**
2	**tablespoons butter**
2	**tablespoons brown sugar**
1	**teaspoon ground ginger**
	Salt, freshly ground pepper, and freshly grated nutmeg

Cut squash in half; scoop out seeds. Cover with foil and place on baking sheet. Bake in 400°F oven for 40 minutes or until tender. Alternatively, place in microwave dish, partially cover, and cook in microwave on High for 7 to 10 minutes. *(continued)*

Drain squash and scoop out pulp; mash or purée with 2 or 3 on-off turns in food processor. Stir in butter, brown sugar, ginger, and salt, pepper, and nutmeg to taste. (Squash can be prepared ahead to this point; transfer to baking dish and reheat, covered, in 350°F oven or microwave until hot.) Makes 6 servings.

Calories per serving: 93
Grams fat per serving: 4
Vitamin A: Excellent
Vitamin C: Good

Barley and Parsley Pilaf

Red onion adds crunch and flavor to this intriguing rice dish.

³/₄ **cup pearl barley**
³/₄ **cup raw brown rice**
¹/₂ **cup hot chicken stock**
¹/₂ **cup chopped red onion or scallion**
 1 **cup chopped fresh parsley**
   Salt and freshly ground pepper

Cook barley in 3 cups boiling water for 30 minutes or until tender; drain.

In another saucepan, bring 2 cups water to a boil; add rice, cover, and simmer for 30 minutes or until rice is tender and water has been absorbed.

In 6-cup casserole, combine rice, barley, chicken stock, onion, parsley, and salt and pepper to taste. (May be prepared in advance to this point.) Bake in 350°F oven for 20 minutes or until heated through. Makes 8 servings.

Calories per serving: 116
Grams fat per serving: 0.6
Fiber: Good
Vitamins A and C: Good

Stir-Fried Vegetables with Ginger and Garlic

The wonderful colors and flavor combinations in this dish complement any meat from chicken and lamb to beef. You need only add rice to complete the main course. For a one-dish meal, add chicken, turkey, shellfish, or ham to the stir-fry and serve over hot pasta.

¼	**pound green beans**
1	**small zucchini**
2	**carrots**
½	**small cauliflower**
1	**large stalk broccoli**
1	**sweet red or yellow pepper (or combination)**
¼	**pound snow peas**
2	**tablespoons vegetable oil**
1	**red onion, thinly sliced**
3	**cloves garlic, finely chopped**
2	**tablespoons finely chopped fresh ginger root**
2	**tablespoons soy sauce**
	Salt and freshly ground pepper

Cut beans on the diagonal into 1½-inch lengths. Thinly slice zucchini and carrots on the diagonal. Cut cauliflower and broccoli into florets. Slice broccoli stem crosswise on the diagonal. Seed peppers and cut into 1-inch squares. Remove flower ends from snow peas.

In large pot of boiling water, blanch beans, carrots, cauliflower, and broccoli separately just until tender-crisp. Drain, and immediately rinse under cold running water to prevent further cooking; drain thoroughly. (Vegetables can be prepared in advance to this point.)

Twenty minutes before serving, heat about 2 teaspoons of the oil in heavy skillet over medium heat. Add onion and 1 clove garlic; stir-fry for 3 to 4 minutes. Add zucchini and some ginger and more garlic; stir-fry for 3 minutes longer, adding more oil if necessary. If pan is full, transfer vegetables to baking dish and keep warm in 250°F oven. Add as many of the blanched vegetables as you can stir-fry at one time, plus some of the garlic and ginger, and cook, stirring, for 2 to 3 minutes or until hot; transfer to baking dish in oven to keep warm and continue stir-frying remaining vegetables, adding a small amount of oil as

Because of its high sodium content, use soy sauce sparingly. Naturally brewed and sodium-reduced soy sauces are lower in sodium than chemically brewed ones.

necessary. Finish with peppers and snow peas, cooking until tender-crisp. Combine all vegetables; toss with soy sauce, and salt and pepper to taste. Makes 8 servings.

Calories per serving: 67
Grams fat per serving: 3
Fiber: Good
Vitamins A and C: Excellent

Orange Sherried Sweet Potatoes

These can be prepared a day in advance, then reheated just before serving. They go well with turkey, goose, or ham. Instead of sherry, you can substitute ginger, maple syrup, or crushed pineapple (adjust amount to taste).

4 large sweet potatoes
1 tablespoon butter
Grated rind of ½ orange
¼ cup orange juice
2 tablespoons (approximate) sherry
2 tablespoons brown sugar
Pinch freshly grated nutmeg
Salt and freshly ground pepper

In pot of boiling water, cook unpeeled potatoes until tender, 30 to 40 minutes. Drain, let cool slightly, then peel. While still warm, mash potatoes with butter, orange rind, orange juice, sherry, sugar, nutmeg, and salt and pepper to taste. Return to saucepan and reheat over medium heat, or refrigerate until 1 hour before serving, then reheat, covered, in 350°F oven for about 25 minutes or until hot. Makes 5 servings.

Calories per serving: 208
Grams fat per serving: 3
Fiber: Good
Vitamins A and C: Excellent

Mashed Turnips with Carrots and Orange

Adding mashed carrots to turnips, along with a pinch of brown sugar and a dollop of butter, mellows the turnip and at the same time adds flavor to the carrots. (See color photograph.)

1	*small yellow turnip (rutabaga)*
4	*carrots*
2	*tablespoons brown sugar*
2	*tablespoons frozen orange juice concentrate (undiluted)*
1	*tablespoon butter or margarine*
	Pinch nutmeg
	Salt and freshly ground pepper
	Chopped parsley (optional)

Peel turnip and carrots. Cut into ¾-inch chunks. Cook in separate pots of simmering water until very tender; drain. Mash each, either with potato masher or in food processor.

Combine turnip, carrots, sugar, orange juice, butter, nutmeg, and salt and pepper to taste. Sprinkle with parsley (if using). Serve immediately or cover and reheat before serving. Makes 8 servings.

Calories per serving: 31
Grams fat per serving: 2
Vitamin A: Excellent

Turnips Paysanne

Either white turnips or a yellow rutabaga can be used in this recipe, but the rutabaga will take longer to cook. To save time, use the food processor to slice the vegetables.

1	**small rutabaga or 4-6 white turnips (about 2 pounds)**
1	**cup sliced celery**
1	**cup sliced carrots**
1	**large clove garlic, finely chopped**
1	**onion, chopped**
1	**cup chicken stock**
1/4	**cup chopped fresh parsley**
1	**tablespoon butter**
	Salt and freshly ground pepper

Peel and dice turnips (or slice in a food processor). In heavy saucepan, combine turnip, celery, carrots, garlic, onion, and stock. Bring to a boil; cover, and simmer until vegetables are tender, about 20 minutes.

Uncover and cook until liquid has reduced to a glaze. Sprinkle with parsley, butter, and salt and pepper to taste. Makes 6 servings.

Calories per serving: 54
Grams fat per serving: 2.4
Fiber: Good
Vitamins A and C: Excellent

Mashed Potatoes with Onions

These everyday vegetables are delicious when mixed; the onions add such flavor to the potatoes that you won't notice the absence of butter. Remember this recipe when you have baked potatoes: Scoop out the center of the potatoes and mix with the rest of the ingredients; spoon it back into the potato skins and reheat in 350°F oven for about 10 minutes. Or, if you are using another filling for the potato skins, use the scooped-out potatoes for this recipe.

6	**potatoes**
2	**teaspoons butter**
2	**onions, finely chopped**
1	**tablespoon water**
½	**cup low-fat milk**
	Salt and pepper

Peel potatoes and cut into quarters. Cook potatoes in boiling water until tender, about 20 minutes.

Meanwhile, in heavy skillet, melt butter; add onions and water and cook over medium-low heat, stirring occasionally, until onions are tender, 10 to 15 minutes, reducing the heat if necessary so onions don't brown.

Drain potatoes and return pan to stove; heat over low heat for 1 to 2 minutes, shaking pan to dry potatoes. Mash potatoes with half of the milk, adding remaining milk to taste (amount of milk needed will vary depending on size and kind of potatoes). Stir in onions, add salt and pepper to taste. Makes 6 servings.

Calories per serving: 123
Grams fat per serving: 2
Fiber: Good
Vitamin C: Excellent
Baked potato stuffed with Mashed Potatoes with Onions:
Fiber: Excellent for large potato

Compare:
For maximum fiber, don't peel potatoes.

	Grams dietary fiber
1 large baked or boiled potato with skin	4
1 large potato, peeled then boiled	2

Curried Fruit with Rice

Light and juicy fruits plus curry make a fresh, pleasing flavor-and-texture combination. Along with rice, they go well with lamb or baked ham. This curry sauce is mildly flavored so as not to overpower the fruit. Add more curry powder for a spicier dish.

New Year's Day or Easter Dinner

Sherry-Braised Ham (page 121) with Curried Fruit with rice
Steamed broccoli
Green salad with Parsley Dressing (page 95)
Poached Pears with Chocolate Sauce (page 205)

2   cups cantaloupe or honeydew melon balls
1   cup diced fresh pineapple
1   banana, sliced
1   cup sliced peaches, strawberries, grapes, or mandarin oranges (or combination)
1   cup chicken stock
1½   teaspoons cornstarch
2   teaspoons curry powder
½   cup finely chopped chutney
¼   cup raisins
2   tablespoons butter
5   cups hot cooked rice
¼   cup slivered toasted almonds*

Combine fruits in bowl; set aside.

In saucepan, combine stock, cornstarch, and curry; mix well. Bring to a boil over medium heat, stirring constantly. (Sauce can be prepared ahead to this point; reheat before continuing with recipe.)

Just before serving, combine chutney, fruits, and raisins; stir to mix. Add to hot curry sauce. Add butter; stir until melted.

To serve: Transfer to serving bowl and sprinkle nuts on top. Place rice in a separate serving dish. Spoon some curried fruit over some of the rice on each person's plate. Or spoon hot rice around edge of shallow serving dish; spoon curried-fruit mixture into center. Makes 8 servings.

Calories per serving (including rice): 268
Grams fat per serving: 6
Fiber: Good
Iron and vitamin C: Good

*To toast almonds, place on baking sheet and roast in 350°F oven for 5 minutes or until lightly golden in color.

Brown Rice with Currants

This flavorful rice dish goes well with chicken, turkey, pork, lamb, and fish.

½ **cup currants**
2 **tablespoons sherry**
1 **teaspoon butter**
1 **onion, chopped**
2 **cups raw brown rice**
4 **cups chicken broth**
1 **teaspoon dried basil leaves**
Salt and freshly ground pepper

Soak currants in sherry and set aside until needed.

In heavy saucepan, melt butter over medium heat; stir in onion and cook, stirring, until tender. Add rice and stir to mix well.

Bring stock to a boil. Pour over rice; stir in basil, and salt and pepper to taste. Simmer, covered, until water has been absorbed, about 40 minutes. Stir in currants and sherry. Makes 8 servings.

Calories per serving: 112
Grams fat per serving: 2.5

Cracked Wheat and Basil Pilaf

Keep this tasty dish in mind for an all-vegetable dinner, or serve with meats or poultry. (See color photograph.)

¾	**cup cracked wheat or bulgur**
1	**tablespoon oil**
1	**large onion, finely chopped**
2	**cloves garlic, finely chopped**
1	**cup thinly sliced mushrooms**
1	**large tomato, diced, or 1 tablespoon each tomato paste and water**
½	**cup chopped fresh basil***
¼	**cup slivered almonds**
½	**teaspoon salt**
	Freshly ground pepper

Rinse cracked wheat under cold running water; place in bowl and add water to cover by at least 2 inches. Soak for 1 hour or until tender. Drain thoroughly.

In heavy skillet, heat oil. Add onion and cook, stirring, over medium heat until tender. Stir in garlic and mushrooms and cook until mushrooms are tender, about 2 minutes.

Stir in tomato, cracked wheat, basil, almonds, salt, and pepper to taste; stir until mixed and heated through. Makes 6 servings (½ cup each).

Calories per serving: 172
Grams fat per serving without almonds: 3
Grams fat per serving with almonds: 6
Fiber: Excellent
Phosphorus, vitamins A and C, and niacin: Good

*If fresh basil is not available, use ½ cup chopped fresh parsley and 1 tablespoon dried basil.

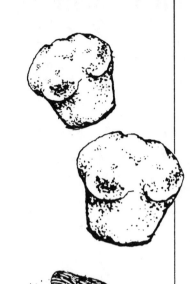

MUFFINS, BREADS, AND COOKIES

NOTHING smells better than freshly baked breads, muffins, and cookies. And nothing tastes better either. Low in fat (if you don't spread on extra butter) and a good source of fiber and carbohydrates, the following make excellent snacks and are an important part of every balanced meal. They also give you a chance to have sweet treats without all the fats, sugars, and refined flours that lurk in most store-bought baked goods.

Moderation is the key to all good eating habits, and this applies to sweets as well. Enjoy them, but eat them in reasonable amounts.

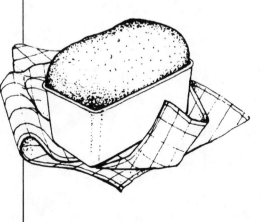

Banana-Apricot Bran Muffins

A good way to start the day. With a glass of milk and fresh fruit, it'll take you through to lunchtime.

1½	cups bran*
1	cup whole wheat flour
1	teaspoon baking powder
1	teaspoon baking soda
½	teaspoon salt
½	cup chopped dried apricots
⅓	cup vegetable oil
⅓	cup packed brown sugar
1	egg, lightly beaten
2	ripe bananas, mashed
1	cup low-fat yogurt

Combine bran, flour, baking powder, baking soda, salt, and apricots; mix lightly.

In large mixing bowl, combine oil, brown sugar, egg, bananas, and yogurt; mix well. Add dry ingredients and mix just until combined.

Spoon batter into paper-lined or nonstick muffin tins. Bake in 400°F oven for 25 minutes or until firm to the touch. Remove from pan and let cool on wire rack. Makes 12 muffins.

Calories per muffin: 173
Grams fat per muffin: 7
Fiber: Excellent
Iron, vitamin A, and niacin: Good

*Bran or natural bran is sold in the grain sections of supermarkets. Because it has some fat, store it in the refrigerator or freezer to prevent it from becoming rancid. Use in muffins, biscuits, bread, and cookies. It is an excellent source of fiber. (Recipes here tested using wheat bran.)

Pumpkin Muffins

Unlike many homemade muffins, these spicy muffins keep well for a few days—though if you have children they will probably eat them all within a day! (See color photograph.)

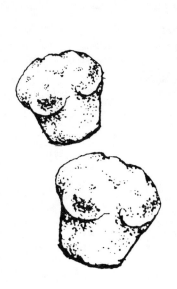

³/₄	cup bran
³/₄	cup whole wheat flour
³/₄	cup granulated sugar
1¹/₂	teaspoons cinnamon
1	teaspoon baking powder
1	teaspoon baking soda
¹/₂	teaspoon salt
1	cup raisins
1	cup mashed or canned cooked pumpkin
2	eggs (unbeaten)
¹/₄	cup vegetable oil
²/₃	cup low-fat yogurt or buttermilk

In bowl, combine bran, flour, sugar, cinnamon, baking powder, baking soda, salt, and raisins; toss to mix. Add pumpkin, eggs, oil, and yogurt; stir just until combined.

Spoon batter into paper-lined or nonstick muffin tins. Bake in 400°F oven for 25 minutes or until firm to the touch. Makes 12 muffins.

Calories per muffin: 160
Grams fat per muffin: 5
Fiber: Good
Vitamin A: Good

Substituting Whole Wheat Flour for All-Purpose Flour in Baking

Whole wheat flour contains 11.4 grams of fiber per 1 cup, while the same amount of all-purpose contains 4.7 grams.

Whole wheat flour is made from the whole grain of wheat. Along with fiber, it also contains some fat. All-purpose flour has had the bran and germ removed from the wheat. It is enriched with the same nutrients naturally present in bran and germ, but it doesn't have the fiber or fat that whole wheat flour does.

Because of the fat content, whole wheat flour doesn't have the same shelf life as all-purpose flour, which will keep for up to 2 years. Whole wheat flour will keep 6 weeks to 6 months, depending on the milling method, before it turns rancid. For this reason, buy whole wheat flour in small amounts unless you use it regularly.

As a general rule, you can substitute whole wheat flour for half the all-purpose flour called for in a recipe. For example, if a recipe calls for 1 cup all-purpose flour, you can use ½ cup all-purpose flour and ½ cup whole wheat flour.

Using all whole wheat flour results in a heavier product. In some cases, such as oatmeal cookies, this is fine; in others such as cakes, it may be undesirable. Experiment with your favorite recipes to see how much whole wheat flour you can substitute.

Refrigerator Bran Muffins

You can mix up this batter and keep it in the refrigerator to have on hand to make delicious hot muffins for breakfast. If you wish, use reconstituted skim milk powder in place of milk. This recipe has less sugar and more fiber than most any other bran muffin recipe.

1	cup vegetable oil
1	cup granulated sugar
6	eggs
⅓	cup molasses
3	cups low-fat milk
5	cups bran
3	cups whole wheat flour
2	teaspoons baking powder
2	teaspoons baking soda
1	teaspoon salt
1	cup raisins or dates

In large bowl, beat together oil, sugar, and eggs until well mixed. Add remaining ingredients and stir until combined. Cover, and refrigerate up to 2 weeks.

Spoon batter into paper-lined or nonstick muffin tins and bake in 425°F oven for 15 to 20 minutes or until firm to the touch. Makes 48 medium muffins.

Calories per muffin: 116
Grams fat per muffin: 5.5
Fiber: Good
Phosphorus, niacin, and iron: Good

Oatmeal Raisin Muffins

Serve these extra-moist muffins with fruit and yogurt or milk for a great quick breakfast. They are also delicious in a packed lunch.

1	cup rolled oats
1¼	cups buttermilk (or 1¼ cup low-fat milk mixed with 2 teaspoons vinegar)
1	cup all-purpose flour (or half whole wheat flour and half all-purpose flour)
1	teaspoon cinnamon
1	teaspoon baking powder
½	teaspoon baking soda
½	teaspoon salt
½	cup raisins or chopped apricots
¼	cup vegetable oil
½	cup packed brown sugar
1	egg, lightly beaten

Stir rolled oats into buttermilk and let stand for 10 minutes.

Mix together flour, cinnamon, baking powder, baking soda, salt, and raisins. Stir oil, sugar, and egg into buttermilk mixture; blend well. Stir dry ingredients into buttermilk mixture, stirring just until combined.

Spoon batter into paper-lined or nonstick muffin tins. Bake in 375°F oven for 20 to 25 minutes or until firm to the touch. Let cool in paper wrapper before removing. Makes 12 muffins.

Calories per muffin: 120
Grams fat per muffin: 5

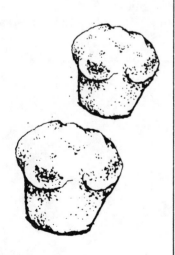

Whole Wheat Pizza Dough

Use this basic dough for any type of pizza. Whole wheat flour adds color, flavor, and fiber.

1	teaspoon granulated sugar
1	cup warm water
1	package active dry yeast or 1 tablespoon
1½	cups all-purpose flour
1½	cups whole wheat flour
1	teaspoon salt
2	tablespoons vegetable oil

In large mixing bowl, dissolve sugar in warm water. Sprinkle yeast over water and let stand for 10 minutes or until foamy. Meanwhile, combine flours and salt.

Stir oil into foamy yeast mixture. Stir in about half the flour mixture. Add more flour, mixing until dough can be gathered into a slightly sticky ball (you may need a little more or less than 3 cups of flour).

On lightly floured surface, knead dough for about 5 minutes or until smooth and elastic, adding more flour as necessary to prevent dough from sticking to counter. Cut dough in half; cover with waxed paper and let rest for 10 minutes.

On lightly floured surface, use a rolling pin to roll each piece of dough into a 12-inch circle, about ¼ inch thick.

Transfer rounds to 2 lightly oiled pizza pans or baking sheets. Using fingers, carefully stretch dough into large circles.

Let dough rise for about 15 minutes before adding toppings. For a thicker crust, let dough rise for 30 minutes. Add toppings just before baking. Makes two 12-inch pizza rounds.

You can use this dough in Deep-Dish Vegetable Pizza (page 148).

Food Processor Variation:

In measuring cup, combine sugar and warm water; add yeast and let stand until bubbly. In food processor bowl combine whole wheat flour and 1 cup all-purpose flour and salt. Add oil to yeast mixture. While processing, pour yeast mixture down feed tube. Process 30 seconds. Turn onto floured board and knead in enough remaining flour to prevent dough from sticking to board. Roll out as in Whole Wheat Pizza Dough.

All-Dressed Pizza

Spread pizza dough with tomato sauce seasoned with oregano and basil. Then finish with your favorite toppings.

Try

- chopped red, yellow, green, or purple peppers

- blanched broccoli florets

- sliced mushrooms

- sliced regular cherry or sun-dried tomatoes

- artichoke halves

- grated part skim mozzarella cheese

Bake in lower half of 450°F oven for 16 to 18 minutes or until crust is golden brown and cheese is bubbly.

▲ *Pork Tenderloin with Rosemary and Thyme (page 120); Asparagus with Red Pepper Purée (page 166).*

▲ *Scallops and Shrimp in Wine Bouillon with Julienne Vegetables (page 134).*

Sole Fillets with Lemon and Parsley (page 129); Herbed Green Beans ▶
with Garlic (page 170); Cracked Wheat and Basil Pilaf (page 183).

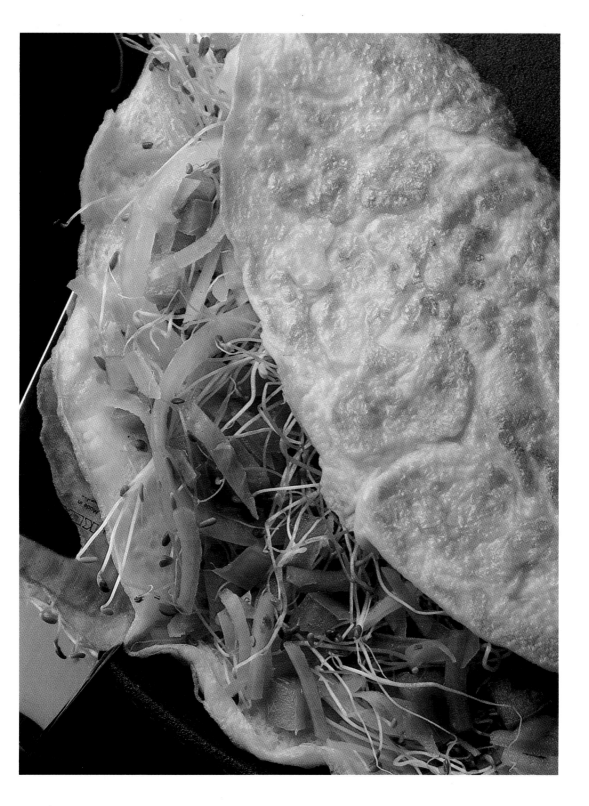

▲ *Omelet à la Jardinière (page 144).*

◀ *Deep-Dish Vegetable Pizza (page 148).*

▲ *Lemon Charlotte with raspberries (page 216).*

◄ *Pumpkin Muffins (page 187); Coconut-Oatmeal Cookies (page 198); Breakfast Bran-and-Fruit Mix (page 237).*

▲ *Peach Blueberry Crisp (page 219).*

Almond Meringues

It's hard to find good-tasting cookies that are low in fat and calories. These are both.

1/4 **cup slivered almonds**
3 **egg whites**
1/2 **cup granulated sugar**
1 **tablespoon cornstarch**
1/2 **teaspoon almond extract**

Place almonds on baking sheet and toast in 325°F oven for 3 minutes or until golden. Let cool. Reduce oven temperature to 225°F.

In large bowl, beat egg whites until soft peaks form. Continue beating, gradually adding sugar, then cornstarch and almond extract; beat until mixture forms stiff peaks. Fold in almonds.

Line baking sheet with foil, shiny side down. Drop batter by small spoonfuls onto prepared pan. Bake in 225°F oven for 1½ hours or until cookies can be easily removed from foil. When cool, store in airtight container. Makes 30 cookies.

Calories per cookie: 22
Grams fat per cookie: 0.5

Old-Fashioned Molasses Bread

Moist and full of flavor, this bread keeps well. Serve for brunch or lunch with salad or soup.

1	cup all-purpose flour
1	cup whole wheat flour
1/2	teaspoon salt
1/2	teaspoon baking soda
2	teaspoons baking powder
2/3	cup skim milk powder
1/3	cup wheat germ
1/2	cup packed brown sugar
1/4	cup chopped nuts
1/2	cup raisins
1/3	cup finely chopped dried apricots
3	eggs
3/4	cup orange juice
1/2	cup vegetable oil
1/2	cup molasses
2	bananas

In a large bowl, combine flours, salt, baking soda, baking powder, skim milk powder, wheat germ, brown sugar, nuts, raisins, and apricots. In food processor with metal blade, in blender, or using electric mixer, whirl eggs until foamy. Add orange juice, oil, molasses, and bananas; process until mixed.

Pour into dry ingredients and stir just until moistened. Pour into two 8 × 4-inch greased pans. Bake in 325°F oven for 1 hour or until firm. Let cool on wire rack, then remove from pan to cool completely. Makes 2 loaves (18 slices per loaf).

Calories per slice: 101
Grams fat per slice: 3.7
Two slices are a good source of fiber.

Whole Wheat Irish Soda Bread

This bread dough can be mixed in a few minutes, then popped into the oven. Serve with any meal from breakfast to dinner.

3 **cups whole wheat flour**
1 **cup all-purpose flour**
2 **tablespoons granulated sugar**
2 **teaspoons baking powder**
1½ **teaspoons baking soda**
1 **teaspoon salt**
2 **tablespoons butter**
1¾ **cups buttermilk (or 1¾ cups low-fat milk,**
 plus 2 tablespoons vinegar)

Combine flours, sugar, baking powder, baking soda, and salt. With pastry blender or two knives, cut in butter until crumbly. Add buttermilk and stir to make a soft dough. Turn out onto lightly floured counter and knead about 10 times until smooth.

Place dough on greased baking sheet; flatten into circle about 2½ inches thick. Cut a large "✗" about ¼ inch deep on top. Bake in 350°F oven for 1 hour or until toothpick inserted in center comes out clean. Makes 1 loaf (about 16 slices).

Calories per slice: 143
Grams fat per slice: 1.7
Fiber: Good

Variation:

Raisin Whole Wheat Soda Bread: Add 1 cup raisins along with flour.

After-Theater Supper

Nova Scotia Seafood Chowder
 (page 60)
Arugula and Radicchio Salad
 with Balsamic Vinaigrette
 (page 76)
Whole Wheat Irish Soda Bread
Lemon Sorbet (page 211)
Coconut-Oatmeal Cookies (page
 198)

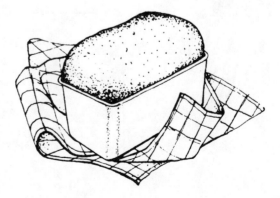

Whole Wheat Raisin Scones

Make these for a late Sunday morning breakfast or to serve with salad or soup for a light supper.

3	tablespoons granulated sugar
1	cup all-purpose flour
1	cup whole wheat flour
1	tablespoon baking powder
1½	teaspoons cinnamon
½	teaspoon nutmeg
½	teaspoon salt
⅓	cup butter or margarine
2	eggs, lightly beaten
⅓	cup low-fat milk
½	cup raisins

Reserve 1 teaspoon of the sugar. In mixing bowl, combine remaining sugar, both flours, baking powder, cinnamon, nutmeg, and salt. With pastry blender or two knives, cut in butter until mixture resembles coarse crumbs.

Reserve 1 tablespoon of the beaten eggs. Stir remaining eggs, milk, and raisins into flour mixture and mix lightly. Turn out onto lightly floured counter and knead about 5 times. Pat into a circle about ¾ inch thick. Cut into 12 wedges and place slightly apart on greased baking sheet.

Brush reserved beaten egg over each wedge; sprinkle with reserved sugar. Bake in 425°F oven for 18 to 20 minutes or until browned. Serve warm. Makes 12 scones.

Calories per serving: 146
Grams fat per serving: 5
Fiber: Good

Date Squares

Sometimes called matrimonial cake, these squares are much healthier than chocolate brownies and most other square recipes that are higher in fat and sugar. Dates are an excellent source of fiber and a good source of iron; if possible, use fresh pitted ones.

DATE FILLING:

2	cups packed chopped pitted dates (²/₃ pound)
1	cup cold coffee
2	tablespoons brown sugar
	Grated rind and juice of ¹/₂ orange
1	tablespoon lemon juice

CRUMB MIXTURE:

1¹/₄	cups all-purpose flour
1	teaspoon baking powder
¹/₂	teaspoon baking soda
¹/₂	teaspoon salt
³/₄	cup butter
1¹/₄	cups rolled oats
³/₄	cup lightly packed brown sugar

Date Filling: In small saucepan, combine dates, coffee, brown sugar, and orange rind; bring to a boil. Reduce heat and simmer, uncovered, until mixture is soft enough to mash and has the consistency of jam (runny but easy to spread), about 10 minutes. Remove from heat; stir in orange and lemon juices. Let cool.

Crumb Mixture: Sift together flour, baking powder, baking soda, and salt. With pastry blender or two knives, cut in butter until mixture is the size of small peas. Stir in rolled oats and sugar. Press half of the crumb mixture firmly into 9-inch-square baking pans. Spread date mixture evenly over crumb mixture and top with remaining crumbs, pressing lightly. Bake in 325°F oven for 25 minutes or until lightly browned. Makes about 25 squares.

Calories per square: 140
Grams fat per square: 5.6
Three squares are an excellent source of fiber.

Almond-Apricot Squares

Apricots add extra flavor to these tasty low-calorie squares.

¾	cup packed dried apricots
½	cup butter
1¼	cups whole wheat flour
¾	cup chopped almonds
¾	cup granulated sugar
¼	cup bran or wheat germ
½	teaspoon cinnamon
2	eggs
½	teaspoon almond extract
½	teaspoon baking powder
½	teaspoon salt

In small saucepan, combine apricots with enough water to cover. Cover and bring to a boil; reduce heat and simmer for 20 minutes. Drain, let cool. Chop apricots finely; set aside.

In mixing bowl, cut butter into 1 cup flour. Mix in ¼ cup of the almonds, ¼ cup of the sugar, bran, and cinnamon. Press half of this mixture into greased 8-inch-square baking pan.

In another mixing bowl, beat remaining ½ cup sugar with eggs and almond extract. Beat in baking powder, salt, apricots, remaining ¼ cup flour, and remaining ½ cup almonds. Pour over layer in pan. Sprinkle with remaining flour-bran mixture. Bake in 350°F oven for 40 minutes. Let cool, then cut into squares. Makes about 18 squares.

Calories per square: 77
Grams fat per square: 4
Two squares are a good source of fiber.

Date Meringue Squares

These go well with frozen desserts such as Grapefruit Ice (page 210) and other fruit sorbets.

1³⁄₄   **cups chopped dates**
 ³⁄₄   **cup water**
 ¹⁄₃   **cup shortening**
 ¹⁄₃   **cup granulated sugar**
  2   **eggs, separated**
  1   **teaspoon vanilla**
 ³⁄₄   **cup all-purpose flour**
 ³⁄₄   **cup whole wheat flour**
  1   **teaspoon baking powder**
 ¹⁄₂   **cup packed brown sugar**
 ¹⁄₄   **cup slivered almonds (optional)**

In saucepan, simmer dates and water until mixture is thick and soft, about 4 minutes.

In mixing bowl, cream shortening; beat in granulated sugar and mix well. Add egg yolks and vanilla; beat until well mixed. Beat in flours and baking powder until mixed. Pat into lightly greased 9-inch square baking pan. Spread date paste on top.

Beat egg whites until stiff peaks form. Continue beating, gradually adding brown sugar; beat until stiff. Spread over date mixture. Sprinkle with nuts (if using). Bake in 350°F oven for 35 to 40 minutes or until golden. Makes about 25 squares.

Calories per square: 125
Grams fat per square: 3.8
Fiber: Good

Coconut-Oatmeal Cookies

These cookies are sure to become a family favorite, but don't eat too many: Coconut is an excellent source of fiber, but it is high in fat. (See color photograph.)

¾	**cup butter or margarine**
¾	**cup granulated sugar**
½	**cup lightly packed brown sugar**
1	**egg**
1	**cup whole wheat flour**
1	**cup rolled oats**
¾	**cup coconut**
¼	**cup wheat germ**
1	**teaspoon baking powder**
1	**teaspoon baking soda**
1½	**cups raisins**

Cream butter, sugars, and egg together thoroughly. Add flour, oats, coconut, wheat germ, baking powder, and baking soda; mix well. Stir in raisins. Drop by spoonfuls onto lightly greased baking sheets. Flatten slightly with floured fork. Bake in 350°F oven for 12 to 15 minutes or until light golden. Makes about 36 cookies.

Calories per cookie: 118
Grams fat per cookie: 5.6
Three cookies are an excellent source of fiber.

Variation:

Raisin Oatmeal Cookies:
   Omit coconut
Calories per cookie: 96
Grams fat per cookie: 4

Wheat Germ Crispy Cookies

Packed with whole grains, these low-fat, low-calorie cookies are good for packed lunches, after-school snacks, and desserts.

1¼	cups whole wheat flour
1	cup wheat germ
1	teaspoon cinnamon
¼	teaspoon ground cloves
¼	teaspoon salt
½	cup butter or margarine
½	cup packed brown sugar
1	egg
1	teaspoon vanilla
2	tablespoons granulated sugar

In bowl, combine flour, wheat germ, cinnamon, cloves, and salt; mix well. In another large bowl, cream butter and brown sugar thoroughly; beat in egg and vanilla. Add mixed dry ingredients to creamed mixture and mix well.

Divide dough in half. On lightly floured counter, roll each half ⅛ inch thick. Cut with 2½-inch round cutter. Place on ungreased baking sheets. Sprinkle with granulated sugar. Bake in 350°F oven for 8 to 10 minutes or until lightly browned. Let cool until firm, then remove from baking sheets. Makes 36 cookies.

Calories per cookie: 57
Grams fat per cookie: 3

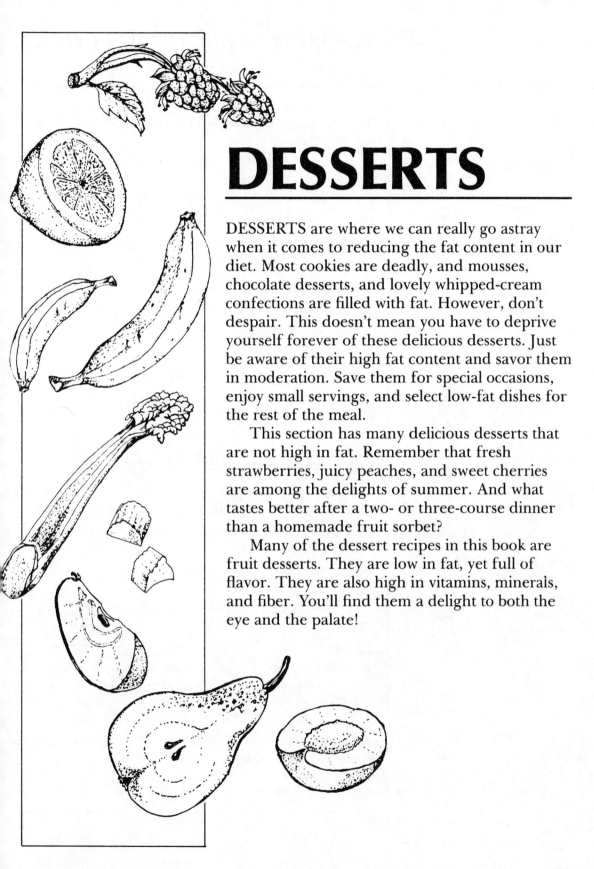

DESSERTS

DESSERTS are where we can really go astray when it comes to reducing the fat content in our diet. Most cookies are deadly, and mousses, chocolate desserts, and lovely whipped-cream confections are filled with fat. However, don't despair. This doesn't mean you have to deprive yourself forever of these delicious desserts. Just be aware of their high fat content and savor them in moderation. Save them for special occasions, enjoy small servings, and select low-fat dishes for the rest of the meal.

This section has many delicious desserts that are not high in fat. Remember that fresh strawberries, juicy peaches, and sweet cherries are among the delights of summer. And what tastes better after a two- or three-course dinner than a homemade fruit sorbet?

Many of the dessert recipes in this book are fruit desserts. They are low in fat, yet full of flavor. They are also high in vitamins, minerals, and fiber. You'll find them a delight to both the eye and the palate!

Blackberries with Orange Cream Sauce

Consider yourself lucky if you live where blackberries grow wild. They're a wonderful summer treat but unfortunately very expensive to buy.

2½   cups fresh blackberries
1   cup Orange Cream Sauce (page 232)

Wash blackberries. Remove any stems. Spoon sauce into individual dessert plates and top with blackberries. Alternatively, spoon blackberries into stemmed glasses and pour sauce over them. Makes 4 servings.

Calories per serving: 126
Grams fat per serving: 0.7
Fiber: Excellent
Vitamin C: Excellent

Compare:

Strawberries served with ¼ cup whipped cream (per serving) instead of with Raspberry-Rhubarb Sauce.

Calories per serving: 146
Grams fat per serving: 10
Fiber: Good
Vitamin C: Excellent

Strawberries with Raspberry-Rhubarb Sauce

Dress up strawberries, cherries, plums, blackberries, or other fresh seasonal fruit with a delicious fruit sauce for a low-fat dessert.

4   cups strawberries
1½   cups Raspberry-Rhubarb Sauce (page 232)

Wash and hull strawberries. Serve them in stemmed glasses and pour Raspberry-Rhubarb Sauce over. Makes 6 servings.

Calories per serving: 97
Grams fat per serving: 0.7
Fiber: Excellent
Calcium and vitamin C: Excellent

Dessert Toppings

Apple pie with cheddar cheese, blueberry pie with vanilla ice cream, pumpkin pie with whipped cream—these innocent toppings can add disastrous amounts of fats and calories.

Ice cream varies considerably in the amount of fat it contains. Do read labels and choose ones with lower fat content.

Compare:
Fat Content of Dessert Toppings

	Grams fat per 1/4 cup
Whipping cream (unwhipped)	24
Whipped cream	12
Dream Whip	7
Cool Whip (frozen)	4
Sour cream (12% fat)	7
Whipped cream (pressurized)	4

	Grams fat per 1/2 cup
Ice cream (vanilla, 16% fat)	12
Ice cream (vanilla, 10% fat)	8
Yogurt (low-fat)	3

1 ounce cheddar cheese has 8 grams fat.

Fat Content of Our Dessert Sauces	*Grams fat per 1/4 cup*
Custard Sauce (page 224)	2
Orange Cream Sauce (page 232)	0.1
Raspberry or Strawberry Purée (page 207)	0.1
Raspberry-Rhubarb Sauce (page 232)	trace
Easy Chocolate Sauce (page 233)	0.1
Sherry Orange Sauce (page 215)	trace

Peaches with Raspberry-Yogurt Sauce

Peaches are a good source, and raspberries an excellent source, of fiber.

You can use fresh or frozen raspberries or strawberries in this sauce. It's good over any fresh fruit.

4 fresh ripe peaches

RASPBERRY-YOGURT SAUCE:
1 cup frozen unsweetened raspberries
½ cup low-fat yogurt
1 tablespoon granulated sugar or honey

GARNISH:
Fresh raspberries or mint

Peel peaches (blanch in boiling water to make peeling easier) and slice.
Raspberry-Yogurt Sauce: In food processor or blender, process raspberries, yogurt, and sugar until smooth. Refrigerate until needed.
Spoon peaches into individual dishes and spoon sauce over peaches. Alternatively, spread sauce on plates and arrange peaches on top. Garnish with fresh raspberries or mint. Makes 4 servings.

Calories per serving: 141
Grams fat per serving: 0.3
Fiber: Excellent
Vitamins A and C: Excellent

Poached Pears with Chocolate Sauce

Many other fruits, such as peaches, plums, apricots, and apples, can also be poached. Serve them with Easy Chocolate Sauce or one of the other fruit dessert sauces in this book, such as Raspberry Purée (page 207).

3	**cups water**
½	**cup granulated sugar**
	Grated rind and juice of 1 lemon
1	**vanilla bean and/or cinnamon stick**
4	**pears**
¼	**cup Easy Chocolate Sauce (page 233)**

In large saucepan, combine water, sugar, lemon rind, lemon juice, vanilla bean and/or cinnamon stick. Bring to a boil, stirring until sugar is dissolved.

Peel, halve, and core pears. Add to boiling syrup. (Pears should be covered in liquid; if not, double the amount of poaching liquid or poach in batches.) Reduce heat to medium-low and simmer gently for 15 to 20 minutes or until pears are almost tender. (Time will vary depending on ripeness and type of pear; remember, pears will continue to cook while cooling.) Remove from heat and let cool in liquid.

Drain pears thoroughly and pat dry on paper towels. Arrange on individual plates. Drizzle with Easy Chocolate Sauce. Serve at room temperature. Makes 4 large servings or 8 small.

Calories per small serving: 168
Grams fat per small serving: 0.8
Fiber: Good
Vitamin C: Good

Poached fruit can be served in the poaching liquid. Remove cooled fruit from liquid and strain liquid. Boil poaching liquid until reduced to 1 cup; let cool, then serve over poached fruit.

Raspberry Sorbet with Strawberry Purée

Don't strain the raspberry mixture; the seeds are an excellent source of fiber. This purée of fruits is used as a sauce.

2 9-ounce packages frozen sweetened
    raspberries, thawed
1 cup water
1 tablespoon lemon juice
1 cup Strawberry Purée (page 207)

In food processor, purée raspberries. Stir in water and lemon juice.

Freezing Instructions:
Method 1—Ice-Cream Machine: Follow manufacturer's instructions.
Method 2—Food Processor: Freeze in metal pan or bowl until hard. Process in food processor until mixture is a hard slush. Return to freezer until needed.
Method 3—Hand Method: Freeze in metal pan or bowl until barely firm. Beat by hand or electric mixer until slushy. Return to freezer until needed.

To Serve: Sorbet should not be rock-hard. If necessary, transfer to refrigerator 15 minutes before serving or process in food processor. To serve, spoon into individual dishes or stemmed glasses and pour sauce over. Alternatively, spoon some sauce onto dessert plates and spoon a scoop or two of sorbet on top of each plate. (This looks very attractive when different kinds of sorbets are served on each plate and are garnished with fresh raspberries or other fresh fruits.) Makes 8 servings.

	Without purée	With ¼ cup purée
Calories per serving:	56	116
Grams fat per serving:	0.1	0.2
Fiber:	Excellent	Excellent
Vitamin C:	Good	Good

Fresh Strawberry Sorbet

Fresh, ripe strawberries make a perfect sorbet. Serve with other fruit ices or sorbets and fresh fruit, or with Orange Cream Sauce (page 232).

1 **cup water**
1 **cup granulated sugar**
4 **cups ripe strawberries, washed and hulled**
  Juice of 2 oranges
  Juice of 1 lemon
  Fresh strawberries for garnish

Bring water and sugar to a boil, stirring, to dissolve sugar; boil for 2 minutes and let cool. In food processor or blender, purée strawberries. Combine strawberries, syrup, orange juice, and lemon juice; mix well.

Freeze and serve according to instructions in Raspberry Sorbet recipe (page 206). Garnish each serving with fresh strawberry. Makes 8 servings.

Calories per serving: 142
Grams fat per serving: 0.4
Vitamin C: Excellent

Raspberry or Strawberry Purée

In blender or food processor, purée 1 9-ounce package frozen raspberries or strawberries. If using unsweetened berries, add confectioners sugar to taste. Makes about 1 cup sauce.

Calories per ¼ cup: 60
Grams fat per ¼ cup: 0.1
Fiber: Excellent (when made with raspberries)

Apple Cinnamon Sorbet with Raspberry Purée

A light, colorful, year-round dessert. This sorbet is full of flavor, and is very good by itself or with Applesauce Whole Wheat Cake (page 227), Pumpkin Muffins (page 187), or the Raspberry Purée (page 207).

1 **cup finely grated, peeled, and cored apple**
2 **tablespoons lemon juice**
2 **tablespoons Calvados or apple brandy (optional)**
½ **teaspoon cinnamon**
2½ **cups water**
1 **cup granulated sugar**
2½ **cups apple juice**
1 **cup Raspberry Purée (page 207)**

In skillet, combine grated apple, lemon juice, Calvados (if using), and cinnamon; cook over medium heat, stirring, until apple is tender, about 3 minutes. In saucepan, bring water and sugar to a boil and cook, until sugar is dissolved. Remove from heat; stir in apple mixture and apple juice.

Freeze and serve according to instructions for Raspberry Sorbet (page 206). Serve with fresh fruit such as grapes, sliced kiwi, or strawberries, plus a fresh mint leaf, or drizzle with Raspberry Purée. Makes 8 servings.

Calories per serving: 158
Grams fat per serving: 0.2
Fiber: Good
Vitamin C: Excellent

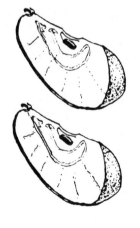

Frozen Lemon Cream

It's hard to tell the base of this creamy dessert is yogurt. Try it with a topping of fresh fruit such as strawberries, blueberries, peaches, bananas, papaya, or kiwi.

3   cups low-fat yogurt
2   teaspoons vanilla
4   teaspoons grated lemon rind
¼   cup lemon juice
½   cup granulated sugar

Combine all ingredients and mix well. Freeze and serve according to instructions for Raspberry Sorbet (page 206). Makes 8 servings.

Calories per serving: 106
Grams fat per serving: 0.2
Calcium and phosphorus: Good

For a festive frozen dessert, use Frozen Lemon Cream as a filling between layers of Orange Sponge Cake (page 225) or sandwiched between Meringues (page 220), and freeze.

Grapefruit Ice

Fresh-squeezed grapefruit juice made into an ice is a delicious, refreshing dessert at any time of year. Arrange scoops of ice on individual plates with fresh grapefruit sections or other fresh fruit, or serve with cookies or squares.

2	**cups granulated sugar**
2	**cups water**
6	**grapefruit**
1/4	**cup lemon juice**

In saucepan, combine sugar and water, stirring to dissolve sugar. Bring to a boil and boil for 5 minutes. Remove from heat. Grate rind from 1 grapefruit (be careful to grate only yellow part—white part is too bitter). Stir rind into syrup and let cool.

Squeeze juice from the 6 grapefruit to measure 4 cups. Stir grapefruit juice and lemon juice into cool syrup.

Freeze and serve according to instructions for Raspberry Sorbet (page 206). Makes 12 servings.

Calories per serving: 171
Grams fat per serving: trace
Vitamin C: Excellent

Lemon Sorbet

A light, refreshing dessert. Compare the fat content of a serving of Lemon Sorbet with that of ice cream: 0.04 grams versus 8 grams.

3   **lemons, juice and grated rind**
2   **cups water**
1   **cup granulated sugar**
1   **egg white**

In saucepan, combine lemon juice, lemon rind, water, and sugar; bring to a boil. Reduce heat and simmer for 5 minutes; let cool. Pour into metal pan and freeze until firm—at least 4 hours. Break frozen mixture into chunks, place in food processor, and process until smooth. Add egg white and process for a few seconds longer. Spoon into freezer container; cover and return to freezer until firm, about 1 to 2 hours. Place in refrigerator for 15 minutes, or until slightly softened, before serving. (To make without using a food processor, omit egg white and freeze according to instructions for Raspberry Sorbet, page 206.)

Calories per serving: 152
Grams fat per serving: trace
Vitamin C: Excellent

Yogurt Fruit Freeze

This is a pleasure for dieters who are dessert lovers. It's also the perfect year-round treat for children.

2½ **cups low-fat yogurt**
2 **small bananas**
⅔ **cup frozen orange juice concentrate (undiluted)**

In food processor or blender, process yogurt, bananas, and orange juice concentrate until smooth. Alternatively, mash bananas and beat in remaining ingredients with electric mixer until smooth. Freeze and serve according to instructions for Raspberry Sorbet (page 206). For kids, freeze in Popsicle containers after processing. Makes 8 servings.

Calories per serving: 100
Grams fat per serving: 0.2
Vitamin C: Excellent
Calcium: Good

Prune Cake

This easy-to-make cake is ideal for packed lunches or for feeding a crowd of kids. Sprinkle it with confectioners sugar or ice with Lemon Icing (page 227).

1½	*cups prunes*
1½	*cups water*
¾	*cup packed brown sugar*
⅓	*cup granulated sugar*
1	*cup low-fat yogurt*
2	*eggs*
1½	*cups all-purpose flour*
1	*cup whole wheat flour*
2	*teaspoons baking powder*
½	*teaspoon baking soda*
1	*teaspoon cinnamon*
½	*teaspoon salt*

In saucepan, combine prunes and water; bring to a boil and simmer for 1 minute. Cover and let stand until cool; drain. Remove pits and chop prunes (you should have about 1½ cups); set aside.

In mixing bowl, combine sugars and yogurt; beat until smooth. Add eggs and beat until well mixed. Add flours, baking powder, baking soda, cinnamon, and salt; beat well. Stir in prunes.

Pour into lightly greased and floured 12 × 8-inch baking pan. Bake in 375°F oven for 30 minutes or until toothpick inserted in center comes out clean.

When cool, ice with Lemon Icing if desired. Makes 18 servings.

	With icing	Without icing
Calories per serving:	182	140
Grams fat per serving:	1.25	1.22
Fiber: Good		

Melon with Blueberries

A quick-to-make, refreshing dessert. Or try it as a first course or breakfast treat. Peaches, grapes, kiwi, or other fresh fruit in season can be used instead of blueberries. If serving as a first course, omit the honey; arrange wedges of melon on individual salad plates, drizzle with lemon juice mixed with liqueur or lime juice, and garnish with blueberries.

- ½ **cantaloupe**
- ½ **honeydew melon**
- 2 **cups watermelon cubes**
- 1 **cup blueberries**
- 2 **tablespoons honey**
- 2 **tablespoons lemon juice**
- 2 **tablespoons melon or orange liqueur or sherry (optional)**
  Fresh mint leaves

Cut cantaloupe and honeydew melon into cubes or balls. In glass serving bowl, combine cantaloupe, honeydew, watermelon, and blueberries.

In small dish, combine honey and lemon juice; stir until mixed. Blend in liqueur (if using). Pour over melons; toss to mix. Cover and refrigerate until serving time.

Serve in stemmed glasses and garnish with mint. Serve at room temperature. Makes 6 servings.

Calories per serving: 122
Grams fat per serving: 0.9
Fiber: Excellent
Vitamins A and C: Excellent

Cantaloupe, Pear, and Grapes with Sherry Orange Sauce

This sauce keeps well in the refrigerator for at least a week. Use any fresh fruit in season. Japanese pears, which look more like apples than pears, are available in the winter; they are very crisp and juicy and add a lot of crunch. Top this dessert with yogurt and brown sugar, or spoon over sherbet for another variation.

    1   cantaloupe
    1   pear (Japanese or domestic), mango, or
          papaya
    1   cup red, green, or black grapes

SHERRY ORANGE SAUCE:
    ½   cup granulated sugar
    1   tablespoon cornstarch
    1   tablespoon grated orange rind
    ½   cup orange juice
    ½   cup medium to dry sherry
    1   tablespoon lemon juice

Cut cantaloupe in half; discard seeds. Cut flesh into cubes or balls. Cut unpeeled pear into cubes (if using mango or papaya, peel and cut flesh into cubes). Cut grapes in half if large and remove any seeds. Spoon into stemmed wine or sherbet glasses.

Sherry Orange Sauce: In small saucepan, blend sugar and cornstarch; stir in orange rind, orange juice, sherry, and lemon juice. Cook, stirring, over medium heat until sauce thickens, bubbles, and becomes clear. Cook for 2 to 3 minutes, stirring constantly. Remove from heat and let cool.

At serving time, spoon sauce over fruit. Makes 6 servings.

Calories per serving: 166
Grams fat per serving: 0.4
Vitamins A and C: Excellent

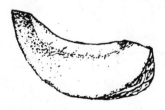

Lemon Charlotte with Strawberries

Top this light, frothy dessert with your favorite kind of fresh fruit. Choose whatever is available—kiwi, raspberries, blueberries, or a combination. (See color photograph.)

7	eggs, separated
1½	cups granulated sugar
¾	cup lemon juice
1	package unflavored gelatin
½	cup water
28	(approximate) ladyfingers*
2	cups strawberries, blueberries, raspberries, or sliced peaches

In mixing bowl, beat together egg yolks and ¾ cup of the sugar until well mixed; beat in lemon juice. Transfer to top of nonaluminum double boiler. Place over simmering water and cook, stirring, until mixture is thick enough to coat back of metal spoon, 8 to 10 minutes.

Meanwhile, sprinkle gelatin over water and let stand for 5 minutes to soften. Stir into hot yolk mixture; let cool, stirring occasionally.

Beat egg whites until frothy; gradually beat in remaining sugar, beating until stiff peaks form. Stir one third of the whites into yolk mixture to lighten, then fold into remaining whites.

Split ladyfingers in half. (If lady fingers are the crisp kind, this is difficult. Use as is.) Line bottom, then sides, of 10-inch springform pan with ladyfingers, cut side in. Spoon in custard mixture. Refrigerate until firm, about 3 hours or overnight. (Cake can be frozen for up to 3 weeks; remove from freezer at least 1 hour before serving.)

Just before serving, place pan on serving platter and remove sides. Arrange fruit on top. Makes 10 servings.

Calories per serving: 326
Grams fat per serving: 6.6
Fiber: Good (Excellent if made with blackberries or raspberries)

*Soft ladyfingers are available in the bread section of some supermarkets, bakeries, and specialty food stores.

Lemon Cloud

This dessert looks like a mousse but contains no cream. This one is easy to make but should be served the day you make it; it can separate slightly if it stands longer than 8 hours.

2	**lemons**
½	**orange**
3	**tablespoons cornstarch**
½	**cup granulated sugar**
1½	**cups hot water**
2	**eggs, separated**

Grate rind from 1 of the lemons and orange half. Squeeze juice from orange and lemons (you should have about ½ cup lemon juice).

In nonaluminum saucepan, combine cornstarch and half the sugar. Stir in water and bring to a boil, stirring constantly. Reduce heat and boil gently for 3 minutes. Beat egg yolks lightly; stir a little hot mixture into yolks; then slowly pour yolk mixture back into saucepan. Cook, stirring, over medium-low heat for 2 minutes. Remove from heat and stir in juices and rinds. Transfer to mixing bowl and refrigerate to cool slightly.

Beat egg whites until soft peaks form; continue beating, slowly adding remaining sugar and beating until stiff peaks form. Fold egg whites into lemon mixture. Spoon into stemmed glasses or serving bowl. Refrigerate until serving time. Makes 6 servings.

Calories per serving: 125
Grams fat per serving: 2
Vitamin C: Excellent

Lemon and Fresh Blueberry Tart

Meringue on the bottom, lemon filling in the center and blueberries on the top make a luscious, low-fat dessert that's lower in calories than a pie with traditional pastry.

MERINGUE CRUST:
- 2 egg whites
  Pinch cream of tartar
- ½ cup granulated sugar
- ¼ teaspoon cornstarch
- ½ teaspoon vanilla

LEMON FILLING:
- ½ cup granulated sugar
- 5 tablespoons cornstarch
- 1½ cups hot water
- 2 egg yolks
  Grated rind and juice of 1 large lemon
  Grated rind of ½ orange

BLUEBERRY TOPPING:
- ¼ cup granulated sugar
- 2 teaspoons cornstarch
- ⅓ cup water
- 1 teaspoon fresh lemon juice
- 2 cups fresh blueberries

Meringue Crust: Line an 8- or 9-inch pie plate with foil; butter foil lightly, sprinkle with flour, and shake off excess flour.

In medium bowl, beat egg whites with cream of tartar until soft peaks form. Beat in sugar, 1 tablespoon at a time, until stiff glossy peaks form. Beat in cornstarch and vanilla. Spread mixture into foil-lined pie plate; bring sides about ½ inch higher than pan. Bake in 300°F oven for 90 minutes or until firm and dry; let cool slightly on rack. While still warm, remove meringue from pie plate and peel off foil. Return meringue shell to pie plate.

Lemon Filling: Grate rind from lemon and ½ orange. Squeeze juice from lemon (you should have about ⅓ cup). In nonaluminum heavy saucepan, mix sugar and cornstarch. Stir in water and bring to a boil over medium heat, stirring constantly. Reduce heat and boil gently for 3 minutes, stirring constantly.

In small bowl, beat egg yolks lightly. Whisk a little hot mixture into egg yolks, then slowly pour yolk mixture back into saucepan, stirring constantly. Cook over medium-low heat, stirring constantly, for 2 minutes. Remove from heat. Stir in lemon juice and grated rinds. Let cool slightly; pour into prepared pie shell.

(continued)

Blueberry Topping: In heavy saucepan, combine sugar and cornstarch. Stir in water and lemon juice. Cook, stirring, over medium heat until mixture thickens, comes to a boil, and becomes clear. Remove from heat and add blueberries, stirring to coat well. Spoon blueberries over lemon filling. Refrigerate for at least 30 minutes before serving. Makes 8 servings.

Calories per serving: 190
Grams fat per serving: 1.5
Fiber: Excellent
Vitamin C: Good

Peach Blueberry Crisp

It's hard to find a better-tasting fall fruit dessert than this one. If you cook it in a microwave, it takes only 10 minutes. (See color photograph.)

  6 **cups peeled, sliced fresh peaches**
  2 **cups blueberries**
 ⅓ **cup brown sugar, packed**
  2 **tablespoons all-purpose flour**
  2 **teaspoons cinnamon**

TOPPING:
  1 **cup quick-cooking rolled oats**
  1 **teaspoon cinnamon**
 ¼ **cup brown sugar, packed**
  3 **tablespoons soft butter**

In 8-cup baking dish, combine peaches and blueberries. In small bowl, combine sugar, flour, and cinnamon; add to fruit and toss to mix.

Topping: Combine rolled oats, sugar, and cinnamon; with pastry blender or two knives, cut in butter until crumbly. Sprinkle over top of fruit mixture. Bake in 350°F oven for 25 minutes or microwave on High for 10 minutes or until mixture is bubbling and fruit is barely tender. Serve warm or cold. Makes 8 servings.

Calories per serving: 255
Grams fat per serving: 5
Fiber: Excellent
Vitamin A: Excellent
Vitamin C: Good

Make-Ahead Summer Dinner

Chilled Melon and Yogurt Soup
(page 47)
Cold chicken
Pasta Salad with Sweet Peppers
and Dill (page 90)
Sliced tomatoes with basil
Whole wheat buns
Raspberry Meringue Torte
(page 220)

Raspberry Meringue Torte

Individually frozen raspberries are available in most supermarkets, making this torte a year-round treat. It's not as complicated as it looks. The meringues can be made well in advance, and the custard sauce early in the day, or even a day in advance; neither procedure takes very long. Use strawberries or other berries when they are in season instead of raspberries.

MERINGUES:

6	*egg whites*
1½	*cups granulated sugar*
1	*teaspoon cornstarch*
1	*teaspoon vanilla*

CUSTARD FILLING:

¼	*cup granulated sugar*
2	*tablespoons cornstarch*
	Pinch salt
2	*cups low-fat milk*
4	*egg yolks*
2	*teaspoons vanilla*
	Pinch freshly grated nutmeg
2	*tablespoons orange or almond liqueur (optional)*

FRUIT LAYERS:

2	*cups blueberries or 3 cups sliced peaches, bananas, kiwi, mangoes, or other fresh fruit*
2	*cups raspberries or strawberries*

Meringues: Line 2 baking sheets with foil; oil foil lightly.

In large bowl, beat egg whites until soft peaks form. Combine sugar and cornstarch. Continuing to beat egg whites, gradually add sugar mixture, beating until stiff peaks form. Stir in vanilla.

Spread meringue mixture over foil-lined baking sheet to form 2 circles about 11 inches in diameter. Bake in 275°F oven for 2 hours or until meringues are firm. Remove from oven; while warm, carefully remove foil. (If foil is difficult to remove, meringues may not be cooked enough or foil wasn't oiled enough.)

Custard Filling: In nonaluminum saucepan or top of double boiler, combine sugar, cornstarch, and salt. Stir in milk. Cook, stirring, over medium-low heat or simmering water until mixture thickens and comes to a simmer; cook for 5 minutes, stirring constantly.

Beat egg yolks until mixed; gradually whisk a small amount of hot milk mixture into yolks. While stirring, pour yolk mixture into hot milk mixture. Stir over low heat for about 2 minutes or until thickened slightly. Remove from heat; stir in vanilla, nutmeg, and liqueur (if using); let cool.

A few hours before serving, place one meringue on serving platter; spread custard over meringue. Arrange blueberries over custard. Place second meringue on top. Arrange raspberries on top. To serve, cut into wedges. Makes 10 servings.

Calories per serving: 240
Grams fat per serving: 3.7
Fiber: Excellent
Vitamin C: Good

Old-Fashioned Peach Cobbler

Make this comforting dessert in the summertime when peaches are juicy and plentiful.

½	*cup packed brown sugar*
½	*teaspoon cinnamon*
1	*teaspoon grated lemon or orange rind*
1	*tablespoon lemon juice*
4	*cups sliced, peeled peaches*
¾	*cup all-purpose flour*
½	*cup whole wheat flour*
1	*tablespoon baking powder*
¼	*cup butter or margarine*
¼	*cup granulated sugar*
1	*egg, lightly beaten*
½	*cup low-fat milk*
½	*teaspoon vanilla*

Lightly butter an 8-cup baking dish. In large bowl, combine brown sugar, cinnamon, grated lemon rind, and lemon juice; mix well. Add peaches and toss to mix; transfer to baking dish.

Combine flours and baking powder. In mixing bowl, cream butter and granulated sugar until light and fluffy; beat in egg. Add dry ingredients alternately with milk. Add vanilla, mixing just until combined. Drop batter by spoonfuls over peach mixture. Bake in 375°F oven for 25 to 35 minutes or until peaches are tender and top is golden brown. Serve warm. Makes 8 servings.

Calories per serving: 212
Grams fat per serving: 5.6
Fiber: Good
Vitamin A: Excellent
Niacin and vitamin C: Good

Pear Crisp with Rolled Oats Topping

You'll enjoy the lemon and ginger flavors of the sauce in this fall or winter dessert. The amount of juice will vary depending on the kind and size of pears used.

8	**pears, cored and sliced**
2	**tablespoons lemon juice**
1	**teaspoon grated lemon rind**
1	**tablespoon grated fresh ginger root or 1 teaspoon ground ginger**
½	**cup granulated sugar**
¼	**cup all-purpose flour**

TOPPING:

½	**cup packed brown sugar**
⅓	**cup whole wheat flour**
⅔	**cup rolled oats**
¼	**cup powdered skim milk**
1	**teaspoon cinnamon**
3	**tablespoons butter**

In mixing bowl, toss pears with lemon juice, lemon rind, and ginger. Mix together sugar and flour; sprinkle over pears and toss to mix. Spoon into lightly buttered 8-cup soufflé or baking dish.

Topping: Mix together sugar, flour, oats, powdered milk, and cinnamon; with pastry blender or two knives, cut in butter until mixture resembles fine crumbs. Sprinkle over pear mixture.

Bake in 375°F oven for 30 to 45 minutes or until pears are tender and mixture is bubbling. Serve hot or warm. Makes 8 servings.

Calories per serving: 271
Grams fat per serving: 5
Fiber: Good
Vitamin C: Excellent

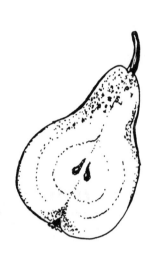

Using powdered skim milk in crumb toppings is an easy way to add calcium and extra protein as well as flavor.

Apricot Clafouti

Clafouti is a French baked-fruit custard dessert. It can be made with almost any kind of fruit besides apricots—cherries, plums, peaches, or whatever is available.

4 **cups fresh apricots**
1 **tablespoon butter**
6 **tablespoons granulated sugar**
3 **eggs**
1⅓ **cups low-fat milk**
⅔ **cup all-purpose flour**
1 **teaspoon grated lemon rind**
½ **teaspoon cinnamon**
2 **teaspoons vanilla**
Pinch salt
Confectioners sugar

Halve apricots, then pit them. Grease an 11-inch glass pie plate or large quiche dish with the butter. Sprinkle with 1 tablespoon of the granulated sugar. Arrange apricots, cut side down, in dish and sprinkle with 2 tablespoons of the granulated sugar.

In blender or food processor, combine remaining sugar, eggs, milk, flour, lemon rind, cinnamon, vanilla, and salt; process until smooth. Alternatively, beat remaining sugar with eggs; add remaining ingredients and beat until smooth. Pour mixture evenly over fruit.

Bake in 375°F oven for 50 to 60 minutes or until top is browned and filling is set. Just before serving, sift confectioners sugar over top. Serve warm or cold. Makes 6 to 8 servings.

	6 servings	8 servings
Calories per serving:	213	162
Grams fat per serving:	5.8	4.4
Fiber: Good	2.7 grams	2.1 grams
Vitamin A:	Excellent	Excellent
Vitamin C:	Good	Good
Niacin:	Good	

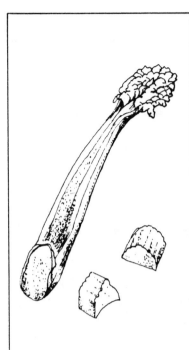

Rhubarb Pudding with Custard Sauce

Tart rhubarb is a wonderful contrast to this light sauce. The tartness will vary, depending on whether you use frozen, hothouse, or home-grown rhubarb, so add more sugar if necessary.

2	pounds fresh or frozen rhubarb
1¼	cups (approximate) granulated sugar
1	teaspoon grated orange rind
2	cups water
2	tablespoons cornstarch
¼	cup cold water
1½	teaspoons vanilla

CUSTARD SAUCE:

2	tablespoons granulated sugar
2	teaspoons cornstarch
	Pinch salt
1	cup low-fat milk
1	egg yolk
1	teaspoon vanilla
	Freshly grated nutmeg

Cut rhubarb into ¾-inch pieces. In saucepan, combine rhubarb, sugar, orange rind, and water. Bring to a boil; reduce heat and simmer, uncovered, until rhubarb is tender, about 10 minutes for fresh, 3 minutes for frozen. Taste, and add more sugar if necessary.

Mix cornstarch with ¼ cup cold water; stir into rhubarb. Cook, stirring, over medium heat until mixture thickens and becomes clear. Boil gently for about 3 minutes. Remove from heat and stir in vanilla. Transfer to serving bowl. Let cool, cover, and refrigerate.

Custard Sauce: In heavy, nonaluminum saucepan or top of double boiler, combine sugar, cornstarch, and salt. Stir in milk. Stir over medium heat; bring to a simmer and cook for 5 minutes or until sauce is thickened slightly. Whisk egg yolk; whisk about ½ cup of hot mixture into yolk. Whisk yolk mixture back into hot milk mixture. Cook, stirring, over low heat for about 2 minutes or until sauce is thickened. Remove from heat; stir in vanilla, and freshly grated nutmeg to taste. Cover, and refrigerate until needed. Makes about 1 cup.

To serve, pour custard sauce over individual servings of rhubarb. Makes 8 servings.

(continued)

Calories per serving (including 2 tablespoons custard sauce): 183
Grams fat per serving (including 2 tablespoons custard sauce): 1.4
Fiber: Good
Vitamin C: Good

Orange Sponge Cake

This cake is great on its own or with fresh fruit, dessert sauces, or sherbets. Make sure you use large eggs at room temperature.

¾ cup granulated sugar
4 eggs, separated
1 tablespoon grated orange rind
½ cup fresh orange juice
1 cup all-purpose flour
1 teaspoon baking powder
Pinch salt
2 teaspoons confectioners sugar

In mixing bowl, combine granulated sugar, egg yolks, orange rind, and orange juice; beat until very light in color. Add flour and baking powder; beat until combined.

In separate bowl, combine egg whites with a pinch of salt and beat until stiff peaks form. Mix a small amount of whites into yolk mixture, then fold yolk mixture into whites.

Pour mixture into ungreased 10-inch tube pan with removable bottom. Bake in 325°F oven for 50 to 55 minutes or until cake is golden brown and springs back when lightly touched. Invert and let cool completely before removing from pan.

Sift confectioners sugar over top, or ice with Orange Icing (page 227), or serve with sherbet or Raspberry Purée (page 207). Makes 12 servings.

Calories per serving: 96
Grams fat per serving: 1.9

Angel food cake is very low in fat because it is made from egg whites only. However, you then have a lot of egg yolks to use up. For this reason, you may want to use a cake mix for making angel food cakes.

Serve wedges of sponge cake topped with Sherry Orange Sauce (page 215) and sections of fresh oranges.

Cinnamon Coffee Cake

Serve this easy-to-make, moist cake with fresh fruit or sorbet for any meal any time of day.

  1 cup low-fat yogurt
  1 teaspoon baking soda
¼ cup butter or margarine
  1 cup lightly packed brown sugar
  1 egg
  1 teaspoon vanilla
1½ cups all-purpose flour
  2 teaspoons baking powder

TOPPING:
½ cup lightly packed brown sugar
  1 tablespoon cinnamon

Grease and flour a bundt pan or 9-inch square baking pan.
  In small bowl, combine yogurt and baking soda; mix well and set aside. (Yogurt mixture will increase in volume.)
  In large mixing bowl, beat butter with sugar until well mixed. Add egg and vanilla; beat well, about 2 minutes. Sift together flour and baking powder; add to butter mixture alternately with yogurt mixture.
  Topping: Combine sugar and cinnamon; mix well.
  Spread half the batter in prepared pan. Sprinkle with half the topping. Cover with remaining batter and sprinkle with remaining topping. Bake in 350°F oven for 45 minutes or until toothpick inserted in center comes out clean. Let cool for 10 to 15 minutes in pan, then invert onto wire rack. Makes 12 servings.

Calories per serving: 172
Grams fat per serving: 3.8

Applesauce Whole Wheat Cake

Full of flavor, this delicious cake looks attractive when made in a bundt or tube pan and keeps well.

Serve cake with fresh fruit desserts, poached pears or sorbets.

Lemon Icing

Using yogurt instead of butter makes a creamy low-fat icing. In mixing bowl, combine 1½ cups confectioners sugar (sifted), 2 tablespoons low-fat yogurt, 1 teaspoon each grated lemon rind and lemon juice; mix until smooth.

Orange Icing

Substitute 1 teaspoon each of grated orange rind and juice for lemon rind and juice.

1¾	cups granulated sugar
¼	cup butter, at room temperature
1	egg
½	cup low-fat yogurt
2	cups applesauce
1	teaspoon grated orange rind
1	teaspoon vanilla
1½	cups all-purpose flour
1¼	cups whole wheat flour
3	tablespoons bran
2	teaspoons cinnamon
2	teaspoons baking soda
1	cup raisins

Butter and flour a 10-inch bundt pan. In mixing bowl, combine sugar and butter; beat until mixed. Add egg and beat until light in color. Add yogurt and beat until mixed. Beat in applesauce, orange rind, and vanilla.

In another bowl, combine flours, bran, cinnamon, baking soda, and raisins; stir to mix. Pour dry ingredients over applesauce mixture and stir just until combined.

Pour into prepared pan and bake in 325°F oven for 70 to 80 minutes or until toothpick inserted in center comes out clean. Remove from oven. Let cool on rack for 20 minutes, then remove from pan and place on wire rack to finish cooling. Makes 16 slices.

Calories per slice: 224
Grams fat per slice: 3.8
Fiber: Good

Rhubarb Crumb Pie

Welcome spring with this pie. A crumb topping reduces the amount of pastry needed. If you are using frozen rhubarb, be sure to thaw it first so there won't be too much liquid.

PASTRY:

- ³/₄ **cup all-purpose flour**
- ¹/₂ **cup whole wheat flour**
- ¹/₂ **teaspoon salt**
- 3 **tablespoons butter or margarine**
- 3 **tablespoons ice water**

FILLING:

- 1 **cup granulated sugar**
- ¹/₄ **cup all-purpose flour**
- 1 **teaspoon grated orange or lemon rind**
- 1 **egg, well beaten**
- 5 **cups sliced fresh or frozen (thawed) rhubarb, cut into ¹/₂-inch pieces**

TOPPING:

- ¹/₃ **cup packed brown sugar**
- 3 **tablespoons rolled oats**
- 3 **tablespoons powdered skim milk (optional)**
- 3 **tablespoons whole wheat flour**
- 1 **teaspoon cinnamon**
- 2 **tablespoons butter**

Pastry: In mixing bowl, combine flours and salt. With pastry blender or two knives, cut in butter until mixture is crumbly. Sprinkle water over mixture and toss with a fork to mix. Press onto bottom and up sides of a 9-inch pie plate.

Filling: Combine sugar, flour, and grated orange rind; mix well. In another bowl, mix egg and rhubarb; add sugar mixture and stir to mix.

Topping: In bowl, combine sugar, rolled oats, powdered milk (if using), flour, and cinnamon. Cut in butter until mixture is crumbly.

Spoon rhubarb filling into pie shell. Sprinkle topping over filling. Bake in 400°F oven for 50 to 60 minutes or until top is golden brown and rhubarb is tender. To prevent top from becoming too brown, cover lightly with foil after 30 minutes of baking. Makes 8 servings.

Calories per serving: 285
Grams fat per serving: 8
Fiber: Good
Calcium: Good

Variation:

Rhubarb Crisp with Oatmeal Topping: Follow Rhubarb Crumb Pie but omit the pastry and reduce flour in filling to 2 tablespoons and omit egg. Combine filling ingredients and spoon into lightly greased 6-cup baking dish. Prepare topping and sprinkle over rhubarb. Bake in 375°F oven for 40 to 50 minutes or until filling is bubbly and top is brown. Makes 6 servings.

Calories per serving: 234
Grams fat per serving: 3.6
Fiber: Good
Vitamin C: Good

Should I Use Butter, Margarine, or Oil?

The question of what kind of fat to use is puzzling and confusing to many people. Research with respect to the link between fat intake and cancer is not conclusive. The most important fact is to lower the total fat content in our diets. However, since saturated fats and cholesterol may also be factors in coronary heart disease, it is prudent to use as little butter, solid vegetable shortening, and lard as possible; they are all high in saturated fats.

Saturated fats are mainly of animal origin, unsaturated fats of vegetable origin. However, it isn't that simple—some vegetable oils are hydrogenated to make them solid, and highly hydrogenated vegetable oils tend to raise blood cholesterol levels. When shopping, look for canola oil and oils and margarines made from corn, sunflower, soybean, or safflower with as little hydrogenated oil as possible. Coconut and palm oils contain saturated fat and should be avoided. When buying margarines, choose the ones with the *lowest* amount of saturated fats and hydrogenated fats. There should be at least twice as many polyunsaturated fats as saturated. If the amounts of fats aren't mentioned on a margarine, don't buy it.

Some margarine labels state "contains no cholesterol." This statement is meaningless since no vegetable oil contains cholesterol.

The answer to what kind of fats to use in cooking is to use a variety but to keep the amounts as low as possible. Try cutting down the fat in your favorite recipes by a tablespoon at a time to determine the minimum amount necessary to produce a good-tasting result. I think you'll be surprised at how good many foods taste with less fat. By cutting out just one tablespoon of butter or margarine you reduce the fat content by 11 grams; cut out a tablespoon of oil and you avoid 14 grams of fat.

What to "butter" is a matter of personal taste, and everyone should make his or her own choice as long as it's in moderation. Consider using a margarine high in polyunsaturated fats instead of butter in baking or cooking. Be conscious of where you are using butter and margarine—often they aren't necessary. Peanut butter sandwiches don't need buttering, for instance, and butter is lost on hot-dog buns smothered with mustard and relish. If you're using toast with jam, try omitting butter or margarine.

Deep-Dish Plum Pie

Make this tasty fruit dessert in summer or fall when plums are plentiful. The yogurt pastry is lower in fat and calories than a traditional pastry and is very easy to roll out.

To reduce calories and fat content, make single-crust or deep-dish pies rather than double-crust pies. Or make a lattice top instead of a full top crust.

PASTRY:

> 3 tablespoons margarine or butter
> 1 cup all-purpose flour
> 6 tablespoons low-fat yogurt

FILLING:

> 1 cup granulated sugar
> 1/4 cup instant tapioca
> 1 teaspoon cinnamon
> 1 lemon, grated rind and juice
> 6 cups pitted and quartered fresh plums

Pastry: In bowl, use two knives or pastry blender to cut butter into flour until mixture is crumbly. Add yogurt and mix thoroughly. Form dough into ball, wrap in plastic, and refrigerate for at least 1 hour. On lightly floured board, roll out dough into circle slightly larger than circumference of baking dish.

Filling: In large bowl, combine sugar, tapioca, cinnamon, and grated rind; mix well. Add lemon juice and plums; toss to mix. Transfer to lightly oiled 6-cup soufflé or deep baking dish. Place dough over filling and press firmly against sides of dish. Cut slits in pastry to vent steam. Place on baking sheet and bake in 400°F oven for 50 to 60 minutes or until top is golden brown and filling is bubbly. If top browns too quickly, cover with foil. Makes 6 servings.

Calories per serving: 288
Grams fat per serving: 6
Fiber: Good
Vitamin C: Excellent
Vitamin A: Good

Cinnamon Applesauce

Applesauce is so simple to make, it isn't necessary to follow a recipe. Treat this one merely as a guide. The amount of sugar and cooking time will vary depending on the kind of apples and how ripe they are. To save time, don't peel or core apples; instead, pass cooked mixture through a food mill or sieve. If you want to keep the skin for more fiber and a chunky sauce, core the apples and chop coarsely; cook until apples are tender, then add sugar to taste. Grated lemon or orange rind or raisins can be added.

6	apples (about 3 pounds)
¼	cup water
1	tablespoon lemon juice
3	tablespoons granulated sugar (optional)
1	teaspoon cinnamon

Cut apples into quarters. In saucepan, combine apples, water, and lemon juice. Bring to a boil; reduce heat and simmer gently, uncovered, until apples are tender, about 20 minutes; stir often.

Place food mill or sieve over mixing bowl. Pass apple mixture through food mill (skin and seeds will stay in top of mill). Add sugar and cinnamon to purée; stir to dissolve sugar. Taste and add more if needed. Amount will vary depending on type of apple. (If sauce is too thin, return to saucepan and cook, stirring, over medium heat until it thickens.) Serve alone or with Applesauce Whole Wheat Cake (page 227). Makes 6 servings.

Calories per serving: 101
Grams fat per serving: 0.5
Vitamin C: Good

Serve this sauce with meats (especially pork) instead of gravy or other high-fat sauces, or as a dessert or breakfast fruit.

When making applesauce, add the sugar after the apples are cooked. If you add the sugar at the beginning, the apples will take longer to cook.

Variation:

Pear and Ginger Sauce: Substitute pears for apples and ginger for cinnamon in Cinnamon Applesauce; increase water to 1 cup; add sugar to taste. (Fiber: Good.) Serve over Old-Fashioned Molasses Bread (page 192).

Raspberry-Rhubarb Sauce

This sauce has a sweet-tart taste that's perfect over ice cream, fresh or frozen yogurt, and sliced peaches or other fresh fruit.

2½ **cups sliced rhubarb, ½-inch slices (fresh or frozen)**
¾ **cup water**
½ **cup granulated sugar**
 Grated rind and juice of 1 lemon
¼ **teaspoon cinnamon**
2 **cups fresh raspberries or 1 cup previously frozen unsweetened raspberries***

In saucepan, combine rhubarb, water, sugar, and lemon rind; bring to a boil over medium heat. Reduce heat and simmer until rhubarb is tender, 10 to 15 minutes. Remove from heat; stir in lemon juice, cinnamon, and raspberries. Let cool. Serve warm or cool over vanilla ice cream. Makes about 3 cups sauce.

Calories per ½ cup sauce: 110
Grams fat per ½ cup sauce: 0.3
Fiber: Excellent
Vitamin C: Good

Orange Cream Sauce

Delicious over Lemon Sorbet (page 211) or with cake, this sauce also makes a creamy base for fresh fruit. For a nouvelle dessert, spread sauce over rimmed individual dessert plates and arrange three kinds of fresh fruit—strawberries, kiwi, sliced peaches, grapes, or blackberries—artistically over the top.

¼ **cup granulated sugar**
1 **tablespoon frozen orange juice concentrate**
 Grated rind of 1 orange
¾ **cup low-fat yogurt**

In small mixing bowl, combine sugar, orange juice concentrate, and orange rind; stir to mix. Stir in yogurt and mix well. Makes 1 cup sauce.

Calories per 1 tablespoon: 21
Grams fat per 1 tablespoon: trace

Compare:

This is a creamy, low-fat dessert sauce; 1 tablespoon whipping cream has 5 grams of fat.

Variation:

Frozen Lemon Cream with Raspberry-Rhubarb Sauce: Spoon Frozen Lemon Cream (page 209) in layers into parfait glasses, alternating with Raspberry-Rhubarb Sauce, or pour the sauce over Frozen Lemon Cream. Use about ¼ cup sauce per person.

Variation:

Orange Cream Dressing: Reduce sugar in Orange Cream Sauce to 2 tablespoons. Use with fruit salads.

*If measuring raspberries while frozen, use 2 cups; if thawed, about 1 cup.

Easy Chocolate Sauce

Spoon this on ice cream, drizzle over bananas, pears, or chocolate cake, or use as a dipping sauce for fresh fruit.

1	cup cocoa
¾	cup granulated sugar
¾	cup water
½	cup corn syrup
1	teaspoon vanilla

In saucepan, combine cocoa and sugar. Whisk in water and corn syrup. Bring to a full boil over medium heat; boil for 2 minutes, stirring constantly. Remove from heat and stir in vanilla. Let cool (sauce will thicken upon cooling). Cover and store in refrigerator. Makes 2 cups sauce.

Calories per 1 tablespoon: 38
Grams fat per 1 tablespoon: 0.3

Cocoa powder is made from solid chocolate with the cocoa butter removed; therefore, it is much lower in fat than chocolate.

Choose chocolate recipes using cocoa powder instead of chocolate if other fat ingredients, such as butter or oil, are in comparatively similar amounts.

Chocolate Milk

Combine 2 tablespoons Easy Chocolate Sauce with ¾ cup milk. Serve hot or cold.

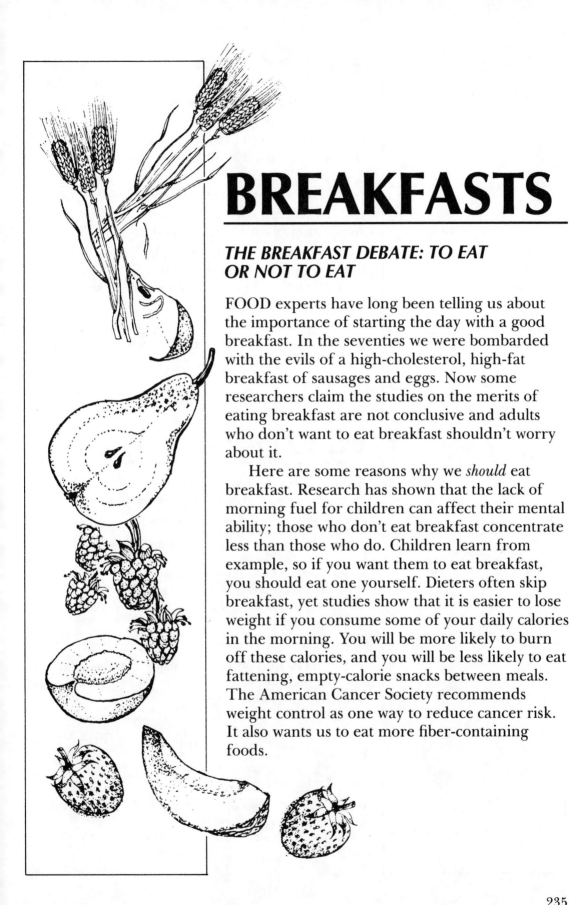

BREAKFASTS

THE BREAKFAST DEBATE: TO EAT OR NOT TO EAT

FOOD experts have long been telling us about the importance of starting the day with a good breakfast. In the seventies we were bombarded with the evils of a high-cholesterol, high-fat breakfast of sausages and eggs. Now some researchers claim the studies on the merits of eating breakfast are not conclusive and adults who don't want to eat breakfast shouldn't worry about it.

Here are some reasons why we *should* eat breakfast. Research has shown that the lack of morning fuel for children can affect their mental ability; those who don't eat breakfast concentrate less than those who do. Children learn from example, so if you want them to eat breakfast, you should eat one yourself. Dieters often skip breakfast, yet studies show that it is easier to lose weight if you consume some of your daily calories in the morning. You will be more likely to burn off these calories, and you will be less likely to eat fattening, empty-calorie snacks between meals. The American Cancer Society recommends weight control as one way to reduce cancer risk. It also wants us to eat more fiber-containing foods.

Breakfast provides an easy way to consume some of the body's needs for fiber, vitamins, and minerals in the form of cereals and fruits; if you don't eat breakfast, it's harder to meet these requirements. On the other hand, breakfast-skippers can pick up nutrients at a morning coffee break if they choose the right foods— fresh fruit, bran muffins, whole wheat bagels, yogurt, cottage cheese, or low-fat cream cheese. Avoid energy-only calories and high-fat items such as Danish pastries, doughnuts, and too much butter. Spread cheese or peanut butter over a bagel rather than butter; these spreads have protein as well as fat.

Because we need fiber from grains as well as from fruits and vegetables, include both grains and fruit in your breakfast.

Blender Breakfast

Keep this in mind for days when you want breakfast on the run; it takes only a minute to make and is packed with nutrients.

> 1   **banana, peach, or nectarine, peeled and**
>   **cut in chunks**
> ½   **cup low-fat milk or low-fat yogurt**
> 1   **teaspoon honey, sugar, or maple syrup**
> 1   **tablespoon natural bran**
> 1   **egg (optional)**

In blender or food processor, combine banana, milk, honey, bran, and egg (if using); process until smooth. Pour into tall glass. Makes 1 serving.

	With Egg	Without Egg
Calories per serving:	296	217
Grams fat per serving:	9	3
Fiber:	Excellent	Excellent
Iron, phosphorus, and niacin:	Excellent	Excellent
Calcium, vitamins A and C, and riboflavin:	Good	Good
Thiamine:	Good	

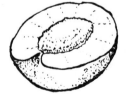

Breakfast Bran-and-Fruit Mix

With this mixture on your kitchen shelf, breakfast can be ready in a jiffy—just add sliced apples, peaches, grapefruit sections, strawberries, or banana, and top with yogurt or milk. (See color photograph.)

2   cups bran flakes
1   cup high-fiber cereal
½   cup sliced or chopped nuts (almonds, walnuts, or pecans) (optional)
½   cup chopped dried apricots
½   cup chopped prunes
½   cup raisins

Combine bran flakes, cereal, nuts, apricots, prunes, and raisins; mix well. Store, covered, in an airtight container. Serve with sliced fresh fruit and either low-fat milk or yogurt. Makes 10 servings (½ cup each).

Calories per ½ cup with ½ cup low-fat milk: 219
Grams fat per serving with ½ cup low-fat milk: 7
Fiber: Excellent
Vitamin A and phosphorus: Excellent
Calcium, riboflavin, thiamine, niacin, and iron: Good

Granola

This is one of the few granola recipes that doesn't use oil. Serve with yogurt and fresh fruit.

4 **cups quick-cooking rolled oats**
1½ **cups whole wheat flour**
1 **cup bran**
¼ **cup toasted wheat germ**
¼ **cup sesame seeds**
¼ **cup sunflower seeds**
½ **teaspoon salt**
1 **cup hot water**
½ **cup honey**
1 **teaspoon vanilla**
1 **cup raisins**

In large bowl, combine oatmeal, flour, bran, wheat germ, nuts, sesame seeds, sunflower seeds, and salt; mix well. In small bowl, mix together water, honey, and vanilla; pour into dry ingredients and stir to mix. Spread on 2 lightly oiled baking sheets and squeeze mixture together to form small clumps. Bake in 325°F oven for 30 minutes or until golden brown, stirring occasionally so granola will brown evenly. Stir in raisins and bake for 5 minutes longer. Let cool completely. Store in airtight containers. Makes 8 cups granola.

Calories per ½ cup: 235
Grams fat per ½ cup: 4
Fiber: Excellent
Iron, phosphorus, and thiamine: Good
Calcium: Excellent, when eaten with ½ cup skim milk.

For other breakfast and brunch dishes, see:

Eggs Florentine (page 143)
Omelet à la Jardinière (page 144)
Baked Zucchini Omelet (page 151)
Broccoli Frittata (page 142)
Muffins and Breads (page 184)
Cinnamon Coffee Cake (page 226)
Applesauce Whole Wheat Cake (page 227)

Whole Wheat Pancakes with Blueberries and Yogurt

Spring Brunch Menu

Grapefruit Juice Spritzer (page 143)
Omelet à la Jardinière (page 144), Baked Zucchini Omelet (page 151), or Broccoli Frittata (page 142)
Arugula and Radicchio Salad with Balsamic Vinegar (page 76) or tossed green salad
Cinnamon Coffee Cake (page 226)
Fresh strawberries

Summer Brunch Menu

Scrambled eggs with fresh basil
Melon with Blueberries (page 214)
Cinnamon Coffee Cake (page 226), or Banana-Apricot Bran Muffins (page 186)

Use any fresh fruit in season as a topping: peaches, strawberries, or raspberries.

3/4 **cup whole wheat flour**
1/2 **cup all-purpose flour**
1 **tablespoon baking powder**
2 **tablespoons granulated sugar**
1/2 **teaspoon salt**
1 **egg, beaten**
1 1/4 **cups skim milk**
2 **tablespoons vegetable oil**

TOPPING:
1/2 **cup low-fat yogurt**
2 **tablespoons maple syrup**
2 **cups blueberries**

In mixing bowl, combine flours, baking powder, sugar, and salt; stir to mix. Pour in egg, milk, and oil; stir until dry ingredients are wet. (Don't worry about a few lumps.)

Heat nonstick skillet over medium heat until hot (a drop of water will sizzle or dance). Lightly grease pan if desired. Using a large spoon, drop batter into skillet to form rounds. Cook until surface is full of bubbles that start to pop and underside is golden brown; turn and brown other side.

Topping: Combine yogurt and maple syrup; mix well. Spoon yogurt mixture over each pancake and top with blueberries. Makes about twelve 4-inch pancakes (2 pancakes per serving).

Calories per serving: 300
Grams fat per serving: 7.5
Fiber: Excellent
Calcium: Excellent
Riboflavin, niacin, and iron: Good

Breakfast Menus

Fresh fruit
Whole-grain cereal
Whole wheat toast
Low-fat yogurt or thin slice
  of low-fat cheese
Milk

Cantaloupe wedges
Bran flakes
Whole wheat toast
Low-fat yogurt

Fresh orange wedges
Whole wheat English muffin
Poached egg
Milk
Coffee

Fresh fruit (melon, apple, or
  berries) topped with low-
  fat yogurt and sprinkled
  with cinnamon sugar and
  wheat germ
Milk

Whole wheat pita bread
  filled with low-fat cottage
  cheese and raisins
Orange Juice
Milk

Hot oatmeal with milk
Half grapefruit
Whole wheat toast
Milk

Whole wheat toast spread
  with low-fat cottage
  cheese and topped with
  freshly grated nutmeg
  and fresh blueberries or
  other fruit
Milk

Swiss Fruit Muesli (page
  241)
Low-fat yogurt and sliced
  peaches or papaya

Quick Breakfast Menus

Orange juice
Granola (page 238) (made
  with bran) topped with
  low-fat yogurt and fresh
  strawberries
Milk

Honeydew melon with
  blueberries
Whole wheat English muffin
  with melted part-skim
  mozzarella cheese
Milk

Orange or apple juice
Breakfast Bran-and-Fruit
  Mix (page 237)
Milk

Refrigerator Bran Muffins
  (page 188)
Tomato juice
Blender Breakfast (page
  236)
Milk

Weekend Breakfast Menus

Whole Wheat Pancakes with
  Blueberries and Yogurt
  (page 239)
Sliced mango with
  grapefruit sections

Fresh fruit or stewed figs
Poached eggs on whole
  wheat English muffins
Tomatoes Provençal (page
  163)
Coffee

Melon with Blueberries
  (page 214)
Whole Wheat Raisin Scones
  (page 194) toasted and
  spread with low-fat cream
  cheese

Swiss Fruit Muesli

This Swiss breakfast is a complete meal in one dish. Soft wheat kernels add extra body and texture.

   ½   **cup soft wheat kernels** *
   ½   **cup rolled oats**
   ½   **cup raisins, chopped apricots, or prunes**
   2   **cups low-fat yogurt or low-fat milk**
       Honey or maple syrup (optional)
       Fresh fruit (sliced peach, pear,
          strawberries, banana, apple, or seedless
          red or green grapes)

In bowl, combine wheat kernels, rolled oats, raisins or other chopped dried fruit, nuts, and yogurt; stir until mixed. Cover and refrigerate overnight. Top with fresh fruit before serving. Makes 4 servings.

Calories per serving: 237 (will vary slightly depending on type of fruit used)
Grams fat per serving: 2
Fiber: Excellent
Calcium: Good
Niacin, thiamine, and iron: Good

---

*Soft wheat kernels or berries are popular in Scandinavian countries. They are available at health food stores; if you can't find them, just omit them and use 1 cup rolled oats.

Winter Brunch Menu

Grapefruit halves
Broccoli Frittata (page 142)
Tossed green salad
Pumpkin Muffins (page 187)
Apple Cinnamon Sorbet with
   Raspberry Purée (page 208)

APPENDICES

To find out the ideal amount of fat you should consume in a day or how many grams of fat you need to cut per day:

1. First estimate how many calories you need in a day. Turn to Table A (Recommended Daily Dietary Allowances) on page 244 and find your energy needs and the corresponding calorie (kcal/day) requirement per day. Note: These are averages only.

In the average American diet, 40 percent of the calories come from fat. The American Cancer Society Diet Guidelines recommend that no more than 30 percent of your calories should come from fat.

---

2. Turn to Table B (Daily Total Fat Intake), page 245; find your closest calorie level. Then look across to the next column at the 30 percent level; the corresponding grams of fat per day are the amount you can consume in order to have 30 percent of your calories from fat. The difference in grams of fat between a 40 percent level and a 30 percent level is the amount you need to cut per day.

    For example, if you are a man consuming about 3000 calories per day with 40 percent from fat, and you want to reduce to 30 percent fat, your desired intake of fat would be 100 grams of fat, or a cut of 33 (133−100) grams.

    If you are a woman consuming about 2200 calories per day with 40 percent from fat, and you want to reduce to 30 percent fat, your desired intake would be 73 grams of fat or a cut of 25 (98−73) grams.

3. The following is another way to find out how many grams of fat you should eat in a day to have 30 percent of your calories from fat:

$$\frac{\text{Daily calorie requirement}}{9} \times .30 = \text{Daily fat intake}$$

Realistically assess the fat content in your diet. If you aren't overweight, rarely eat meat or rich desserts, use little butter, margarine, oils, or mayonnaise, and stay away from fried foods, you already probably consume 30 percent or fewer calories from fat in your diet and don't need to reduce it any further.

The energy allowances for the young adults are for men and women doing light work. The allowances for the two older age groups represent mean energy needs over these age spans, allowing for a 2 percent decrease in basal (resting) metabolic rate per decade and a reduction of activity of 200 kcal/day for men and women between 51 and 75 years, 500 kcal for men over 75 years, and 400 kcal for women over 75. The customary range of daily energy output is shown for adults in parentheses, and is based on a variation in energy needs of 400 kcal at any one age, emphasizing the wide range of energy intakes appropriate for any group of people.

Table A: Recommended Daily Dietary Allowances

Mean Heights and Weights and Recommended Energy Intake

Category	Age (years)	Weight (kg)	(lb)	Height (cm)	(in)	Energy Needs (with range) (cal)
Infants	0.0–0.5	6	13	60	24	kg × 115 (95–145)
	0.5–1.0	9	20	71	28	kg × 105 (80–135)
Children	1–3	13	29	90	35	1300 (900–1800)
	4–6	20	44	112	44	1700 (1300–2300)
	7–10	28	62	132	52	2400 (1650–3300)
Males	11–14	45	99	157	62	2700 (2000–3700)
	15–18	66	145	176	69	2800 (2100–3900)
	19–22	70	154	177	70	2900 (2500–3300)
	23–50	70	154	178	70	2700 (2300–3100)
	51–75	70	154	178	70	2400 (2000–2800)
	76+	70	154	178	70	2050 (1650–2450)
Females	11–14	46	101	157	62	2200 (1500–3000)
	15–18	55	120	163	64	2100 (1200–3000)
	19–22	55	120	163	64	2100 (1700–2500)
	23–50	55	120	163	64	2000 (1600–2400)
	51–75	55	120	163	64	1800 (1400–2200)
	76+	55	120	163	64	1600 (1200–2000)
Pregnancy						+300
Lactation						+500

From: Recommended Dietary Allowances, Revised 1979. Food and Nutrition Board, National Academy of Sciences—National Research Council, Washington, D.C.

Table B: Daily Total Fat Intake According to Percentage of Total Calories

Calorie intake	Percent calories from fat	Grams fat per day
	20	27
1200	30	40
	40	53
	20	40
1800	30	60
	40	80
	20	49
2200	30	73
	40	98
	20	56
2500	30	83
	40	111
	20	67
3000	30	100
	40	133
	20	71
3200	30	107
	40	142

Table C: Fat and Calorie Content of Meat, Fish, and Poultry

Type and/or cut	Portion 4 ounces		Portion 8 ounces	
	Grams fat	Calories	Grams fat	Calories
Beef				
Cross rib roast, lean only, braised	12	252	24	504
Cross rib roast, lean + fat, braised	33	418	67	835
Prime rib roast, lean only, roasted	11	241	23	482
Prime rib roast, lean + fat, roasted	41	467	81	934
Rump roast, lean only, roasted	8	213	16	426
Rump roast, lean + fat, roasted	26	355	52	710
Brisket, lean only, simmered	9	223	17	446
Brisket, lean + fat, simmered	42	484	83	968
Flank steak, braised	7	214	15	429
Club steak, lean only, broiled	11	243	21	486
Club steak, lean + fat, broiled	37	446	74	891
Porterhouse, lean only, broiled	8	221	16	441

(continued)

Type and/or cut	Portion 4 ounces		Portion 8 ounces	
	Grams fat	Calories	Grams fat	Calories
Porterhouse, lean + fat, broiled	45	499	89	999
T-bone steak, lean only, broiled	8	223	16	446
T-bone steak, lean + fat, broiled	44	495	89	990
Round steak, lean only, broiled	7	212	14	423
Round steak, lean + fat, broiled	17	292	35	585
Sirloin steak, lean only, broiled	6	205	12	410
Sirloin steak, lean + fat, broiled	31	395	62	791
Ground beef, lean, cooked	13	245	25	491
Ground beef, regular, cooked	23	320	45	641
Veal, cutlet or chop (boneless)	14	262	28	524
Pork				
Ham, roasted, lean only	10	176	20	419
Ham, roasted, lean + fat	19	272	38	544
Pork loin chop, lean only, broiled	17	289	34	578
Pork loin chop, lean + fat, broiled	25	354	50	708
Pork loin roast, lean only	16	269	32	538
Pork loin roast, including fat	27	357	54	715
Spareribs	34	445	68	889
Bacon, sliced, broiled	67	686	134	1372
Bacon, Canadian, broiled	21	309	42	618
Bacon, sliced, 4 slices, cooked (3 ounces)	18	184		
Bacon, Canadian, 4 slices, cooked (1 ounce)	16	234		
Lamb				
Lamb shoulder, lean only	11	230	22	459
Lamb shoulder, including fat	30	379	60	757
Lamb leg, lean only	8	208	16	417
Lamb leg, including fat	21	312	42	625

Type and/or cut	Portion 4 ounces		Portion 8 ounces	
	Grams fat	Calories	Grams fat	Calories
Lamb loin chop, lean only	9	211	17	421
Lamb loin chop, including fat	33	402	66	804
Poultry				
Chicken breast with skin, fried	11	252	20	503
Chicken breast without skin, fried	5	212	11	424
Chicken breast with skin, roasted	9	223	18	446
Chicken breast without skin, roasted	4	187	8	374
Chicken, light meat with skin, roasted	12	252	25	503
Chicken, dark meat with skin, roasted	18	287	36	574
Chicken, light meat without skin, roasted	5	196	10	392
Chicken, dark meat without skin, roasted	9	232	22	465
Turkey, light meat without skin, roasted	5	186	10	372
Turkey, dark meat without skin, roasted	8	206	16	413
Duck, without skin, roasted	13	228	25	456
Goose, without skin, roasted	14	270	29	540
Processed Meats				
Hot dog (2 hot dogs)	20	248		
Bologna (8 slices, 3 inches in diameter)	32	320		
Salami (4 slices, 4 inches in diameter)	28	352		
Fish				
Sole fillets, cooked, steamed	2	72	4	145
Tuna in water	1	142	2	284
Tuna in oil	23	323	46	645
Trout	16	242	32	484
Shrimp	1	130	2.5	260
Salmon, fresh	8	204	16	408
Cod	6	190	12	381
Mackerel	18	264	35	529

4-ounce portion = 3 × 3 × ¾-inch chop
= 4 × 2 × ½-inch slice
= 2 pieces 4 × 2 × ¼ inch

Table D: Fat and Calorie Content of Cheese

Type	Grams fat per 1 ounce	Calories per 1 ounce
Cheese spread	5.9	81.2
Cheese spread (skim)	1.7	53.8
Blue cheese	8.1	98.9
Brick cheese	8.4	103.9
Brie	7.8	93.6
Camembert	6.7	84.0
Cheddar	9.2	112.9
Processed slices	8.7	105.0
Processed slices (skim)	1.7	53.5
Colby	8.9	110.4
Cottage cheese, 1% fat	.3	21.0
Cottage cheese, 2% fat	.6	25.2
Cottage cheese, creamed, 4.5% fat	1.4	28.9
Cream cheese	9.8	97.8
Edam cheese	7.8	100.0
Feta	6.2	76.1
Gouda	7.8	101.6
Gruyère	8.9	115.7
Monterey	8.4	104.5
Mozzarella	7.0	89.1
Mozzarella, part skim	4.8	78.4
Parmesan, grated	8.4	127.7
Ricotta, made with whole milk	3.6	48.7
Ricotta, part skim	2.2	38.7
Roquefort	8.7	103.4
Swiss	7.6	105.3

28 grams = 1 ounce = ¼ cup of grated or chopped or crumbled cheddar or other hard cheese = ⅛ cup of cottage or cream cheese

USDA Handbook #8

Table E: Fat Content of Dairy Products, Fats, and Oils

	Grams fat per 1 tablespoon
Butter	12
Margarine	12
Half-and-half	1.7
Whipping cream	5.6
Sour cream	2.5
Sour cream (low-fat)	1
Yogurt (low-fat)	trace
Oils (corn, safflower, olive)	14
Salad Dressings	
French	6
Blue/Roquefort	8
Mayonnaise	11
Miracle Whip	7
Oil & Vinegar (Kraft)	7.5
Oil and vinegar (homemade)	10
Low-calorie	2.0 (or less)
Miracle Whip, Light	4
Thousand Island	8

	Grams fat per 1 cup
Milk, Ice Cream, Frozen Desserts	
Whole milk (3.3% fat)	8
Milk (2% fat)	5
Milk (1% fat)	2.4
Skim milk (0.2% fat)	0.4
Ice milk (vanilla)	10.6
Ice milk (strawberry)	4
Ice cream (10% fat)	14
Ice cream (16% fat)	24
Fruit ice	0
Sherbet	0 to 4
Ice cream bar (vanilla, chocolate-coated)	11

Table F: Breakfast Cereals by Fiber Content

Excellent Sources of Fiber
(over 4 grams of fiber per 1-ounce serving)

Cereal Name	Grams Fiber per 1 ounce = 1 serving
Fiber One (General Mills)	12
All-Bran (Kellogg's)	9
Bran Chex (Ralston Purina)	5
Corn Bran (Quaker)	5
Natural Bran Flakes (Post)	5
Nabisco Shredded Wheat N' Bran	4
Fruitful Bran (Kellogg's)	4
Cracklin' Oat Bran (Kellogg's)	4
Bran Flakes (Kellogg's)	4
Fruit & Fiber (Post)	4

Good Source of Fiber
(2 to 3.9 grams of fiber per 1-ounce serving)

Cereal Name	Grams Fiber per 1 ounce = 1 serving
Cheerios (General Mills)	2
Frosted Mini-Wheats (Kellogg's) (with brown sugar)	3
Grape-Nuts (Post)	2
Grape-Nuts Flakes (Post)	2
Shredded Wheat (Nabisco) (spoon-size or biscuit)	3
Total (General Mills)	2
Wheaties (General Mills)	2

Under 2 grams of Fiber per 1-ounce Serving

Cereal Name	Grams Fiber per 1 ounce = 1 serving
Apple Jacks (Kellogg's)	trace
Cap'n Crunch (Quaker Oats)	trace
Cocoa Puffs (General Mills)	trace
Corn Flakes (Kelloggs's)	trace
Crispy Wheat 'n Raisins (General Mills)	trace
Fruit Loops (Kellogg's)	trace
Frosted Flakes (Kellogg's)	trace
Honeycombs (Post)	trace
Life (plain) (Quaker Oats)	trace
Lucky Charms (General Mills)	trace
Product 19 (Kellogg's)	trace
Rice Crispies (Kellogg's)	trace
Special K (Kellogg's)	trace
Corn Pops (Kellogg's)	trace
Trix (General Mills)	trace

Fiber Values from Consumer Reports, Ready-to-eat Cereals, October 1986

Table G: Vegetable Fiber Values

Vegetable	Serving size (approximate)	Grams dietary fiber per serving	Dietary fiber per 100 grams
Beans, white, cooked;	½ cup	6	7
green or yellow, cooked	½ cup	2	3
Beets, red, cooked	2	3	3
Broccoli, fresh or frozen, cooked	1 cup	4	4
Brussels sprouts, cooked	4	2	3
Cabbage, red or green, raw, chopped	½ cup	1	3
Carrots, sliced, cooked;	½ cup	2	3
raw	1	2	3
Cauliflower, raw, chopped	½ cup	1	2
Celery, raw, inner stalks	3	1	2
Chard, Swiss, cooked	½ cup	5	6
Corn kernels, frozen, cooked	½ cup	2	2
Cucumber (not peeled) (8 × 2 inches)	1		1
Lentils, cooked	½ cup	3	4
Lettuce (iceberg)	1 wedge	1	2
Parsnips, cooked, mashed	½ cup	2	3
Peas, green frozen, cooked	½ cup	3	5
Pepper, sweet, red or green, raw;	1 large	2	1
cooked	1 large	1	1
Potatoes, boiled in skin;	1 long	5	2
peeled, boiled	1 long	2	1
Spinach, fresh, frozen or canned, cooked, drained	½ cup	10	6
Squash, summer (zucchini and crookneck), cooked	½ cup	1	1
Squash, winter, all varieties, cooked, baked	½ cup	2	2
Sweet potato, boiled in skin	1 large	4	2
Tomato, ripe, raw, unpeeled	1 medium	2	2
Turnip, boiled, mashed	½ cup	2	2

Dishes Containing an Excellent Source of Vitamin C

(More than 15 milligrams per serving)

Soup Dishes
Chicken and Leek Chowder
Chilled Yogurt and Melon Soup
Corn and Tomato Chowder with Tarragon
Cream of Broccoli Soup
Fish Chowder, Family Style
Fresh Tomato and Basil Soup
Gazpacho
Portuguese Collard Soup
Potage Vert
Spa Vegetable Soup
Summer Garden Italian Soup with Pesto
Tomato-Bean Chowder

Salads
Artichoke-Tomato Salad
Arugula and Radicchio Salad with Balsamic
    Vinaigrette
Bermuda Bean Salad
Broccoli Buffet Salad
Chicken and Melon Salad
Chick-Pea Salad with Red Onion and
    Tomato
Coleslaw with Apple and Onion
Cracked Wheat with Peas and Onions
Greek Salad
Julienne Vegetable Salad with Lemon
    Vinaigrette

Melon and Bean Salad
Pasta Salad with Sweet Peppers and Dill
Red Potato Salad with Sour Cream and
    Chives
Spinach and Red Cabbage Salad with Blue
    Cheese Dressing
Spinach Supper Salad
Tabbouleh
Tomato Raita
White Kidney Bean Salad

Vegetables
Asparagus with Red Pepper Purée
Braised Red Cabbage
Braised Red Peppers and Leeks
Broccoli Frittata
Broccoli and Sweet Pepper Stir-Fry
Glazed Brussels Sprouts with Pecans
Mashed Potatoes with Onions
Orange Sherried Sweet Potatoes
Scalloped Cabbage au Gratin
Stir-Fried Vegetables with Ginger and Garlic
Tomatoes Florentine
Tomato Raita
Tomatoes Provençal
Two-Cabbage Stir-Fry
Turnips Paysanne

Dishes Containing an Excellent Source of Vitamin A

(More than 1,200 I.U. per serving)

Soups
Chicken and Leek Chowder
Chilled Melon and Yogurt Soup
Cream of Broccoli Soup
Fish Chowder, Family Style
Fresh Tomato and Basil Soup
Nova Scotia Seafood Chowder
Portuguese Collard Soup
Red Lentil Soup
Spa Vegetable Soup
Summer Garden Italian Soup with Pesto

Salads and Vegetables
Asparagus with Red Pepper Purée
Baked Squash with Ginger
Baked Zucchini Omelet
Braised Red Pepper and Leeks
Broccoli and Sweet Pepper Stir-Fry
Broccoli Frittata
Foil-Steamed Spring Vegetables
Lemon-Ginger Carrots
Mashed Turnips with Carrots and Orange
Orange Sherried Sweet Potatoes
Stir-Fried Vegetables with Ginger and Garlic
Tabbouleh
Tarragon Carrots
Tomatoes Provençal
Turnips Paysanne

Sauces
Tomato-Basil Sauce
Tomato Salsa

Main Courses
Almond Chicken
Beef and Vegetable Stew
Breast of Chicken Florentine

Bulgar Wheat, Tofu, and Sweet Peppers
Chinese Pork and Vegetables
Creamy Pasta with Broccoli, Cauliflower,
 and Mushrooms
Deep-Dish Vegetable Pizza
Eggs Florentine
Fettucine with Fresh Tomatoes and Basil
Ginger-Apricot Stuffed Lamb with Kumquats
Microwave Fillets Provençal
Microwave Tarragon Chicken with Julienne
 Vegetables
Mexican Pork Stew
Mussels Sicilian Style
Navarin of Lamb
Pot au Feu
Scallops and Shrimp in Wine Bouillon with
 Julienne Vegetables
Sole Florentine
Souvlakia of Lamb
Tex-Mex Chili
Tomato Sauce Provençal with Veal on Pasta
Tuscan White Kidney Bean and Tomato
 Casserole
Winter Vegetable Stew

Desserts
Apricot Clafouti
Cantaloupe, Pear, and Grapes with Sherry
 Orange Sauce
Deep-Dish Plum Pie
Melon with Blueberries
Old-Fashioned Peach Cobbler
Peach Blueberry Crisp
Peaches with Raspberry-Yogurt Sauce

Dishes Containing an Excellent Source of Fiber

(Over 4 grams of fiber per serving)

Breakfast Dishes
Banana-Apricot Bran Muffins
Blender Breakfast
Breakfast Bran-and-Fruit Mix
Melon with Blueberries
Refrigerator Bran Muffins
Swiss Fruit Muesli

Lunch*
Chicken and Leek Chowder
Eggs Florentine
Portuguese Collard Soup
Potage Vert
Summer Garden Italian Soup with Pesto
Tomato-Bean Chowder
Tri-Color Bean Soup

Salads*
Bermuda Bean Salad
Broccoli Buffet Salad
Chick-Pea Salad with Red Onion and
   Tomato
Mediterranean Lentil Salad
Melon and Bean Salad
Spinach Supper Salad
White Kidney Bean Salad

Dinner
Almond Chicken
Baked Zucchini Omelet
Beef and Vegetable Stew
Breast of Chicken Florentine
Broccoli Frittata
Bulgur Wheat, Tofu, and Sweet Peppers
Chinese Pork and Vegetables
Cracked Wheat and Basil Pilaf
Cracked Wheat with Peas and Onions
Creamy Pasta with Broccoli, Cauliflower,
   and Mushrooms
Deep-Dish Vegetable Pizza
Navarin of Lamb
Sole Florentine
Tex-Mex Chili
Tomatoes Florentine
Tuscan White Kidney Bean and Tomato
   Casserole

Desserts
Banana-Apricot Bran Muffins
Blackberries with Orange Cream Sauce
Coconut-Oatmeal Cookies (3)
Lemon and Fresh Blueberry Tart
Peach Blueberry Crisp
Peaches with Raspberry-Yogurt Sauce
Raspberry Purée
Raspberry Meringue Torte
Raspberry Sorbet
Strawberries with Raspberry-Rhubarb Sauce

*Also suitable for dinner

REFERENCES

American Cancer Society, 1986 Cancer Facts and Figures (pamphlet).

Burkitt, Dennis P. "Etiology and prevention of colorectal cancer." *Hospital Practice,* February 1984, pp. 67-77.

"Cancer Prevention Research: Summary—Nutrition." Mimeographed. National Cancer Institute, 1984.

Carroll, K.C.; Braden, L.M.; Bell, J.A.; and Kalamegham, R. "Fat and Cancer." *Cancer, A Journal of the American Cancer Society.* (Supplement.) Vol. 58, number 8 (October 1986): 1818-25.

Cummings, John H., and Stephen, Alison M. "The role of dietary fibre in the human colon." *CMA Journal* 123:1109-14.

Dietary Standard for Canada. 3rd ed. Canada Bureau of Nutritional Sciences, Department of National Health and Welfare, Ottawa, 1975.

"Does fiber-rich food containing animal lignan precursors protect against both colon and breast cancer? An extension of the 'fibre hypothesis.'" Editorial. *Gastroenterology* 86:761-74.

Eastwood, M. A., and Passmore, R. "Nutrition: The changing scene." *The Lancet,* 23 July 1983, pp. 202-06.

"Facts on Cancer and Diet." Toronto: Canadian Cancer Society, 1986.

Goldsmith, G. A.; Miller, O. N.; and Unglaub, W. G. "Efficiency of tryptophan as a niacin precursor in man." *Journal of Nutrition* 73: 173-76, 1961.

Gori, Gio Batta. "Dietary and nutritional implications in the multifactorial etiology of certain prevalent human cancers." *Cancer* 43 (1979): 2151-61.

Handler, Semour. "Dietary fibre: Can it prevent certain colonic diseases?" *Postgraduate Medicine* 73 (1983): 301-07.

Kritchevsky, David. "Diet, Nutrition and Cancer: The Role of Fiber." *Cancer, A Journal of the American Cancer Society.* (Supplement.) Vol. 58, number 8 (October 1986): 1830-36.

——. "Fibre, steroids, and cancer." *Cancer Research* 43: 2491S-5S.

Meyskens, Frank. "Vitamin A and Its Derivatives (Retinoids) in the Prevention and Treatment of Cancer." Mimeographed.

Miller, A. B. "Diet, Nutrition and Cancer. An epidemiological overview." *Journal of Nutrition Growth and Cancer.* Vol. II: 159-71, 1985.

National Research Council. *Executive Summary: Diet, Nutrition, and Cancer.* Washington, D.C.: National Academy Press, 1982.

Nutrition and Cancer: Cause and Prevention. American Cancer Society, 1984.

Procedures for Calculating the Nutritive Values of Home Prepared Foods, Agriculture Research Service, U.S. Department of Agriculture, 1966.

Rietz, P. Wisso, and Weber, F. "Metabolism of vitamin A and the determination of vitamin A states." *Vitamins and Hormones* 32:234-49, 1974.

Rozen, Paul, et al. "The low incidence of colorectal cancer in a 'high-risk' population: Its correlation with dietary habits." *Cancer* 48 (1981): 2692-95.

Schatzkin, Arthur, et al. "Alcohol Consumption and Breast Cancer in the Epidemiologic Follow-Up Study of the First National Health and Nutrition Examination Survey." *The New England Journal of Medicine* 316 (May 1987): 1169-73.

USDA Composition of Foods, Agriculture Research Service, Agriculture Handbook #8, 1-12.

U.S. Department of Health and Human Services. *Diet, Nutrition & Cancer Prevention: A Guide to Food Choices.* Washington, D.C.: U.S. Government Printing Office, 1985.

Willett, Walter C., and MacMahon, Brian. "Diet and cancer: An overview. Part I." *The New England Journal of Medicine 310* (8 March 1984): 633–38.

——. "Diet and cancer: An overview. Part II." *The New England Journal of Medicine* 310 (15 March 1984): 697–703.

Willett, W.C., et al. "Moderate Alcohol Consumption and the Risk of Breast Cancer." *The New England Journal of Medicine* 316 (May 1987): 1174–81.

——. "Dietary Fat and The Risk of Breast Cancer." *The New England Journal of Medicine* 316 (January 1987): 22–28.

Williams, R. R., et al. "Cancer incidence by levels of cholesterol." *Journal of the American Medical Association* 245: 247–52.

Wynder, E. L.; Rose, D. P.; Cohen, L.A. "Diet and Breast Cancer in Causation Therapy." *Cancer, A Journal of the American Cancer Society.* (Supplement.) Vol. 58, number 8 (October 1986): 1804–13.

ACKNOWLEDGMENTS

I would like to thank the American Cancer Society, especially Dr. Diane Fink and Irving Rimer. Thanks also to the Ontario division of the Canadian Cancer Society, especially Karen Hanley. A huge thanks to dietitian Shannon Graham for her help in testing recipes. Thanks to Carol Ferguson, Marg Fraser, and Elizabeth Baird of *Canadian Living* magazine.

Thanks to Kathy Vanderlinden for her help with the introduction. Thanks also to Pam Verdier, Dr. A. B. Millar, Dr. Meera Jain, Dr. Peter Scholefield, Cheryl Moyer, Fred Bird, Maggie McDonald, and Linda McKnight.

Most of all, thanks to my family—my parents, Hugh and Marion Elliott, my husband, Bob, and my children, Jeff, John, and Susie, for being my best critics and putting up with me while my life revolved around writing this book.

ANNE LINDSAY
Toronto 1988

Index